Quiet Water New Hampshire and Vermont: Canoe and Kayak Guide

2d edition

John Hayes and Alex Wilson

Appalachian Mountain Club Books

Boston, Massachusetts

Cover Photographs: Harry Lichtman and Marny Ashburne

All photographs by the authors unless otherwise noted.

Cartographers: Vanessa Gray, Nadav Malin

Illustrations: Cathy Johnson

Cover Design: Mac & Dent

Book Text Design: Carol Bast Tyler; Layout: Elisabeth Brady

Distributed by The Globe Pequot Press, Inc., Guilford, CT

Library-of-Congress Data is available.

The paper used in this publication meets the minimum requirements of the
American National Standard for Information Science—Permanence of Paper
for Printed Library Materials, AANSI Z39.48–1984.

**Due to the changes in conditions,
use of the information in this book
is at the sole risk of the user.**

Printed on recycled paper using soy-based inks.

Printed in the United States of America.

10 9 8 7 6 5 4 3 2 1   01 02 03 04 05 06 07

Contents

Natural History Essays

Southern New Hampshire

Central New Hampshire

Northern New Hampshire

Southern Vermont

Central Vermont

Northern Vermont

Preface to
Second Edition

The first edition of the *Quiet Water Canoe Guide: New Hampshire/Vermont*, written by Alex Wilson and published in January 1992, launched a series that now includes guides to Massachusetts/Connecticut/Rhode Island, Maine, New York, and New Jersey. John Hayes, co-author with Alex of the Maine and New York guides, has co-authored this second edition.

Though the first edition enjoyed great success, lake and pond descriptions inevitably go out of date with time, necessitating a new edition. Also, we took this opportunity to add new material, nearly doubling the amount of water covered. The first edition contained 63 entries covering 74 bodies of water; for the second edition, we dropped six of those entries that covered eight bodies of water because of limited access, development, or overuse (Dan Hole Ponds, Shellcamp Pond, White Lake, Knapp Brook Ponds, Lake Groton, Lake Willoughby, and Spectacle Pond); and added 55 new bodies of water. The new entries comprise 45 percent of the 121 total. We also combined some entries: Branch Pond and Grout Pond, and Kettle Pond and Osmore Pond.

We combined some new entries with first-edition entries: Hopkinton Lake and Stumpfield Marsh with Everett Lake; Lake Francis with First Connecticut Lake; and Bomoseen Lake with Glen Lake and Half Moon Pond. We also expanded some first-edition entries: we added another section to the Dead Creek entry, and we included a section of the Contoocook River in the Powder Mill Pond entry.

We rechecked all original bodies of water to make sure that new housing developments had not crowded the shores, and we revised directions to reflect new road names. When possible, we tried to avoid bodies of water with substantial development, but for the most part, we worry more about the effect of personal watercraft and high-speed boating on fragile loon, bald eagle, osprey, otter, and other wildlife populations—and on paddlers' feelings of solitude. If we care about preserving these species and their habitat for future generations, we will demand that elected and appointed officials make wildlife preservation and ecosystem protection a higher priority.

We heartily applaud the state of New Hampshire for banning lead sinkers and jigs, fishing devices the Tufts University Wildlife Veterinary Clinic has implicated in more than 50 percent of loon mortality in its freshwater breeding grounds. And we commend Vermont for making substantial boating restrictions—especially on personal watercraft—on hundreds of small bodies of water since the first edition's publication.

My co-author, Alex, led the successful effort in 1994–95 to ban personal watercraft and water-skiing and to impose a 10 MPH speed limit on Somerset Reservoir—one of southern Vermont's longest and most primitive bodies of water. Through publication of this expanded guide, we hope to draw attention to the need to preserve these wonderful places. All quietwater paddlers should work together at local and state levels to bring added protection to these precious resources.

John Hayes
Marlboro, VT

November 2000

Acknowledgments

For the second edition, we owe special thanks to those who contacted us about new bodies of water to include, and to those who pointed out problems in the first edition. In particular, we thank Peter Thompson of the Cornell University Geology Department; Janet Brown; Dick and Daniel Allen; Bill Laliberte; Linda Robinson; Malcolm Moore; and Linda Rice. We thank Vanessa Gray, who did the cartography for the second edition, and the Spiral Shop Studios in Brattleboro for the photographic prints. We thank new paddling partners Andrew Hayes, Vanessa Gray, Philip Demay, and Bob Engel. We also thank Beth Krusi and the staff at the Appalachian Mountain Club (AMC) for their assistance in the preparation of the second edition.

From the first edition (please note that many affiliations have changed) we thank: Alex's family—Jerelyn, Lillian, and Frances Wilson—and other paddling partners (many of whom continue to paddle with us), including Sally Andrews, Malcolm Moore, Jay Falk, Betsey Copp, Ron Svec, Jim Williams, Sumner Grey, and Mark Kelley. For suggestions of lakes and ponds to explore, we thank Tom Howe of the Lakes Region Conservation Trust; Anne McCullough and Paul Doscher of the Society for the Protection of New Hampshire Forests; David Sobel; Red Barber of the Vermont Department of Forests, Parks, and Recreation; and Drew Gillett. For help with finding information, we thank Jerry Carbone at Brooks Memorial Library in Brattleboro, Vermont; Marc DesMeules at the Vermont Nature Conservancy; Virginia Garrison and Susan Warren at the Vermont Agency of Natural Resources; Paul Wellenberger at the Great Bay National Estuarine Reserve; and helpful folks at both the Green Mountain and White Mountain National Forests.

We are also indebted to Jennifer Ramstetter of Marlboro College, who reviewed the first-edition wildlife write-ups; Sheila Roth, a fine photographer in Brattleboro, for helpful photographic tips and the photographic printing; Cathy Johnson for the wildlife illustrations; Carol Bast Tyler for the book design; Hanson Carroll and Stephen Gorman for the cover photographs; and Alex's business associate Nadav Malin, who produced the first-edition maps. Finally, we offer a special thanks to the Appalachian Mountain Club, and particularly our good friend Gordon Hardy, who saw the potential in the series of quietwater paddling guides Alex envisioned and who carried out that vision in launching the series.

While we received a lot of help from these and other individuals, we accept responsibility for any errors, inaccuracies, or misleading information. We would be most grateful to readers who let us know of any problems so that they can be corrected in future editions. Write to us care of AMC Books, 5 Joy Street, Boston, MA 02108. Thank you, and enjoy your paddling.

John Hayes
Alex Wilson

Introduction

Quiet waters—lakes, ponds, estuaries, and slow-flowing streams—seem to receive much less attention than whitewater rivers. If you seek the adrenaline rush of paddling cascading rivers, there are plenty of excellent resources—but this is not one of them. This guide will help you find peaceful and quiet places. It will lead you to wood ducks swimming through early-morning mists, to old-growth white pine towering above crystal-clear ponds where you can imagine what our forests looked like centuries ago, to the loon's haunting wail wafting off the water as afternoon settles into dusk.

With quietwater paddling, you can focus on *being* there instead of *getting* there. You do not need a lot of fancy high-tech gear—though a light canoe or kayak makes portaging into out-of-the-way places a lot easier. Binoculars and field guides to fauna and flora make up our most important gear.

We logged thousands of miles by car and hundreds of miles by canoe and kayak, searching for the best places to paddle. Some trips proved fruitless, as the pond we sought turned out to be inaccessible, off-limits to boating, ringed with cabins, or chock-full of speedboats. Other efforts yielded wonderful surprises—places that looked uninteresting on maps or seemed inaccessible turned out to be real gems.

This guide will not only lead you to a body of water but also describe why you might want to paddle it. We hope that our research will allow you to spend your valuable time paddling instead of driving around for hours trying to find an elusive access. We designed this book, and others in this series of AMC Quiet Water Guides, for paddlers of all experience levels, to help you better enjoy New Hampshire's and Vermont's wonderful water resources.

How We Selected These Lakes, Ponds, and Rivers

This guide includes only about 10 percent of the nearly one thousand lakes and ponds in New Hampshire and Vermont. In our selection process, we looked for: nice scenery; limited development; not too many motorboats and personal watercraft; a varied shoreline with lots of coves and inlets to explore; and interesting plants, animals, and geological formations.

We included a variety of water types: big lakes, for longer excursions; and small, protected ponds and marshes, for when you have limited time, your children lack the patience for extended outings, or weather conditions preclude paddling big lakes. We wrote this book not only for vacationers planning a week-long trip hundreds of miles from home but also for local residents wanting to do some paddling on their afternoon off.

For the first edition, Alex included a representative sampling of small and large bodies of water from the two-state region. He found these bodies of water by asking people about the best places to paddle and by consulting DeLorme's *New Hampshire Atlas and Gazetteer* and *Vermont Atlas and Gazetteer.* For the second edition, in addition to consulting with others, we followed the procedure used in the southern New England, Maine, and New York guides: we systematically searched the U.S. Geological Survey (USGS) 7.5-minute topographic maps of the two states—all 350-plus. From our initial list of a few hundred lakes, ponds, streams, and tidal estuaries, we paddled those that looked good from the boat access. In all, we found 121 suitable for inclusion in this book's 92 sections.

We have by no means included all the very best places. During our research, we constantly discovered new places—either through someone's tip, a re-examination of the maps, or just coincidence. If anyone has suggestions of other lakes and ponds, please let us know (John Hayes or Alex Wilson, c/o AMC Books, 5 Joy Street, Boston, MA 02108). Also, please bring to our attention suggestions for improvements, inaccuracies, and clarifications to make future editions better.

Do We Really Want to Tell People about the Best Places?

Throughout this project, many people asked us how we could, in good conscience, tell others about our favorite hidden lakes and ponds—the more remote, pristine places, still unspoiled by too many people. After all, increased visitation would make these places less idyllic. We spent many an hour grappling with this difficult issue as we paddled along.

We believe that by getting more people out enjoying these places—people who value wild, remote areas—support will build for greater protection of these waters. For many lakes and ponds, protection will mean purchase of fragile surrounding areas by state or local governments, or private organizations such as The Nature Conservancy. On other bodies of water, restricting high-speed boating offers the best form of protection.

We hope you will help protect our most treasured water resources. For many lakes and ponds, water-skiers and users of personal water-craft—people who have the greatest negative impact on these delicate environments—are often the most vocal. Policy makers need to hear from low-impact users as well.

We had hoped we could report that many of these waters have more protection now than they did when the first edition was published in 1992, and there are some wonderful successes. The state of Vermont banned water-skiing and personal watercraft and limited boating speeds to 10 MPH on Somerset Reservoir—one of the largest bodies of water in southern Vermont—and placed restrictions on personal watercraft and speeding on many smaller lakes and ponds. New Hampshire has also banned personal watercraft from some important bodies of water. The land around a number of our most treasured water resources has received protection from development forever. While The Nature Conservancy and land trusts continue to protect more of the shoreline along a few key ponds and lakes, most other bodies of water suffer from continued development and more high-speed boating. When we update this guide in a few years, we hope to report a lot more progress in protecting these lakes and ponds.

Safety First

Your attraction to quiet water rather than quick water might result from having small children or not liking dangerous places—such as raging whitewater—or not wanting to concentrate too much on your paddling skills. So you turn to lakes and ponds, envisioning tranquil paddling on mirror-smooth water that reflects the surrounding hills.

You certainly will find these places—the idyllic, mist-filled, mirror-smooth surfaces of quiet ponds at daybreak. But if you spend appreciable time paddling, you will also encounter some quite dangerous conditions.

Be sure that children always wear properly fitting life vests.

Strong winds can arise quickly, turning tranquil lakes into raging, whitecapped inland seas. On big lakes, strong winds can whip up two- to three-foot waves in no time—waves big enough to swamp an open boat. If you capsize in cold water, hypothermia, a cooling of the body's core that can lead to mental and physical collapse, can set in quickly.

New Hampshire and Vermont require people to carry U.S. Coast Guard–approved personal flotation devices, or PFDs, for every person in the boat. We recommend that everyone wear PFDs at all times on the water; both states require children to wear PFDs. With children in the boat, you too should wear a PFD so that if the boat capsizes you can help the children better. A foam- or kapok-filled PFD will also keep you warmer in cold water. If you do not normally paddle wearing a PFD, at least don it in windy conditions, when crossing large lakes, or when you may encounter substantial motorboat wakes. It may make you a little hotter, it may interfere with your paddling, but it could save your life.

Also, if you have just driven five hours to reach a particular lake and find it dangerously windy, choose a more protected body of water, or go hiking instead. We include small ponds and streams near many of the larger, better-known lakes for just this reason.

On some shallow, marshy waters included in this guide, waterfowl-hunting season brings an influx of activity. Avoid these areas during waterfowl-hunting season, especially if you see blinds and decoys in the water. For hunting-season dates, contact the New Hampshire Fish and Game Department (603-271-3212) or the Vermont Department of Fish and Wildlife (802-241-3700).

Starting Out Right: Equipment Selection

For quietwater paddling, most any canoe or sea kayak will do, but avoid high-performance racing or tippy whitewater models. Borrow a boat before buying; selection will be easier with a little experience.

Whether canoe or kayak, look for a model with good initial and secondary stability. A boat with good initial stability and poor secondary stability will tip slowly, but once it starts it may keep going. The best canoes for lakes and ponds have a keel or shallow-V hull and fairly flat keel line to help track in a straight line, even in a breeze. Kayaks perform extremely well in rough water, particularly if equipped with a foot-operated rudder. To keep from taking on water in rough water, they require a sprayskirt.

If you like out-of-the-way paddling requiring portages, get a Kevlar boat if you can afford it. Kevlar is a strong carbon fiber, somewhat like fiberglass but much lighter. We paddle a rugged, high-capacity, 18' 4" Mad River Lamoille canoe that weighs just 60 pounds, a 15' 9" Mad River Independence solo canoe that weighs less than 40 pounds, a 14' Wenonah Wigeon kayak that weighs 38 pounds, and a 14' Wilderness Systems Chaika kayak that weighs 32 pounds. If you plan to go by yourself, consider a sea kayak or a solo canoe, in which you sit (or kneel) close to the center of the boat. You will find paddling a well-designed solo canoe far easier than a two-seater used solo. The touring or sea kayak, with its long, narrow design; low profile to the wind; and two-bladed paddling style, is faster and more efficient to paddle than canoes.

A padded portage yoke in place of the center thwart on a canoe is essential if you plan on much carrying. With unpadded yokes, wear a life vest with padded shoulders. Attach a rope—called a "painter"—to the bow so you can secure the boat when you stop for lunch, line it up or down a stream, and—if the need ever arises—grab onto it in an emergency. We both have embarrassing stories about not using a painter to secure the boat—wind can cause Kevlar boats to disappear very quickly!

Choose light and comfortable paddles. For canoeing, we use a relatively short (50-inch), bent-shaft paddle, handmade in West Danby, New York (Hilltop Paddles). Laminated from various woods, the paddle has a special synthetic tip to protect the blade. Bent-shaft paddles allow more efficient paddling, because the downward force converts more directly into forward thrust. However, straight-shaft paddles also work well, and we used them for years. Always carry at least one spare paddle per group, particularly on longer trips, in case a porcupine happens to get a hold of one and decides to gnaw on it.

As mentioned above, the law requires PFDs for everyone in the boat. The best life preserver is Coast Guard–approved Type I, II, or III. A floating cushion (Type IV) is less effective than a life vest that you wear. A good PFD keeps a person's face above water, even if he or she loses consciousness. Children must wear their PFDs, and they must be the right size so that they will not slip off; adult PFDs are not acceptable for children. Although the law does not require adults to wear PFDs, we strongly recommend that you do so, especially when paddling with children.

As for clothing, plan for the unexpected. Even with a sunny-day forecast, a shower can appear by afternoon. On trips of more than a few hours, we bring along rain gear. On longer trips, we also carry extra dry clothes in a waterproof stuff sack. Along with rain coming up unexpectedly, temperatures can drop quickly, especially in the spring or fall, making conditions ripe for hypothermia. Lightweight nylon or polypropylene clothing dries more quickly than cotton, and wool still retards heat loss when wet. Remember that heads lose heat faster than torsos—bring a hat.

Paddling with Kids

When canoeing with kids, try to make it fun. Try to keep calm. Your kids will do better, and you will have a better time. Even though you may be plenty warm from paddling, children may get cold while sitting in the bottom of the boat. They will also require protection from the sun and biting insects. Watch for signs of discomfort. On long paddling excursions, set up a cozy place where young children can sleep. After the initial excitement of paddling fades, the gently rolling canoe often puts children to sleep, especially near the end of a long day.

Paddling Technique

On a quiet pond, does it matter if you use the proper J stroke, the sweep stroke, the draw, or the reverse J? No. Learning some of these strokes, however, can make a day of paddling more relaxing, enjoyable, and less fatiguing. We watch lots of novices zigzagging along, frantically switching sides while shouting orders fore and aft. People have told us about marriage counseling sessions devoted to paddling technique. . . .

Paddling does not have to be difficult. If you want to learn canoeing or kayaking techniques, buy a book or participate in a paddling workshop, such as those offered by the AMC (www.outdoors.org), equipment retailers, and boat manufacturers. Among the books we recommend on canoeing are *Beyond the Paddle* by Garrett Conover (Tilbury House, 1991); *The Complete Wilderness Paddler* by Davidson and Gugge (Vintage, 1983); *Basic Essentials Canoeing, 2d ed.*, by Cliff Jacobson (Globe Pequot Press, 1999); and *Basic Essentials Canoe Paddling, 2d ed.*, by Roberts and Salins (Globe Pequot Press, 2000). For kayaking, good books include *The Essential Sea Kayaker* by David Seidman (International Marine Publishers, 1997); *Basic Book of Sea Kayaking* by Derek Hutchinson (Globe Pequot Press, 1999); and *Complete Book of Sea Kayaking, 4th ed.*, by Derek Hutchinson (Globe Pequot Press, 1995). Also look for *Paddling with Kids* by Bruce and Karen Lessels to be published in fall 2001 by the Appalachian Mountain Club.

Start out on small ponds. Practice paddling into, with, and across the wind. On a warm day when you are close to shore, you might even want to practice capsizing. Intentionally tipping your canoe or kayak will give you an idea of its limits and how easily it can tip over. Try to get back into the boat when you are away from shore. Getting the water out of a kayak while treading water is impossible without a hand pump; you can have one mounted permanently on your boat or you can carry a portable one. You should be able to right a canoe with two people, getting most of the water out (keep a bailer fastened to a thwart). Getting back in is another story. . . . Good luck!

Public Access and Camping

We have listed only public access locations; however, private property bounds most bodies of water. Never launch your boat from private land without getting permission first, and do not get out along the shore on land posted as private. Never camp on posted land. Disputes between recreational users of land and private property owners can get tense. Cooperation will help keep bodies of water open to paddlers.

Fortunately, within the Green Mountain and White Mountain National Forests and throughout the two states, several hundred thousand acres of public lands and many hundreds of bodies of water remain open for all to enjoy. New Hampshire and Vermont also maintain several dozen public campgrounds and camping areas. Campgrounds charge modest fees, and some camping areas—particularly in the national forests—are free. Note, however, that national forests increasingly require display of a recreation permit when you park your vehicle.

For some lake entries, we have included contact information for nearby public camping areas. For information on private campgrounds, see the extensive lists in the DeLorme atlases.

Respect for the Outdoors

Our wetlands are extremely important ecosystems and home to many rare and endangered species. Even a low-impact pastime such as canoeing or kayaking can substantially affect fragile marsh habitat. Portaging boats can damage plants and erode narrow trails, particularly in the spring and when using portage carts. An unaware paddler can disturb nesting loons and eagles, rare turtles, and fragile bog orchids. And even a canoe or kayak can carry invasive weeds and zebra mussels from one body of water to another—use care to clean off your boat before you visit other bodies of water.

You can go even further than the old adage "Take only photographs; leave only footprints." Carry along a trash bag and pick up the leavings of less thoughtful individuals. If each of us does the same, we will enjoy more attractive places to paddle. While motorboaters tend to have a bad reputation when it comes to leaving trash, paddlers should try to have the opposite reputation—which could come in handy when seeking restrictions on high-impact resource use.

For information on low-impact camping and other uses of fragile habitats, see *Soft Paths: How to Enjoy the Wilderness without Harming It* by Bruce Hampton and David Cole (Stackpole Books, 1995), or *Ultimate Guide to Backcountry Travel* by Michael Lanza (AMC Books, 1999). Also visit Leave No Trace—an organization dedicated to teaching people about how to leave minimal impact on the areas they visit—at www.LNT.org.

What You Will See

Diverse wetlands—among the richest readily accessible ecosystems—provide wonderful opportunities to learn about nature. You can visit saltwater tidal marshes; deep, crystal-clear mountain ponds; and unique bog habitats. You can observe hundreds of species of birds; dozens of species of mammals, turtles, and snakes; and literally thousands of plants. Some quite rare species—such as a delicate bog orchid or a family of otters—provide a real treat when you observe them. But even ordinary plants and animals lead to exciting discoveries and can provide hours of enjoyable observation.

We have described a few interesting plants and animals that you might encounter. We included these descriptions—and accompanying pen-and-ink illustrations by Cathy Johnson—throughout. By learning a little more about these species, you will find them all the more fun to observe—well, maybe not the black flies and mosquitoes.

Have a Great Time

Our goal is to help you find good places to paddle and to appreciate the outdoors. We hope you enjoy using this book as much as we have enjoyed researching and writing it. Let us know what you like or dislike about the places we have described, and tell us about any others you think should be included.

Finally, this guide should not limit the areas you visit; it is a starting point. Other lakes and ponds—literally hundreds more—offer excellent quietwater paddling. Buy some maps and explore. You will find, as we did, that some ponds have no public access. Others bristle with summer homes. But many waters—hidden beaver ponds, quiet meandering channels of slow-moving streams, old millponds with ruins of long-abandoned mills, and bird-filled estuaries—will offer hours of discovery. You can reveal their wonderful secrets, or keep them to yourself. And that is as it should be.

How to Use This Book

For each lake or pond included in this book, we have provided a short description and map. Most maps show roads or highways that provide access to the body of water, as well as boat-launch sites. Some launch sites have boat ramps suitable for trailered motorboats as well as canoes and kayaks, but many require a carry to the water—we have not distinguished between these types of launch sites on the maps.

We have designed the maps and descriptions in this guide to accompany road maps. If unfamiliar with your destination, you should also use a good highway map or the DeLorme Mapping Company's *New Hampshire Atlas and Gazetteer* (12th ed., 1999) or *Vermont Atlas and Gazetteer* (10th ed., 2000); www.delorme.com. We have keyed each lake to these atlases, which divide each state into thirty-six 10" x 15" maps. These detailed, 1:100,000-scale maps include most—but not all—boat-access locations, road names, campgrounds, parks, and other pertinent information. For more detail and information on topography, marsh areas, etc., refer to the 7.5-minute, 1:24,000-scale USGS topographic maps that we have listed at the beginning of each section.

Happy paddling!

Map Legend

⌂	Tent site
♟	Lean-to
🎪	Picnic area
Å	State or federal campground
⛺	Private campground
⌣	Boat access
P	Parking area
⸬	Marsh
☼	Peak
━━━	Interstate highway
───	State highway
·-·-·-·	Paved road
═══	Less-traveled road
= = = =	Rough dirt road
··········	Footpath
═══	River
───	Stream

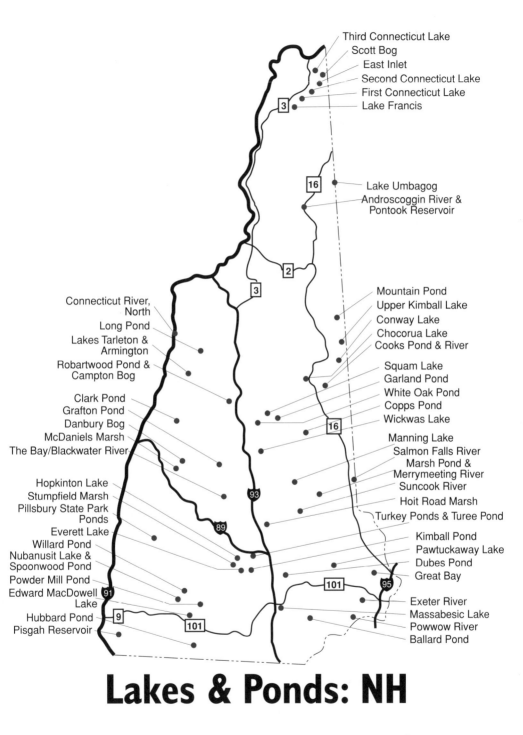

Third Connecticut Lake
Scott Bog
East Inlet
Second Connecticut Lake
First Connecticut Lake
Lake Francis

Lake Umbagog
Androscoggin River &
Pontook Reservoir

Connecticut River,
North
Long Pond
Lakes Tarleton &
Armington
Robartwood Pond &
Campton Bog

Clark Pond
Grafton Pond
Danbury Bog
McDaniels Marsh
The Bay/Blackwater River

Hopkinton Lake
Stumpfield Marsh
Pillsbury State Park
Ponds
Everett Lake
Willard Pond
Nubanusit Lake &
Spoonwood Pond
Powder Mill Pond
Edward MacDowell
Lake
Hubbard Pond
Pisgah Reservoir

Mountain Pond
Upper Kimball Lake
Conway Lake
Chocorua Lake
Cooks Pond & River

Squam Lake
Garland Pond
White Oak Pond
Copps Pond
Wickwas Lake

Manning Lake
Salmon Falls River
Marsh Pond &
Merrymeeting River
Suncook River
Hoit Road Marsh
Turkey Ponds & Turee Pond

Kimball Pond
Pawtuckaway Lake
Dubes Pond
Great Bay

Exeter River
Massabesic Lake
Powwow River
Ballard Pond

Lakes & Ponds: NH

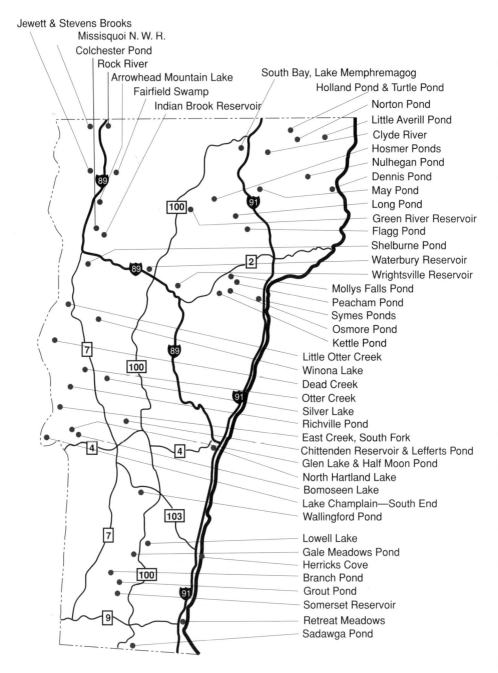

Jewett & Stevens Brooks
Missisquoi N. W. R.
Colchester Pond
Rock River
Arrowhead Mountain Lake
Fairfield Swamp
Indian Brook Reservoir

South Bay, Lake Memphremagog
Holland Pond & Turtle Pond
Norton Pond
Little Averill Pond
Clyde River
Hosmer Ponds
Nulhegan Pond
Dennis Pond
May Pond
Long Pond
Green River Reservoir
Flagg Pond
Shelburne Pond
Waterbury Reservoir
Wrightsville Reservoir
Mollys Falls Pond
Peacham Pond
Symes Ponds
Osmore Pond
Kettle Pond
Little Otter Creek
Winona Lake
Dead Creek
Otter Creek
Silver Lake
Richville Pond
East Creek, South Fork
Chittenden Reservoir & Lefferts Pond
Glen Lake & Half Moon Pond
North Hartland Lake
Bomoseen Lake
Lake Champlain—South End
Wallingford Pond
Lowell Lake
Gale Meadows Pond
Herricks Cove
Branch Pond
Grout Pond
Somerset Reservoir
Retreat Meadows
Sadawga Pond

Lakes & Ponds: VT

Pisgah Reservoir
Winchester, NH

MAPS

New Hampshire Atlas: Map 19

USGS Quadrangle: Winchester

INFORMATION

Area: 110 acres

Prominent fish species: Smallmouth bass, pickerel, and crappie

Contact information: For more information and a trail map, call Pisgah State Park—603-239-8153

Hidden deep in the hills of 13,000-acre Pisgah State Park in the southwestern corner of New Hampshire, Pisgah Reservoir remains one of the most remote bodies of water included in this book. When you reach the end of Reservoir Road, you still have a steep half-mile carry with switchbacks. With a light, 40-pound canoe, the hike in takes about 20 minutes. If you have a heavy boat, or one without a good portage yoke, plan on frequent rests. When you get to the very steep switchback, you are almost there. At the trail intersection, turn left to get to the dam for launching, or simply head through the woods to the lake, which you will see from the trail. All the hard work is worth it!

This gorgeous reservoir, small but highly varied, offers many islands, deep inlets, and hidden coves to explore. With a total length of about a mile and a half, the reservoir offers more than five miles of shoreline to paddle—through quite deep, exceptionally clean, and unspoiled water. The surrounding heavily wooded shoreline supports

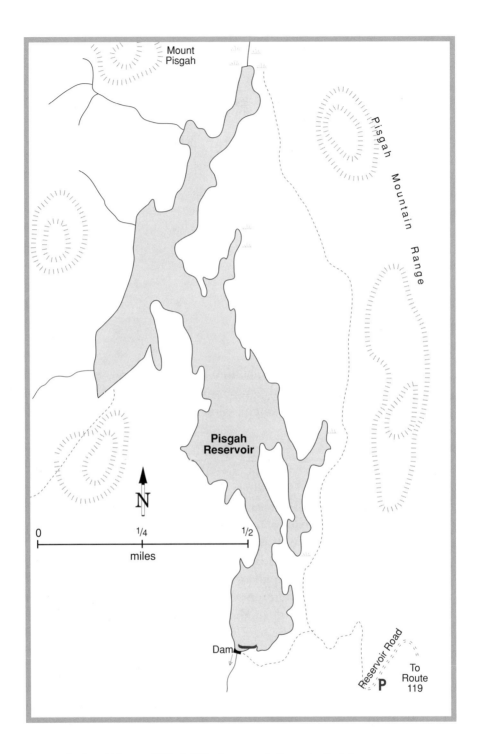

Mount
Pisgah

Pisgah Mountain Range

Pisgah
Reservoir

N

0   1/4   1/2
miles

Dam

Reservoir Road

P   To
Route
119

hemlock and white pine as the dominant species, interspersed with various hardwoods, including red oak, beech, red maple, and yellow and white birch. At the water's edge, the banks often grow thick with blueberry bushes. Most of the shoreline is rocky, with some marshy areas in the longer inlets, where you might see nesting ducks during the spring. At the extreme northern end and in some of the shallow inlets, pond vegetation can grow fairly thick, but most of the lake remains open.

Besides the main reservoir, Pisgah State Park sports a number of smaller ponds, including Fullam, Lily, Baker, Tufts, and Kilburn. Most are located in the northern half of the park, reachable via hiking trails or unimproved dirt roads. Access points to Pisgah State Park occur on all sides, with a half-dozen parking areas at trailheads. Pick up a trail map in the mailbox at the end of Reservoir Road, or at one of the other access points to the park.

GETTING THERE

From Hinsdale, go east on Route 119 and turn left onto Reservoir Road 2.4 miles east of the junction with Route 63 north. The gate is open daily, from 9:00 A.M. until usually around dusk, from the end of mud season until snow makes passage difficult. During the week, the gate is sometimes left open all night, allowing a much earlier start in the morning.

Hubbard Pond
Rindge, NH

MAPS
New Hampshire Atlas: Map 20
USGS Quadrangle: Peterborough South

INFORMATION
Area: 187 acres
Prominent fish species: Smallmouth bass and pickerel

Hubbard Pond, a hidden treasure in southern New Hampshire, offers much to the quietwater paddler. Surrounded on three sides by Annett State Forest, Hubbard Pond presents a wonderful place to visit in any season. We prefer spring and autumn, because wildlife viewing peaks in the spring, and fall foliage blends against the spectacular backdrop of Mount Monadnock—and you will not have to share the pond. You might want to visit in midsummer anyway, when the prolific highbush blueberries ripen.

Hubbard Pond seems a lot larger than it appears at first glance because of the many marshy inlets and islands. Weeds choke most of the shallow lake, making it a great spot for painted turtles, ducks, wading birds, beaver, and the occasional otter, which we have seen here in both spring and fall. In the spring, we watched a pair of large snapping turtles mating and an osprey wheel overhead, searching the water for fish. By midsummer, though, vegetation can make the going pretty difficult on the pond's shallowest parts.

White pine, hemlock, and other conifers dominate the wooded shoreline. Hummocks, covered with leatherleaf, also support lots of pitcher plant, tamarack, and black spruce, trees typical of more

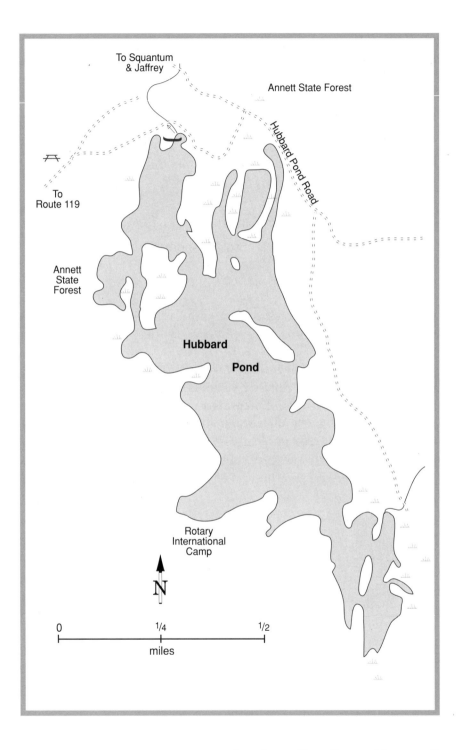

To Squantum
& Jaffrey

Annett State Forest

Hubbard Pond Road

To
Route 119

Annett
State
Forest

Hubbard

Pond

Rotary
International
Camp

N

| 0 | 1/4 | 1/2 |

miles

The northern pitcher plant, *Sarracenia purpurea*, has the widest distribution of all the North American pitcher-plant species.

northerly locations. Despite the marshiness along much of the shore, the ground rises quickly on the eastern shore and most islands, so you can get up on solid ground for a picnic lunch. Up on the high banks you will see plenty of evidence of beaver cutting saplings.

Getting There

From the junction of Route 119 and Cathedral Road in Rindge (1.6 miles east of where Route 119 crosses over Route 202), take Cathedral Road northeast (follow signs for Cathedral of the Pines and Annett State Forest). After passing the entrance to Cathedral of the Pines, turn right onto the access road at a sharp curve (2.3 miles from Route 119 or 0.7 mile beyond the Cathedral of the Pines entrance). Go 0.4 mile to the access at the outlet.

Edward MacDowell Lake
Dublin and Peterborough, NH

MAPS

New Hampshire Atlas: Map 20

USGS Quadrangles: Marlborough and Peterborough North

INFORMATION

Area: 165 acres

Prominent fish species: Largemouth bass and pickerel

Camping: All state-park campground reservations—603-271-3628 or www.nhparks.state.nh.us; Greenfield State Park—603-547-3497; Monadnock State Park—603-532-8862

Contact Information: U.S. Army Corps of Engineers—603-924-3431

Though MacDowell Lake does not even appear on some maps, we found a picturesque place with ample room to paddle, especially early in the season. Maintained by the Army Corps of Engineers, the whole area consists of sinewy channels that penetrate a shallow marshland with lots of floating islands, inlets, and channels to explore. The northern channel twists and winds with tight turns. We saw Canada geese, tree swallows, several great blue herons, wood duck, yellow pond lily, and some swamp rose. Fragrant waterlily, pickerelweed, and buttonbush line many of the channels.

If you paddle around to the right from the boat access, you come to a little waterfall and riffle with lots of rounded boulders. If you feel adventuresome, carry up over this and paddle upstream a distance. You will come to some beaver dams that impound more water. Few people come up here to this very scenic area. Mind you, you might regret

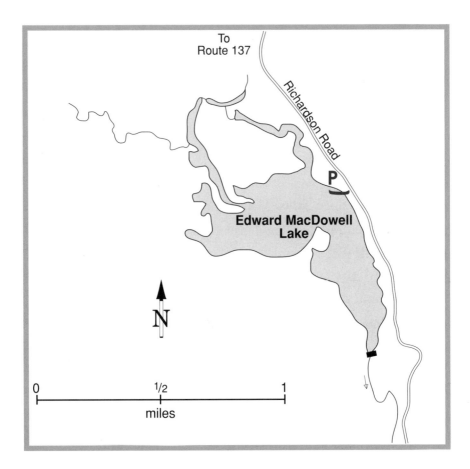

trying to drag your boat through the riffle or through the poison ivy in the woods, but we felt it was well worth the effort.

Though the Army Corps allows motors, the swampy, shallow, weedy nature of the place will preclude much activity. We saw only canoes and kayaks when we paddled here and felt it was quite easy to find solitude.

GETTING THERE

From the junction of Routes 123 and 137 in Hancock, travel south on Route 137. Two miles after passing Sargent Camp Road, turn left onto Spring Road at a sharp bend in Route 137. Go 0.4 mile to Richardson Road on the right; the access is off Richardson Road in another 0.5 mile.

From Route 101, travel north on Route 137 for a little more than a mile. Watch for Spring Road going off to the right, and follow as above.

Nubanusit Lake and Spoonwood Pond

Hancock and Nelson, NH

MAPS

New Hampshire Atlas: Map 20

USGS Quadrangles: Marlborough and Stoddard

INFORMATION

Nubanusit Lake area: 645 acres

Spoonwood Pond area: 144 acres

Prominent fish species: Smallmouth bass, perch, pickerel, smelt, brook trout, brown trout, lake trout, rainbow trout, and landlocked salmon

Camping: All state-park campground reservations—603-271-3628 or www.nhparks.state.nh.us; Greenfield State Park—603-547-3497; Monadnock State Park—603-532-8862

Conservation education: The Harris Center, Kings Highway, Hancock, NH 03449—603-525-3394

Nubanusit Lake would be one of southern New Hampshire's real gems if motorboating were more restricted (personal watercraft are not allowed). On a summer weekend, the speedboats and water-skiers can be oppressive and even dangerous. The lake also can suffer from large wind-driven waves. Fortunately, one can paddle northwest from the boat launch and then around the bend to the southwest. At the dam, carry your boat a short distance over to the outlet of Spoonwood Pond, and you are free at last.

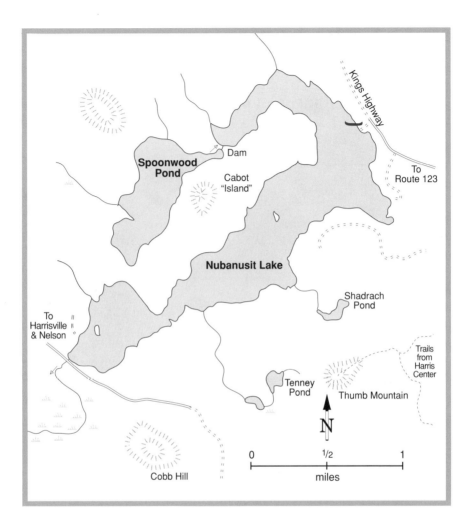

Spoonwood Pond is well protected, inaccessible by car and off-limits to motorboats. Like Nubanusit, Spoonwood has a rocky shoreline, and in some places giant slabs of granite extend down to and into the water. Large crystals of feldspar, mica, and garnet, along with iron deposits, poke out of the granite, making it look almost like a conglomerate rock. From Spoonwood Pond, you can hike through heavily wooded, rocky terrain on Cabot "Island" (not really an island), owned by Keene State College. You can cross over to the southern end of Nubanusit Lake if you want to watch motorboats, or you can stick to the eastern side of the lake and hike on wilderness land managed by the Harris Center.

Bald eagles, *Haliaeetus leucocephalus*, are beginning to breed once again in New Hampshire and Vermont.

Both Nubanusit and Spoonwood have exceptionally clean water. The considerable depth (96 feet in Nubanusit and 70 feet in Spoonwood) and lack of surrounding marshland make the waters oligotrophic, having very low biological productivity, allowing you to peer into the depths of the crystal-clear water. The lakes show almost no evidence of tannic and other organic acids that result from plant decay and turn the water yellowish brown. Both have excellent reputations for coldwater fishing, including for several species of trout.

In late June, mountain laurel blooms in huge, ten-foot-tall clumps, along with sheep laurel and many other densely packed shoreline shrubs. We saw a red-breasted merganser with a raft of young and watched two adult bald eagles fish Spoonwood Pond. Bald eagles did not nest in New Hampshire from 1949 to 1988; in 1989, eagles began nesting successfully on Umbagog Lake. Then in 1998 a pair started to build a nest near Spoonwood Pond. They hatched two chicks in May

1999, but the chicks fell prey to raccoons. In 2000, the chicks again failed to survive, this time succumbing to either a May heat wave or a winged predator, such as a great horned owl.

If you want to visit the Harris Center for Conservation Education, drive a few minutes down Kings Highway from the boat access. The Harris Center includes a network of hiking trails and a wonderful old estate where it holds educational programs. A trail from the Harris Center leads to Thumb Mountain, which overlooks Tenney and Shadrach Ponds.

GETTING THERE

From Route 9 in South Stoddard, take Route 123 southeast 4.8 miles. Make a sharp right onto Hunt's Pond Road. Go another 0.4 mile and turn right onto Kings Highway, which is not much of a highway (a sign to the Harris Center points to the left here). The access is on Landing Road on the left, 1.1 miles down Kings Highway. Parking is at a premium—a reason to visit midweek or before Memorial Day or after Labor Day.

Powder Mill Pond and Contoocook River

Bennington, Greenfield, and Hancock, NH

MAPS

New Hampshire Atlas: Map 20

USGS Quadrangle: Peterborough North

INFORMATION

Area: 200 acres

Prominent fish species: Largemouth bass and pickerel

Camping: All state-park campground reservations—603-271-3628 or www.nhparks.state.nh.us; Greenfield State Park—603-547-3497; Monadnock State Park—603-532-8862

A dam on the Contoocook River in Bennington, New Hampshire, holds back unspoiled Powder Mill Pond. A few unobtrusive old farms front the western shore. The main drawback: road noise from Route 202, which runs quite close to the pond at the northern end. Since Powder Mill is a public water supply, gasoline-powered motorboats are prohibited, leaving exceptionally clean water, as evidenced by the shells of freshwater mussels along the shore—probably left by raccoons or otters. You will find lots of deep inlets and marshy eddies to explore along the nearly three-mile stretch from the covered bridge on Forest Road at the southern end of the pond to the dam at the northern end.

Close to the northern end of the lake, two islands harbor six or seven unmaintained campsites. (We have not been able to verify if camping is permitted.) Another campsite can be found on the eastern side of the lake, just south of the railroad trestle. You can see the island

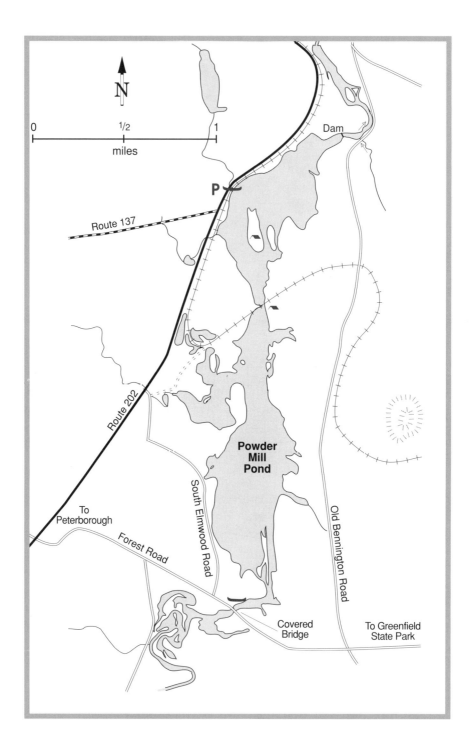

campsites fairly easily from the water; the site on the eastern shore may require more scouting.

You can also paddle south (upstream) under the covered bridge and up the Contoocook River. This section of the river twists and folds tightly, leaving many islands and oxbow curves to explore. Red maple lines the shore, along with oak, hemlock, and other trees. Red maple always has red on it: red buds in the winter, red flowers in the spring, red stems on the leaves in summer, and red leaves in fall. Look for beaver activity in the swamps. We watched a muskrat harvest grass and saw several kingfishers. When you get to the point where the current picks up, lots of barely submerged boulders—hard to see and hard to avoid—will impede your progress.

GETTING THERE

From Peterborough, take Route 202 north. To reach the southern access point, go about 1.0 mile north of the junction with Route 123 west, turn right onto Forest Road, and go 1.2 miles to the covered bridge. Here you can pull over and carry your boat down to the water. To reach the northern access, continue north on Route 202 to just past the junction with Route 137 west, where Route 202 comes quite close to the pond. Park on the west side of the road, just north of the most obvious put-in spot.

Ballard Pond
Derry, NH

MAPS

New Hampshire Atlas: Map 22

USGS Quadrangles: Derry, Salem Depot, Sandown, and Windham

INFORMATION

Area: 89 acres

Prominent fish species: Pickerel

Camping: All state-park campground reservations—603-271-3628 or www.nhparks.state.nh.us; Bear Brook State Park—603-485-9874; Pawtuckaway State Park—603-895-3031

The Division of New Hampshire Forests and Lands maintains the boat access at Ballard State Forest, Taylor Mill Historic Site. Ernest K. Ballard restored the site in 1940. Prior to 1865, Taylor Brook powered a reciprocating sawmill here—a technology invented by the Shakers and later replaced by a more efficient circular saw. Because this popular fishing site gets a lot of traffic, you may drop off your boat by the mill, but you need to park your vehicle back across the road. As we moved the vehicle the second time we paddled here, we helped a small snapping turtle negotiate the traffic. We don't recommend that you do this, but if you pick up one of these beasts, do it by the tail, not the carapace; otherwise its long neck can reach your hands. Even a relatively small snapper can do serious damage to your digits.

As we paddled out on a perfectly still morning with glasslike water, a family of Canada geese cast rippling Vs as they beat a hasty retreat ahead of us. This wonderful spot, free from development, hosts many

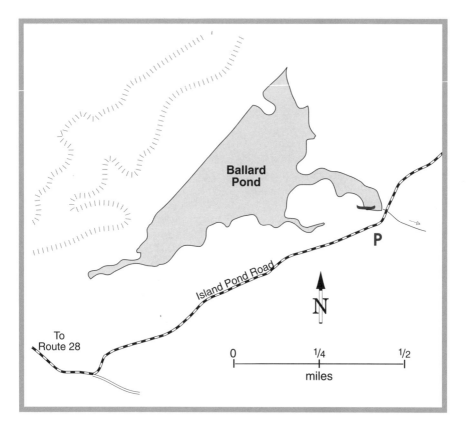

nesting waterfowl. The small millpond hides the main pond from view. Portage up over the remains of an old concrete bridge at the end of the millpond and down into a vast expanse of aquatic vegetation. We thought of Monet as we paddled through a sea of huge, fragrant water-lily blossoms during our late-August visit, but a thick carpet of aquatic vegetation hampered our explorations. Paddling here certainly would be easier in the spring, before the emergent vegetation lays claim to the water's surface.

This shallow pond harbors huge amounts of aquatic vegetation that eventually dies back each fall, accumulating more rapidly than it can break down and settling to the bottom to decompose anaerobically. Your paddle may stir up methane-rich marsh gas and the sulfury smell of hydrogen sulfide. The decaying plant matter also releases tannic acids, which stain the water a yellow-brown.

Large patches of fragrant waterlily, _Nymphaea odorata_, cover the surface of Ballard Pond in the summer.

As we paddled by, large numbers of painted turtles and frogs dove for cover under the water shield, pickerelweed, and lily pads. If you paddle here midsummer, look for the meandering channel—probably the old stream bed that is too deep for pickerelweed—that wends its way back up the pond to the end. Finding this channel may take a few minutes, but it will make your paddling easier.

GETTING THERE

From Derry, take either Route 28 or Bypass 28 to the point where they meet east of town. At the stoplight at this junction, take Island Pond Road east for 3.7 miles. The boat access is on the left at the site of the old Taylor Mill. Pull in here to drop off your boat, then drive back across the road to park your car in the large parking area.

Massabesic Lake
Auburn and Manchester, NH

MAPS

New Hampshire Atlas: Map 22

USGS Quadrangles: Candia, Derry, Manchester North, and Manchester South

INFORMATION

Area: 2,512 acres

Prominent fish species: Largemouth bass, smallmouth bass, pickerel, northern pike, perch, brook trout, brown trout, and rainbow trout

Camping: All state-park campground reservations—603-271-3628 or www.nhparks.state.nh.us; Bear Brook State Park—603-485-9874; Pawtuckaway State Park—603-895-3031

Because Massabesic Lake serves as the water supply for the city of Manchester, the city prohibits swimming and water-skiing, and a portion of the lake remains off-limits to all boating. Despite this—and in part because of it—Massabesic offers superb paddling. The extremely clean and crystal-clear water, with its rocky bottom, supports an excellent smallmouth bass fishery. The limited development along the shore seems even less intrusive because of the prohibition on swimming. Indeed, it is a real surprise to find such a large and relatively pristine lake so close to New Hampshire's largest city.

Because of its smaller size and greater shoreline variation, we prefer paddling the lake's southern section. The generally rocky shoreline gives way to dense woods farther inland. White pine, red pine, red maple, white birch, and red oak dominate, but you will also see some

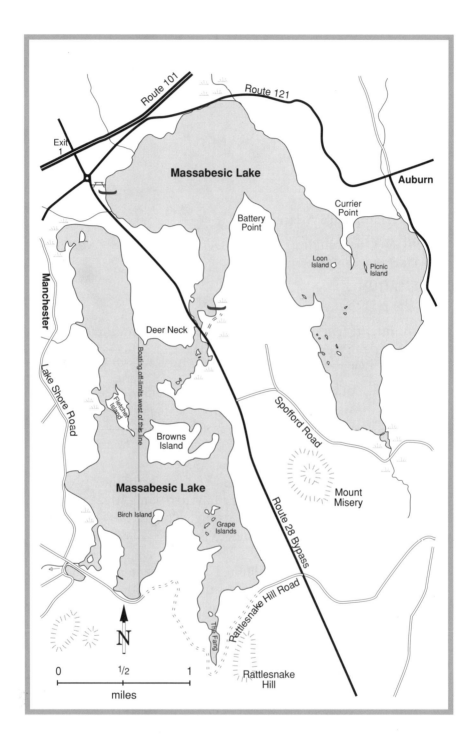

Route 101

Route 121

Exit
1

Massabesic Lake

Auburn

Currier
Point

Battery
Point

Loon
Island

Picnic
Island

Manchester

Deer Neck

Boating off-limits west of this line

Lake Shore Road

Fletcher
Island

Browns
Island

Spofford Road

Massabesic Lake

Birch Island

Grape
Islands

Mount
Misery

Route 28 Bypass

Rattlesnake Hill Road

The Fang

Rattlesnake
Hill

N

0   1/2   1

miles

black gum (*Nyssa sylvatica*) growing along the water's edge. One of the first trees to turn red in the fall, black gum's brilliant foliage really stands out. A few surviving American chestnut trees also grow here. If you visit in midsummer, you should find lots of highbush blueberry. Also keep an eye out for loons, which often nest here. Be careful not to disturb them.

The Grape Islands near the southern end of the lake offer superb paddling, as does the deep cove called the Fang at the southern tip. Near the inlet from the upper section of Massabesic, close to Route 28 Bypass, a small marshy area usually can be paddled. Watch for great blue herons, wood ducks, other assorted water birds, and possibly beaver here.

Because of the many motorboats and sailboats that ply the waters of Massabesic, we would avoid the upper end of the lake, especially on busy summer weekends. On a breezy day, either stick to the more protected southern end or paddle one of the smaller bodies of water in the region.

GETTING THERE

The best access to the southern section is from a channel connecting the lake's two halves. From the junction of Route 28 Bypass and Route 101 (Exit 1), drive south on Route 28 Bypass for 1.7 miles. The pullout is on the left, just after crossing the bridge over the channel. You can quickly paddle south under the bridge to reach the quieter southern section.

Access to the upper section is at a large park and picnic area on the east side of Route 28 Bypass, just south of the circle where Route 121 intersects.

Powwow River
Kingston, NH

MAPS
New Hampshire Atlas: Map 23

USGS Quadrangle: Kingston

INFORMATION
River length: 2 miles

Prominent fish species: Smallmouth bass and pickerel

Standing at the boat access, a sea of aquatic vegetation spreading out over a wide expanse of marsh greets you. From here, just across the road from Powwow Pond, you can paddle down through a channel in the vegetation to Country Pond. We have chosen not to include either Powwow Pond or Country Pond, because of shoreline development and boat traffic, but to focus instead on the Powwow River section that connects the two. Except for a power line, this marsh remains fairly pristine. We paddled here totally alone on a bright Saturday in mid-June.

It took us all morning to paddle down and back, mostly because we spent time identifying much of the flora along the way and exploring side channels. We suspect that the going will be more difficult late in the summer. Besides huge patches of fragrant waterlily, pickerelweed, water celery, water shield, and various species of sedge and pondweed, we found some nice patches of yellow crowfoot, *Ranunculus flabellaris*, in bloom. It has typically gorgeous yellow buttercup flowers, but the very finely divided underwater leaves look like those of water marigold (aster family) or coontail. In some deeper water, we also found floating heart (*Nymphoides cordata*), a waterlily-like member of the gentian

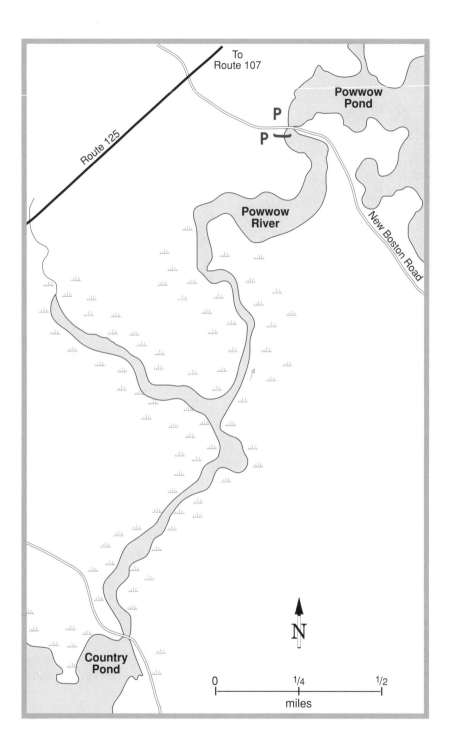

To
Route 107

Powwow
Pond

P
P

Route 125

Powwow
River

New Boston Road

N

Country
Pond

0	1/4	1/2
miles

A painted turtle, *Chrysemys picta*, basks on a sunny day on the Powwow River.

family, in bloom. What struck us most, perhaps, was the decidedly pinkish cast to the usually pure-white flowers of the fragrant waterlilies.

On this sunny day, painted turtles sunned themselves wherever they could clamber out of the water, and we spotted two water snakes (*Nerodia sipedon*), one of them very fat, out sunning. Bullfrogs tried to hide among the lily pads as we passed by. All the typical marsh birds appeared in profusion; we especially noted the large number of common yellowthroats calling from the brushy shores.

GETTING THERE
From Kingston at the junction of Routes 107 and 125, take Route 125 south for 1.0 mile, turn left onto New Boston Road, and go 0.4 mile to the access on the right. Park on either side of the road.

Exeter River
Exeter, NH

MAPS

New Hampshire Atlas: Map 23

USGS Quadrangle: Exeter

INFORMATION

Length: 6 miles

Prominent fish species: Brook, brown, and rainbow trout

Huge trees drape out over the water of this meandering, slow-moving stream. Neither we nor the several other canoes and kayaks that shared this water with us on a June Saturday could detect any current. We could not get over the size of the trees, particularly the white oak and white pine. Some of these stately trees certainly exceed 100 feet in height. High tree-species diversity kept us occupied as we identified red and white oak, basswood, beech, and shagbark hickory, among others.

Except for the campground along Route 108, which does not intrude all that much, the Exeter River corridor provides a pretty serene place to paddle. The lack of development here helps explain why we heard a continuous chorus of orioles singing their melodious song from the treetops as we paddled several miles upriver from Exeter's Gilman Park put-in. Both the main and side channels provide opportunities for exploring.

We spotted a few different species of pondweed, one with a very long leaf lying flat along the surface of the water (look for brownish leaves with veins parallel to the leaf's long axis). Viburnum bloomed along the banks. Dead trees provided perching areas for birds and lent a somewhat somber character to the banks. Beaver cuttings crowded the

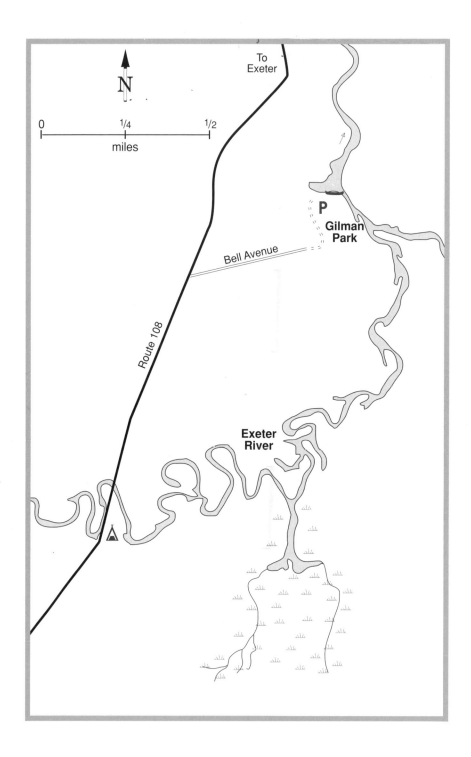

A gorgeous rose, a garden escapee, blooms in profusion on the banks of the Exeter River near Route 108.

shoreline in places. While pondweed seemed to dominate the water's surface near shore, buttonbush held sway on the banks. Up near Route 108, along the right shore, we found an escaped rose in electric bloom, with clusters of 25 or so blossoms at the end of each branch, some hanging over the water and some actually in the water. The small white blossoms of this truly gorgeous plant had a slight pink cast and a faint odor.

Bird-species diversity is also high along this lowland riverine area, so it would be a good idea to bring your binoculars, though you might have to crane your neck to catch a glimpse of the orioles and other tree-top species.

GETTING THERE

From the junction of Routes 27, 101, and 108 in downtown Exeter, head south on Route 108. Go 0.7 mile, passing Phillips Exeter Academy, and turn left on Bell Avenue, just after a bridge. The entrance to Exeter's Gilman Park, open from dawn to dusk, is 0.3 mile down this road.

Pillsbury State Park Ponds
Washington, NH

MAPS

New Hampshire Atlas: Map 26

USGS Quadrangle: Lovewell Mountain

INFORMATION

May Pond area: 149 acres

Prominent fish species: Largemouth bass and pickerel

Camping: All state-park campground reservations—603-271-3628 or www.nhparks.state.nh.us; Pillsbury State Park—603-863-2860

The string of four small ponds in Pillsbury State Park, the headwaters of the Ashuelot River, offers superb quietwater paddling, particularly if you camp here overnight. Butterfield Pond, the farthest downstream, extends from a dam next to Route 31. A narrow, rocky strait connects Butterfield to May Pond, the largest and deepest of the lakes. We saw loons on both May and Butterfield.

A dozen or so camping sites occur along the northern shore of May Pond, some beautifully situated on the water. They remain open year-round and are free of charge in the off-season.

Near the eastern end of May Pond, you can portage along an open trail and road up to Mill Pond, or you can drive. Mill Pond, quite small and shallow, has much of its surface covered with aquatic vegetation during the summer months, making paddling difficult. But you should see more wildlife here, such as the pair of hooded mergansers we watched feeding in late April.

The adventurous can take out at the inlet into Mill Pond and portage up to North Pond, the most remote of the four ponds. Take out on the right side of the inlet (facing upstream) and carry a few dozen

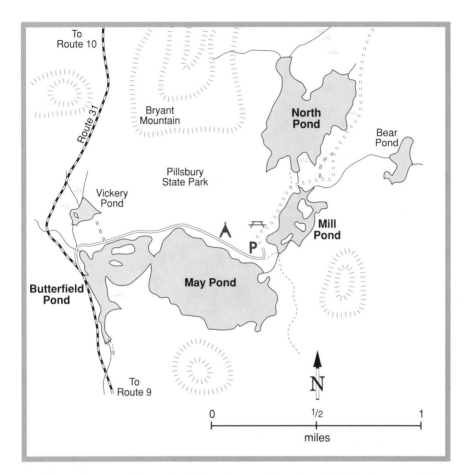

yards to the woods road. Take the road to the left (back toward the parking area at Mill Pond), cross the bridge, and then take the trail to the right after 50 or 60 yards. This trail leads a few hundred yards to North Pond. You also can portage up from Mill Pond, with a longer carry.

North Pond, a rich fen, has the feel of northern Canadian wilderness, with birds galore and one of the most curious of plant species: the northern pitcher plant. Look for these insect-eating reddish plants on the numerous low islands, sphagnum-moss hummocks, or shoreline amid the dense creeping cranberry bushes and other heaths. Like Mill Pond, North Pond sports a fairly thick mat of summer vegetation, but that should not stop you from enjoying this bit of wilderness.

When you tire of paddling, you can enjoy some of the wonderful trails around these ponds and through the hills, including hikes into the

The most remote of the four ponds in Pillsbury State Park, North Pond has a nice picnic area along the northeastern shore.

smaller Vickery and Bear Ponds. Pick up a map at the park office, just as you turn into the park from Route 31.

GETTING THERE

From Hillsborough, take Route 9 west and turn north onto Route 31. The park entrance is on the right about 13.5 miles from Route 9.

From Goshen, take Route 10 south and turn left onto Route 31. The park entrance is on the left in about 4.7 miles.

Willard Pond
Antrim, NH

MAPS

New Hampshire Atlas: Map 26

USGS Quadrangle: Stoddard

INFORMATION

Area: 98 acres

Prominent fish species: Brook trout and rainbow trout

Contact information: Audubon Society of New Hampshire—603-224-9909

Hidden in the southwestern part of New Hampshire, protected by an Audubon Society preserve, Willard Pond is simply breathtaking. The Audubon Society prohibits gasoline-powered motorboats and restricts the fishing to loons, kingfishers, and fly fishers. The one privately owned house at the southern end of the pond, set back from the water, does not intrude on the pond.

Moss-covered granite boulders dot the shoreline, and the forested hillsides harbor mountain laurel, aspen, yellow birch, beech, red oak, red maple, and white pine. The crystal-clear water allows you to see the bottom through at least 15 feet of water. The clarity of the water actually is disconcerting, because at first glance a boulder two feet underwater seems lodged just under the surface film—then you glide right over it.

A wildlife preserve owned and managed by the New Hampshire Audubon Society nearly surrounds the entire area. In addition to observing birds from the boat, birders can make use of two trails that circle a substantial portion of the pond. The singing of warblers,

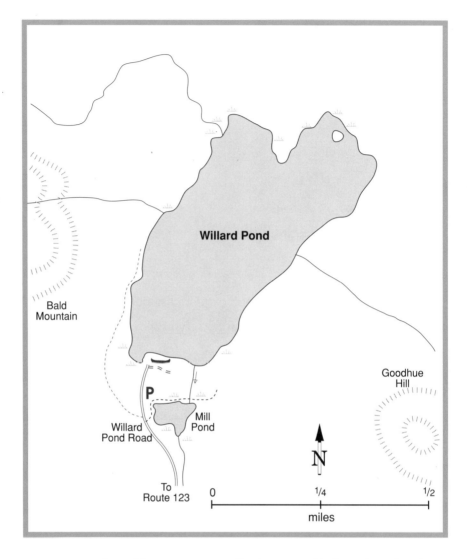

Willard Pond

Bald
Mountain

Goodhue
Hill

P

Mill
Pond

Willard
Pond Road

To
Route 123

N

0   1/4   1/2

miles

sparrows, and a wide assortment of other songbirds makes the shore
come alive. You may also hear the enchanting wail of the pond's nesting loon pair (be very careful not to disturb nesting loons). Several
marshy inlets provide ideal habitat for ducks and herons. The property
obviously is well managed; in fact, we had a lot of trouble finding a
piece of trash to take out.

Though small, Willard Pond is one of the most pristine bodies of water in southern New Hampshire—perfect for a quiet morning of solo paddling.

GETTING THERE

In Hancock, at the junction of Routes 123 and 137, take Route 123 northwest for 3.1 miles. Turn right, going nearly straight, onto Davenport Road. Davenport intersects with Willard Pond Road in 0.7 mile, and the pond is another 1.0 mile down this road.

In Stoddard, at the junction of Routes 123 and 9, go southeast on Route 123 for 3.2 miles and turn left onto Willard Pond Road; the access is 1.5 miles down this road.

You can drive right to the water to unload your boat, but you must drive back and park your vehicle at the large parking lot.

Stumpfield Marsh, Hopkinton Lake, and Everett Lake

Hopkinton and Weare, NH

MAPS

New Hampshire Atlas: Map 27

USGS Quadrangles: Henniker, Hopkinton, and Weare

INFORMATION

Stumpfield Marsh area: 95 acres

Hopkinton Lake area: 500 acres

Everett Lake area: 150 acres

Prominent fish species: Largemouth bass and pickerel

Camping: All state-park campground reservations—603-271-3628 or www.nhparks.state.nh.us; Bear Brook State Park—603-485-9874; Pillsbury State Park—603-863-2860

Clough State Park: Entrance fee is $2.50/person—603-529-7112

Stumpfield Marsh. Of the three locations presented here, Stumpfield Marsh is the smallest and feels the most remote. No development encroaches on the layered hillsides surrounding this wide, shallow marsh. After banging into a few barely submerged stumps, the reason for the marsh's name becomes apparent. Because the shallow waters of the marsh support abundant vegetation, paddling here can be a challenge in summer and early fall.

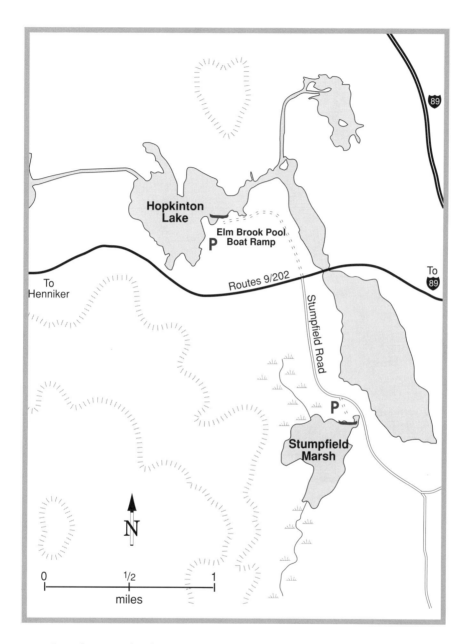

Standing at the boat access, note the dead trees with great blue heron nests out in the middle of the marsh. We paddled here twice, once in October and once in late April when herons were on their nests.

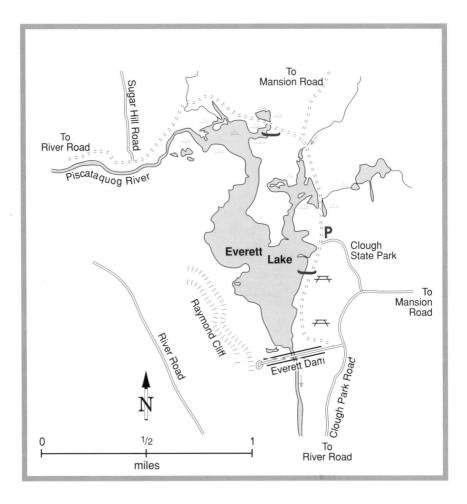

Though fall colors and light-colored dead trees reflecting on the pond make paddling here in the fall gorgeous, we definitely prefer the spring. Not only do you get to see the herons, but you can also paddle farther back into the marsh.

We also saw lots of ducks and geese, in spring with young and in fall during migration. Mallards, red-breasted mergansers, wood ducks, Canada geese, and other waterfowl stop off here. Note the spent shells of huge aquatic snails in the shallows and the workings of the active beaver colony.

Hopkinton Lake. The varied scenery and forested hillsides of Hopkinton Lake, along with diversity of aquatic habitat, make it an

Nearly fully fledged great blue herons, *Ardea herodias*, wait to be fed.

enjoyable place to paddle, if you can ignore the noise from Routes 9/202 and I-89, which run close by. We prefer the northeast arm and the long connector that leads to it; we could hear I-89 off in the distance, but it did not intrude too much—on us or the resident beaver colony. Yellow pond lily and fragrant waterlily cover the shallow, marshy areas, along with pondweed and other aquatic plants. In the northeast arm, aquatic vegetation covered perhaps 50 percent of the surface area. We found quite a bit of buttonbush, other shrubs, and fern growing in the understory.

When we paddled here on a bright sunny October day, we encountered only canoes, kayaks, and one lone eight-horsepower motorboat. Because of shallow water, barely submerged stumps, and abundant aquatic vegetation, this place may not suffer from too much high-speed motor traffic in the summer. We imagine that fishing must be good, with all of the drowned stumps providing cover.

Everett Lake. Created in 1962 by an Army Corps of Engineers flood-control dam on the Piscataquog River, Everett Lake offers pleasant paddling, picnicking, and swimming. Clough State Park oversees the facilities and prohibits motors on the 150-acre lake; the only development consists of the dam and recreational facilities. Though the large 250-foot-high dam looms over much of the lake, if you paddle toward the northern end, through the winding, marshy channels full of pickerelweed and waterlily, it looks and feels much more natural, with lots of nooks and crannies to explore.

On the marshy northeastern end you should see great blue herons, painted turtles, and various ducks. On the larger, northwestern arm of the lake, you reach a sandy-bottomed inlet creek lined with alder and willow, but this creek is too shallow to paddle more than a few hundred feet. Most of the lake shoreline is open and sandy with white pine on the higher land. Many potential picnic sites dot the shores.

GETTING THERE

Stumpfield Marsh. The unmarked access is hard to find. From I-89, Exit 5, go west on Routes 9/202 for 1.7 miles and turn left onto Stumpfield Road 0.1 mile after crossing Hopkinton Lake far below. The very-hard-to-see access road goes off through the woods after 0.8 mile.

Coming from the west from Henniker on Routes 9/202, Stumpfield Road goes right 2.3 miles after Route 127 goes off left (north) to Hopkinton Dam.

Hopkinton Lake. From I-89, Exit 5, follow the directions as above; however, turn right 0.1 mile after crossing Hopkinton Lake at a sign that says Elm Brook Pool Boat Ramp (across from Stumpfield Road). The access is 0.6 mile down this road.

Everett Lake. From Goffstown, where Routes 13 and 114 split, take Route 114 west. Follow signs for the dam and state park. Turn right onto Parker Station Road. Take the right fork after 1.2 miles and turn right onto Clough Park Road in another 2.6 miles. The entrance to the park is another 2.2 miles on the left. After paying the entrance fee, turn right at the T.

When Clough State Park is closed, you can get onto the lake by continuing past the park entrance (passing Alexander Road to the left) for 1.9 miles and bearing left onto Mansion Road. In just over 0.5 mile, Mansion Road curves sharply to the right; continue straight on a poorly maintained road marked: HOP-EV Parking. This road leads into a road and trail network for off-road vehicles. Continue on the main road south toward the lake for 1.5 miles. A fork to the left leads into one arm

Large numbers of fragrant waterlily blossoms make paddling Stumpfield Marsh and Hopkinton and Everett Lakes a real pleasure.

of the lake, but there may be a gate here. If you turn right instead, cross over a small inlet to the lake in 0.2 mile. You can pull over by the little bridge and carry your boat down to the water (on the left side of the road). A short paddle past a beaver lodge leads into the main lake. This road winds around the reservoir and leads back to River Road in 2.6 miles.

Turkey Pond, Little Turkey Pond, and Turee Pond

Bow and Concord, NH

MAPS

New Hampshire Atlas: Map 27

USGS Quadrangle: Concord

INFORMATION

Turkey and Little Turkey Ponds area: 339 acres

Prominent fish species: Largemouth bass and pickerel

Turkey and Little Turkey Ponds. This beautiful spot, where St. Paul's School protects much of the land on the east side, lies just outside of Concord. A wonderful biking and hiking path circles the ponds. Though I-89 bisects the two ponds—and provides a fair amount of road noise—we still enjoyed paddling among the fractured granite boulders and tree-lined shores. Several tree-covered islands dot the waterways, adding to the ponds' picturesque beauty. You will find the occasional motorboat here, but we encountered mostly canoes and kayaks at this popular recreational area during our October visit.

We watched a kingfisher dive for fish, fattening up for its soon-to-come journey, and studied flocks of ducks and geese that had stopped off in their fall migration. Various species of aquatic vegetation covered Little Turkey Pond, especially fragrant waterlily, yellow pond lily, and water shield.

Turee Pond. Though we enjoyed paddling on the Turkey Ponds, Turee Pond presents more of a wilderness-type experience for the adventurous paddler. At first glance from the boat access, you see a small, round, seemingly uninteresting pond with lots of open water.

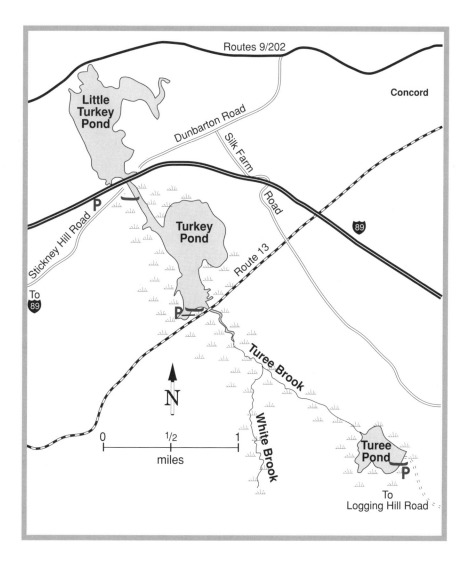

Look carefully at the far shore, though—it is an extensive marsh with sphagnum hummocks covered with tamarack, black spruce, and red maple. If you hanker for a "wilderness" adventure right outside of Concord that includes portaging over several beaver dams, paddle northwest across the pond and down Turee Brook toward Turkey Pond, some two miles distant. We would not attempt this in times of low water.

With an extensive marshland as a backdrop, a massive beaver lodge crowds the channel on Turee Brook.

You will paddle alone among the arrowhead and a diverse assemblage of shoreline shrubs. Red-winged blackbirds will accompany you for the distance, along with yellowthroats and swamp-loving sparrows. We hauled a large snapping turtle partially out of the water to check for leeches—it had two—and saw huge numbers of painted turtles. Several species of fern crowd the bank, along with sundew, leatherleaf, and sweet gale. One large beaver lodge we passed had so much brush stored for winter in the narrow channel that we could barely squeeze by.

As we paddled back to the access and then drove back out the road, past a noisy soccer match, we reveled in the knowledge that such a wonderful and productive spot exists so close to Concord. However, do not go here unless you are willing to work at it—and probably get your feet wet.

Getting there

Turkey Ponds. There are three access points, one just off I-89, Exit 3; one at the southern end on Route 13 (I-89, Exit 2); and the third on the north end off Routes 9/202. The Exit 3, I-89, access is available only to westbound traffic. After exiting and passing under I-89, turn sharply left. The unmarked access is 0.2 mile from the exit, at the dead end on Stickney Hill Road. Carry your boat along the hiking path, veering off to the right just before the bridge over the connecting arm, and head steeply down to the water.

The Exit 2, I-89, access is 1.0 mile south on Clinton Street/ Route 13. Immediately after crossing the bridge leading from Turee Pond, look for an unmarked woods road off to the right.

We did not measure the mileage to the northern access point.

Turee Pond. Turee Pond is located behind Bow High School. From I-89, Exit 1, go south on Logging Hill Road (which becomes Bow Center Road) for 0.8 mile and turn right onto White Rock Hill Road. In 0.4 mile, turn right onto Turee Pond Road. Turn right into the high school and keep to the right until you reach the access.

Kimball Pond
Dunbarton, NH

MAPS

New Hampshire Atlas: Map 27

USGS Quadrangle: Goffstown

INFORMATION

Area: 52 acres

Prominent fish species: Largemouth bass and pickerel

This small, scenic pond, nestled among the hills just to the south of Concord, provides an outstanding place to paddle. Numerous marshy coves and islands await exploration, as does the Great Meadows marsh, which expands out to the north. Conifers dominate the wooded shoreline, with occasional red oak, white birch, and other deciduous trees.

We portaged up into Great Meadows over a beaver dam and enjoyed the solitude, listening to ravens calling their hoarse cries off in the woods as a sharp-shinned hawk alternately flapped and glided overhead. Exploring here and in the marshy coves back on the main pond, expect to find waterlily, water celery, water shield, pickerel-weed, arrowhead, and lots of other aquatic vegetation growing in profusion. Shrubs—including leatherleaf, sweet gale, buttonbush, and lots of sheep laurel—dominate the understory and the marshy islands. We found a large beaver lodge with many red oak cuttings.

We shared the pond with a couple of canoes and kayaks, but because of the islands and the Great Meadows, you can get off by yourself to explore and to enjoy this wonderful, picturesque site.

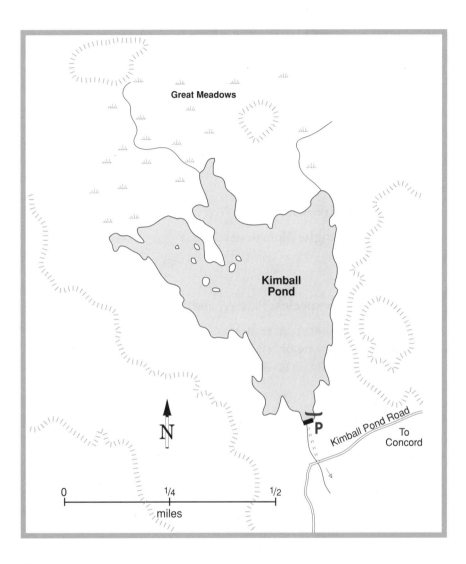

Great Meadows

Kimball
Pond

N

Kimball Pond Road

To
Concord

P

0   1/4   1/2

miles

GETTING THERE

From I-89, Exit 1, go south on Logging Hill Road (which becomes, in turn, Bow Center, Wood Hill, and Twist Hill Roads) for 5.8 miles to Morse Road on the right; watch for a boat-launch sign just before the turn; follow the signs to the access. Take Morse Road for 0.7 mile and turn left onto Montalona Road at the T. Turn right onto Kimball Pond Road in 0.3 mile and go 0.8 mile to the access on the right.

Dubes Pond
Hooksett, NH

MAPS

New Hampshire Atlas: Map 28

USGS Quadrangle: Manchester North

INFORMATION

Area: 111 acres

Prominent fish species: Pickerel and perch

Camping: All state-park campground reservations—603-271-3628 or www.nhparks.state.nh.us; Bear Brook State Park—603-485-9874; Pawtuckaway State Park—603-895-3031

We paddled here twice, once in April and once in June. Dubes Pond, just a short distance from Manchester, can be described only as outstanding. Unfortunately, a housing development along the western side was under construction when we paddled here most recently (April 2000). Though nothing could be seen from the pond, we could hear the sounds of road and house construction. If this development impinges on the pond, it will represent an extraordinary loss to the few remaining undisturbed wetlands of New Hampshire.

Dubes Pond gets very little boat traffic, which is good, given the very large great blue heron rookery that dominates the farthest reaches. If you paddle here when the herons nest, please stick to the edges of the pond, giving the stand of dead nesting trees in the middle a wide berth. The rookery is actually on a different pond, which has a small earthen dike separating it from the western arm of Dubes Pond. There does not seem to be a great way to portage over the dike; we used four different approaches, none really satisfactory. Out in the western pond, fragrant

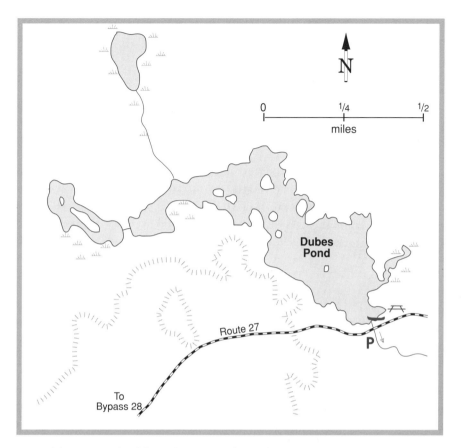

waterlily, water shield, and water celery abound in the clear water. We also saw a large snapping turtle.

Back on Dubes Pond itself, especially in the northwest, sphagnum hummocks support a large array of shrubs, but leatherleaf, with small, nondescript, bell-like flowers hanging down, appears to dominate. If you look carefully, you might find orchids growing on these hummocks. In other areas, granite boulders—some barely submerged, some out of water, some forming boulder islands—are the dominant theme. Some larger islands support stands of white pine, making this quite a picturesque pond. We found hours going by as we explored the many coves and islands.

If you paddle into the bay immediately to the right after leaving the boat access, you will find it choked with fragrant waterlily, with lots of round-leafed sundew tufts on rotting stumps and small hummocks.

This tiny carnivorous plant, which grows in rosettes only a couple of inches across, captures hapless insects that alight on its glistening sticky hairs. The plant then secretes enzymes that help digest the insects.

We saw another carnivorous plant growing here: yellow-flowered bladderwort. In contrast with sundew, bladderwort captures prey underwater in tiny air-filled sacs. Small aquatic organisms bump into the trigger hairs, and the sac deflates, sucking in the surrounding water and its prey.

As we paddled back to the boat access late in the day, watching beaver swim about and listening to rufous-sided towhees call from the brushy shores, we reveled in how this wild, pristine place can exist just 10 minutes from the center of New Hampshire's largest city. Let us hope that it remains wild for future generations to enjoy.

GETTING THERE

From Manchester, take Routes 3/28 north and turn right onto Route 27. The boat access is on Route 27 on the left, 2.3 miles beyond the junction with Bypass 28. Drive up by the fire hydrant and drop off your boat. Then drive back across the outlet stream and park in the very large lot on the opposite side of the road. There is a small picnic area at the boat launch.

Hoit Road Marsh
Concord and Loudon, NH

MAPS

New Hampshire Atlas: Map 28

USGS Quadrangle: Penacook

INFORMATION

Area: 206 acres

Prominent fish species: Largemouth bass and pickerel

Though Hoit Road borders part of the southern edge of the marsh, as you leave the boat access and paddle around to the left, civilization all but disappears. A few cars pass by at regular intervals, but they really don't intrude on the solitude once you have paddled off into one of the many arms of this wonderful and productive marsh.

Wood ducks and Canada geese, and possibly other ducks, nest in this shallow marsh maintained by the New Hampshire Fish and Game Department. The wetland also provides habitat for myriad other marsh birds, insects, mammals, and plants. Water shield, fragrant waterlily, pickerelweed, and other aquatic plants cover most of the surface. As these plants die back each fall, the decaying vegetation stains the water a yellow-brown. The many small islands harbor loads of sweet gale, purple iris, sheep laurel, and many other small shrubs. One large island on the northern end has a nice stand of white pine, and at the foot of the island we found a large new beaver lodge.

Besides numerous wood ducks, we saw a pair of Canada geese beginning to nest when we paddled here in the spring. An adult bald eagle soared overhead, while numerous damselflies and dragonflies patrolled the surface. As we listened to the chorus of several frog

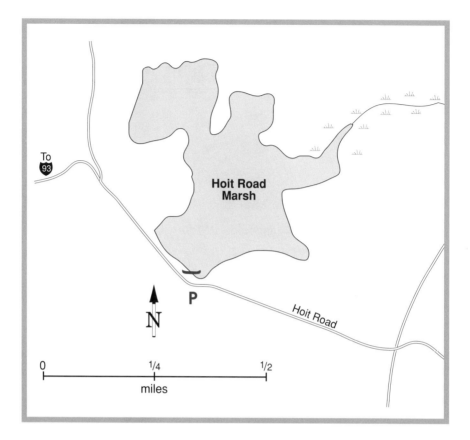

species, we reveled in how special this place is—all the more remarkable because of its close proximity to New Hampshire's capital city. Its many nooks and crannies, wooded shoreline, and shrubby islands offer hours of exploration. Paddle here in the early morning or late evening when wildlife is active. You will be free from motorboats here—and their noise, which so dominates New Hampshire's larger lakes.

GETTING THERE

From I-93, take Exit 17, Hoit Road east, for 2.4 miles. You can see the water from the road; parking is on either side of the road.

Pawtuckaway Lake
Nottingham, NH

MAPS

New Hampshire Atlas: Map 29

USGS Quadrangles: Epping and Mount Pawtuckaway

INFORMATION

Area: 903 acres

Prominent fish species: Largemouth bass, smallmouth bass, black crappie, yellow perch, white perch, and pickerel

Camping: All state-park campground reservations—603-271-3628 or www.nhparks.state.nh.us; Pawtuckaway State Park—603-895-3031

Pawtuckaway Lake, a large body of water well known for its bass fishing, boasts a highly varied shoreline with numerous coves, inlets, and islands to explore. Unfortunately, the eastern shore and the southern end suffer from heavy development and boat traffic. For the best paddling, we recommend that you stick to the northern end, especially Fundy Cove. There is no development in this cove and almost none around the northern end down to Log Cabin Island. South of the island, both seasonal and year-round houses dot the eastern shore and its numerous coves.

From the boat access, paddle south into Fundy Cove and then east into the main lake. White pine, red maple, white birch, and hemlock dominate the heavily wooded shoreline. The generally open understory provides easy access onto the shore for a picnic lunch or a rest. In mid- to late summer, a profusion of highbush blueberry growing along the shores may impede your progress. Most of the marshy inlets offer good birding habitat. We also saw lots of yellow bladderwort floating in

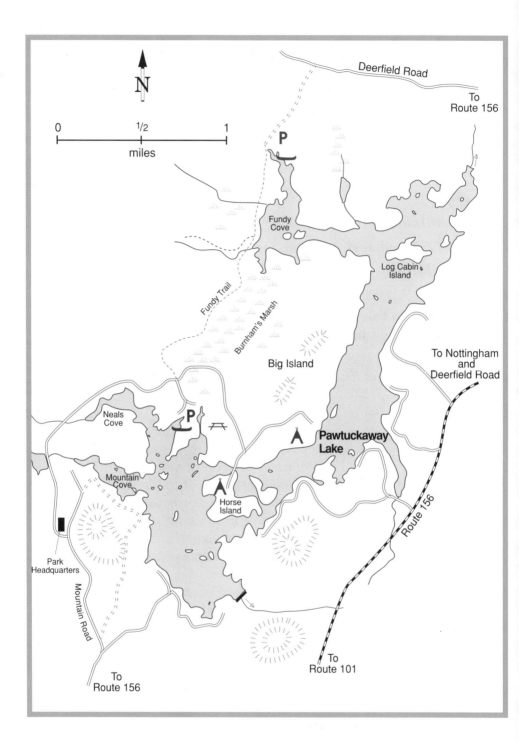

Several islands offer plenty of opportunity for exploration on the northern end of Pawtuckaway Lake.

the water, along with water celery, with its narrow leaves lying flat on the water's surface.

When paddling here, be careful of large rocks at or just below the surface. Out with his dog one day, Alex managed to hang himself up on a somewhat concave boulder that lurked an inch or two beneath the surface of the water and had quite a time getting off—fortunately, his dog was patient. While paddling here on another occasion in a group, we all managed to paint a few rocks.

At the northeast tip of the lake, the town of Nottingham maintains a nice beach (unfortunately the town limits swimming to residents) very near the north outlet dam (not to be confused with the south outlet dam).

If you venture down to the south end, you can explore around some very pretty islands. You will never feel very remote at the southern end of the lake, however, because of all the houses across the lake and the large number of motorboats in use during the summer months. We much prefer the northern end of the lake for paddling, though we saw canoes and kayaks all up and down the lake on a busy summer weekend.

Numerous hiking trails course through Pawtuckaway State Park, including the Fundy Trail, which extends from the main park road near the picnic area, along Burnham's Marsh, to the boat launch at the northern end of the lake. Farther west in the park, trails take you over several small mountain peaks, along a unique boulder field of glacial erratics, and into Round Pond. Pawtuckaway State Park is extremely popular during the summer months. In fact, long lines of cars often form, waiting to get into the park. If you can visit in September, though, this is a great spot.

GETTING THERE

To reach the northern boat access from Route 27, turn north onto Route 156 in Raymond, go 5.4 miles, and turn left onto Deerfield Road. Go another 1.9 miles to the boat access on the left. You will find plenty of parking on all but the busiest weekends (on a beautiful Saturday in late August, we counted 49 vehicles at the boat access).

To get to Pawtuckaway State Park, where there is a large campground and another boat launch, go back down Route 156 for 4.0 miles to Mountain Road. Turn right, following signs to the park, which is approximately 2.0 miles up this road. From the south, follow Route 156 approximately 1.3 miles north from Route 27, and turn left onto Mountain Road.

Carnivorous Plants
The Table is Turned

Carnivorous plants are fascinating—and a common sight as you paddle through the bogs and marshes of New England's lakes and ponds. Specialized adaptations make them one of nature's true wonders and make us wonder how their meat-eating habit evolved.

Carnivory in plants apparently resulted from convergent evolution: the taking on of similar traits among unrelated species. Carnivory in plants exists in many different, completely unrelated plant families on nearly every continent. These plants have two characteristics in common: almost all live in mineral-poor soils and supplement meager soil nutrients with those from animals, and they use modified leaves to trap food.

Two main capture strategies have evolved: active and passive. Most people recognize the active capture strategy of the Venus' flytrap, a plant that grows in sandy soils in a narrow band along the coastal border between North Carolina and South Carolina. Few other carnivorous plants have adopted active capture strategies, but one of them grows abundantly—sometimes forming dense mats—in the quiet, shallow marshes and bogs of New England: bladderworts of the genus *Utricularia*. Bladderwort

leaves consist of minute bladders that, upon stimulation, inflate and ingest insect larvae and other organisms, to be digested by the plant's enzymes.

Passive capture strategies have taken two main paths among the remaining carnivorous plants. Pitcher plants—*Sarracenia purpurea*—collect rainwater in their funnel-shaped modified leaves. Insects, attracted to nectar secreted around the top of the pitcher, fall in. The plant's stiff, downward-pointing hairs keep most insects from climbing back out. Eventually the insects drown, and a combination of plant and bacterial enzymes reduces the insects to absorbable nutrients.

Another passive-capture plant uses sticky surfaces to ensnare insects. Sundews (genus *Drosera)* form tiny rosettes that protrude from a central root. Stalked glands of two types cover the modified-leaf surface. One type secretes a sticky substance that glistens like dew in the sun, giving the plant its name. Entrapped insects, drawn initially by the nectarlike secretions, are digested by enzymes secreted by the second set of glands.

Each of the plants described above—bladderwort, pitcher plant, and sundew—captures its intended victims in a different way, but they all do so because, in nutrient-poor marshes and bogs, absorbing nitrogen and other minerals from insects and other prey gives them a selective advantage over other plants.

Do not be fooled by the black, fertile-looking soils of marshes and swamps. Black dirt like this in Iowa means fertile soil, but in bogs it means black carbon from undecomposed plants. The tea-colored water, laden with organic acids from decaying vegetation and supplemented by acid rain, effectively washes out the minerals necessary for plant growth. Although two primary nutrients supporting plant growth—carbon dioxide and water—remain plentiful, nitrogen, phosphorus, potassium and other important elements get leached out or bound up in underlying layers of sphagnum and peat. Carnivorous plants, with their diet of insects and other organisms, supplement the lost nutrients, making them effective competitors in the bog ecosystem.

Bladderworts. Bladderworts grow in quiet, shallow waters or in shoreline muck. Keep an eye out for their small yellow or purple snapdragon-like flowers, leading on short stalks to their carnivorous underwater bladders. The vast majority of the plant lives underwater in dense, feathery mats, bearing hundreds of tiny (0.02 to 0.1 inch long), bulbous traps that are the plant's leaves. The bladders have two concave sides and a trap door. When an insect larva or other small organism bumps into the door's guard hairs,

the bladder's sides pop out, creating suction; the door swings open; and water and the hapless critter get sucked in. All of this occurs in an instant, followed by slow digestion by plant enzymes.

In most ponds, mosquito larvae form the bulk of the plant's diet, but it also ingests other larvae, rotifers, protozoans, small crustaceans, and even tiny tadpoles. The digested animal remains are absorbed by plant tissues, causing the trap's sides to go concave again, readying the plant for its next meal. With large prey, such as a tiny tadpole, the door will close around the organism, and part of it will get digested. The next time the hairs get triggered, the plant ingests more of the organism, eventually sucking it all in.

Several species of bladderwort grow in our area, including two with purple flowers, one aquatic and one terrestrial, and as many as 10 species with yellow flowers, mostly aquatic but including at least two terrestrials. We usually notice the presence of these plants when we see their snapdragon-like flowers protruding a few inches above the water's surface. Their dense underwater mats attest to their successful adaptation to nutrient-poor waters. If you lift a mat out of the water slowly and listen carefully, you may hear crackling as the bladders suck in air instead of their intended prey.

Pitcher plants. Although several other species of *Sarracenia* pitcher plants exist in North America, the northern pitcher plant, *Sarracenia purpurea*, has the widest distribution, growing from British Columbia to Nova Scotia, southward through the Great Lakes region, and down the eastern coastal plain, crossing the Florida panhandle to the Mississippi River. Initially green in the spring, the pitcher plant's funnel-shaped leaves turn progressively more purple, becoming deep maroon in the fall, and return to green again in the spring. During midseason, the red veins of the hood stand in stark contrast to the mostly green pitchers. Flowering occurs in June and July in New England, and single reddish flowers, borne on stout stalks, tower a foot or more above the cluster of pitchers.

In contrast to most other species, the northern pitcher plant does not have a hood to keep rain out. The curved pitchers recline, allowing rain to fall freely into the open hood. Because of dilution of the pitcher's contents, insects drown well before digestion occurs. The stiff, downward-pointing hairs in the plant's throat keep insects from climbing back out, and the relatively narrow funnel leaves little room for airborne escape. The upper pitcher walls sport a waxy coating, making for slippery footing. A combination of plant and bacterial enzymes degrade the unlucky insects, and their nutrients pass easily through the unwaxed surface of the lower pitcher.

Amazingly, several different types of organisms can live in the pitchers, unharmed by the digestive juices. One genus of mosquito harmless to humans, *Wyeomyia*, lives the aquatic part of its life cycle in the pitcher, and other insects can escape by walking up the waxy cuticle and out over the downward-pointing hairs.

Sundews. To find sundews, look for tiny glistening drops at the ends of their traps. Because they are so small—the smallest plants may measure only an inch across—sundews are easily overlooked. Four species occur in our area, and we describe the most common species here: roundleaf sundew (*Drosera rotundifolia*).

This remarkable plant grows mainly in sphagnum bogs, from Alaska to northern California, across the Canadian Rockies and plains, through the Great Lakes, north throughout Labrador, south to the Chesapeake Bay, and down through the Appalachians. The same plant grows in Europe as well; Darwin devoted much of his book *Insectivorous Plants* to this one species. The entire plant averages about three inches across and about an inch high, with all of its leaves modified into sticky traps. A short leaf stalk ends in a flattened oval pad covered with red, stalked glands. The longer glands secrete a sticky fluid, while the shorter glands secrete digestive enzymes. Insects, attracted to the nectar-like secretions, become trapped. Slowly, imperceptibly, the pad edges roll over slightly, placing the insect in contact with digestive juices.

The usually white (but sometimes pink) flowers hover well above the plant's leaves, borne on a slender stalk. Although easy to miss, a little careful looking on sphagnum mats will show up many of these reddish rosettes. You should see several small insects in various stages of digestion. And you, too, can wonder about how these plants developed the incredible ability to supplement the meager amount of nutrients available from the soil with those from insect prey.

Great Bay
Durham, Greenland, Newington, Newmarket, and Stratham, NH

MAPS

New Hampshire Atlas: Map 30

USGS Quadrangles: Newmarket and Portsmouth

INFORMATION

Area: 4,500 acres

Prominent fish species: Coho, chinook, Atlantic salmon, striped bass, bluefish, and rainbow smelt

Great Bay is a large tidal estuary in southeastern New Hampshire near Portsmouth. Though located near heavily populated areas, the shoreline has only sparse development, and because of its shallowness and variable water level, few motorboats venture out on it. Most of the bay lies within Great Bay National Estuarine Research Reserve, which includes more than 4,000 acres of tidal waters and mud flats and some 48 miles of high-tide shoreline.

Because of tidal influences, Great Bay is quite unlike any other body of water covered in this book. It changes constantly, with the shoreline migrating in and out twice daily on changing tides. At high tide, Great Bay swells to more than twice the low-tide size. While constant change makes it a great place to explore—one where you could spend several days paddling—some special precautions are in order. You could easily get stranded on mud flats as the tide goes out, and you need to time the tides carefully, as you may find yourself paddling against strong tidal currents. Strong winds, common over the great expanse of the bay, can make paddling even more difficult. So in planning your visit to Great Bay, make sure you have a tide chart.

Changing tides on Great Bay offer unique challenges for quietwater paddlers.

Great Bay's large size provides dozens of places to explore. Among the best: Adams Point, Woodman Point, and Squamscott River inlet. To reach these from the Adams Point access, paddle south around the point separating Great Bay from Little Bay. Because of the quite narrow channel, tidal currents can be very strong. If possible, launch from Adams Point into Great Bay as the tide comes in and return as the tide goes out. You can usually tell tide direction by looking at which way the boats moored at Adams Point face. The boats face upstream, so when the tide goes out they face south, and when the tide comes in they face north. If you get caught fighting tidal current, stay close to shore where it will be a lot weaker.

From Adams Point, you can paddle across Furber Strait to the Estuarine Research Reserve. The eastern shore along here has picturesque bluffs overlooking the bay, with stands of large red pine above and rocky, seaweed-covered coves below. Woodman Point, at the southern tip of the reserve, is spectacular. A trail leads out to the point, which

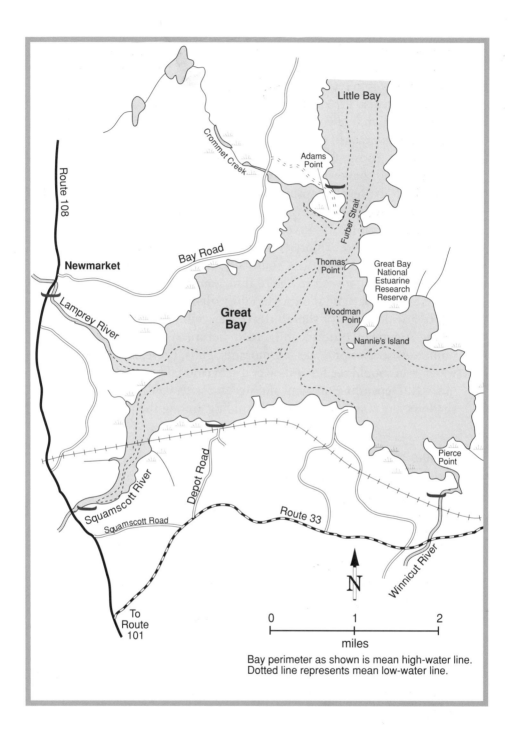

Little Bay

Crommet Creek

Adams
Point

Route 108

Furber Strait

Bay Road

Newmarket

Thomas
Point

Great Bay
National
Estuarine
Research
Reserve

Lamprey River

Great
Bay

Woodman
Point

Nannie's Island

Pierce
Point

Squamscott River

Depot Road

Route 33

Squamscott Road

Winnicut River

To
Route
101

N

0   1   2

miles

Bay perimeter as shown is mean high-water line.
Dotted line represents mean low-water line.

overlooks Nannie's Island, where common terns (a state-listed endangered species) nested as recently as 1980. Be careful of the particularly lush poison ivy at Woodman and Thomas Points.

You can also explore the western shoreline southwest toward Newmarket. At high tide you can paddle into Crommet Creek, but note that this area has exposed mud flats at low tide. During the winter months, bald eagles roost along this shore and across at the reserve. The shoreline and shallows south of Adams Point have the most productive oyster beds in New Hampshire and are often one of the only areas in the state not closed to oystering because of pollution.

The Squamscott River inlet into the bay provides another interesting area to explore. Except for the narrow Squamscott River channel, though, this entire south side of the bay consists of exposed mud flats during low tide. Again, time your trip carefully.

At Great Bay and the surrounding salt-marsh areas, you can expect to see a wide range of shorebirds (lesser yellowlegs, glossy ibis, snowy egret, American bittern, and green heron, to mention just a few), numerous species of ducks, cormorants, gulls, geese, and others. In the water, you should see horseshoe crabs, hermit crabs, oysters, and ribbed mussels. Depending on wind and water clarity, you can paddle over the shallows and watch for marine life hiding among the prolific eelgrass.

GETTING THERE

To reach the Adams Point boat access, go north on Route 108 to Newmarket. Just after crossing the Lamprey River, turn right and go 3.9 miles on Bay Road to the entrance to Adams Point and Jackson Lab. For birders, there is an excellent spot for wading birds just on the other side of the road from this boat launch.

The boat launch on the Squamscott River is off Route 108 just south of the bridge. Be careful turning off here, as the access road is in poor shape. You can also launch your boat at the end of Depot Road. From the intersection of Routes 33 and 108 north, go 1.7 miles east on Route 33 and turn left onto Depot Road. Drive in about 1.0 mile, turn left at the T, and park across the tracks.

Another launch site is in downtown Newmarket on the Lamprey River. Heading south, turn left off Route 108, just after crossing the bridge over the river.

The Loon
Voice of the Northern Wilderness

No animal better symbolizes the northern wilderness than the loon, whose haunting cry resonates through the night air on many northern lakes. The bird seems almost mystical, with its distinctive black-and-white plumage, daggerlike bill, and piercing red eyes. But like our remaining wilderness, the loon is threatened over much of its range. As recreational pressures on lakes and ponds increase, the loon gets pushed farther away. We who share its waters bear the responsibility for protecting this wonderful bird and its habitat.

Along with its status as a symbol of northern wilderness, the common loon, *Gavia immer*, is a most extraordinary bird. A large diving bird that lives almost its entire life in the water, it visits land only to mate and to lay eggs. Loons have a very difficult time on land because their legs, positioned quite far back on their bodies to aid them in swimming, prevent them from walking.

Loons have adapted remarkably well to water. Unlike most birds, which have hollow bones, loons have solid bones, enabling them to dive to great depths. They also have an internal air sac, which they compress or expand to control how high they float. By compressing this sac, a loon can submerge gradually, with barely a ripple, or swim with just its head above water.

Their heavy bodies and rearward legs make takeoff difficult. A loon may require a quarter-mile of open water to build up enough speed to lift off, and it may have to circle a small lake several times to build enough altitude to clear nearby hills or mountains. When migrating, a loon flies rapidly—up to 90 MPH—but cannot soar.

Loons generally mate for life and can live for 20 to 30 years. The female lays two eggs in early May, and both male and female—indistinguishable to the casual observer—take turns incubating the oblong, moss-green eggs. If loons leave eggs unattended, the embryos can die in just a half-hour. Because loons cannot walk on land, they always build their nests very close to shore—where a passing paddler can scare birds away and a motorboat wake can flood the nest with cold water. Loons most often nest on islands to hide the eggs from predators such as raccoons and skunks. On some lakes and ponds, you will see floating nesting platforms built by concerned individuals or organizations to improve the chances of nesting success. On reservoirs with varying water levels, these platforms take on special importance because they rise and fall with water levels, reducing the likelihood of flooding or stranding a nest.

Loon chicks hatch fully covered in black down, and they usually enter the water a day after hatching. Young chicks often ride on a parent's back to conserve heat and to avoid predators. They grow quickly on a diet of small fish and crustaceans; by two weeks of age, they reach half the adult size and can dive to relatively deep lake bottoms, covering more than 30 yards underwater. Loon chicks remain totally dependent on their parents, however, for about eight weeks and do not fly until 10 to 12 weeks of age. After leaving the nest a day after hatching, loons do not return

to land for three or four years—until they reach breeding age. The young mature on the sea, having followed their elders to saltwater wintering areas.

Loons in New Hampshire and Vermont have achieved only moderate nesting success in recent years. According to surveys conducted at the time of this book's first edition in 1991, 102 pairs nested in New Hampshire, producing 85 surviving chicks. In Vermont, where the state lists the loon as endangered, only 15 pairs nested, producing 14 surviving young. In Vermont in 1998, according to the Vermont Institute of Natural Science, 30 chicks survived. In New Hampshire in 2000, according to the Loon Preservation Committee, 128 chicks survived. For an animal that has received quite a bit of attention, population recovery has proceeded slowly.

Besides encroachment by humans and nest predation by raccoons and skunks, loons suffer mortality in many other ways. According to the Tufts University Wildlife Veterinary Clinic, chicks die primarily from collisions with personal watercraft and motorboats, and adults die primarily from ingestion of lead sinkers and jigs. As with other diving waterfowl, ingestion of lead sinkers and shotgun pellets poisons loons. The New Hampshire legislature took the forward-looking step of banning lead sinkers and jigs effective January 1, 2000. Other Northeast states should follow New

Hampshire's example. A total ban is needed on lead shotgun pellets in wetland areas. And anglers must avoid leaving spent monofilament line behind, as it also causes loon deaths.

As development encroaches on more lakes and recreational use increases, loons become increasingly at risk. We should ban noisy, polluting, accident-causing personal watercraft from any water with loons. We must also stop further shoreline development—perhaps the main cause of the loon's long decline.

Because paddlers can easily disturb loons when nesting, we must watch for warning displays during the nesting season, early May through mid-July. (If a nest fails, loons may try up to two more times, though the later a chick hatches, the lower its chance of survival.) If you see a loon flapping its wings and making a racket during the nesting season, steer clear. When you see a nest site marked with buoys or warning signs, as is done on many lakes and ponds, keep your distance.

Loons have lived in this area longer than any other bird—an estimated 60 million years. Let's make sure this wonderful species remains protected so future generations may listen to its enchanting music on a still, moonlit night. For information on loons, contact the Loon Preservation Committee in New Hampshire (a project of the Audubon Society in Moultonborough—603-476-5666), or the Vermont Institute of Natural Science (Woodstock—802-457-2779; www.vinsweb.org).

McDaniels Marsh
Springfield, NH

MAPS

New Hampshire Atlas: Map 34

USGS Quadrangle: Enfield Center

INFORMATION

Area: 513 acres

Prominent fish species: Pickerel and perch

Just a short distance north of popular Sunapee Lake, McDaniels Marsh offers an out-of-the-way, less-traveled treasure for the quietwater paddler. Beautiful hills rise in the distance as you wend your way through islands toward the line of spruce and tamarack that marks the end of this deceptively long marsh. Pitcher plants grow in profusion on sphagnum-laden hummocks and floating islands. A small spillway raises the water level a few feet, barely submerging many stumps and granite boulders.

We visited twice: once in late April and once in early August. In April, before aquatic vegetation emerged from dormancy, we easily reached the far corners of the marsh, teeming with bird life—especially wood ducks that had recently returned to the dozens of nesting boxes placed by the state. Hundreds upon hundreds of migrating tree swallows darted about, replenishing their energy stores from a dense hatch of emergent insects.

In August, vegetation covered perhaps 90 percent of the water surface, restricting paddling somewhat, but we found the experience just as enjoyable. A sea of lavender from the blooming pickerelweed bathed

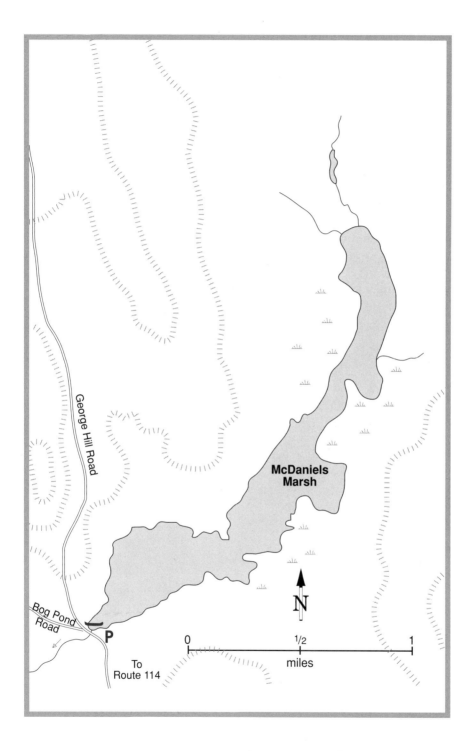

George Hill Road

McDaniels
Marsh

Bog Pond
Road

P

N

To
Route 114

0   1/2   1
miles

much of the marsh's northeastern end. Billowy white blooms of tawny cotton grass (*Eriophorum virginicum*), a member of the rush family (round stems), formed equally beautiful expanses of white. At this time of year, one has to work to find a passage to the northeast, but we found a relatively open, winding channel all the way to the far end (about two miles from the access). You also will see extensive areas of cattails and occasional arrowhead with its waxy white blooms. Floating-leafed and submergent plants also grow here in profusion: white and yellow pond lily, water shield, pondweed (*Potamogeton spp.*), bur-reed, water celery, and bladderwort.

Look for insectivorous pitcher plant and sundew on the thick sphagnum hummocks, along with the dominant leatherleaf, sweet gale, and steeplebush (*Spiraea*). You may also find rose pogonia orchids—we spotted a cluster of several dozen of the delicate pink flowers on one boggy hillock. Paddling through the shallow, universally ruddy brown, tannin-stained water, expect to stir up the mucky bottom, releasing strong-smelling marsh gas that results from incomplete decomposition of the abundant vegetation in this highly productive marsh.

Besides the usual mix of red maple, birch, white pine, balsam fir, and spruce, toward the northeast end tamarack dominates the boggy shore. Along with wood ducks and tree swallows, we saw Canada geese, blue-winged teal, black ducks, great blue herons, red-winged blackbirds, kingfishers, osprey, yellow-rumped warblers, chickadees, phoebes, and cedar waxwings; we heard a winter wren singing from the dense underbrush. There are lots of painted turtles here and at least one active family of beavers (though quite a few abandoned lodges). You also may be lucky enough to spot a moose or otter, both frequently seen here.

GETTING THERE

From I-89, Exit 13, go south on Route 10 for 0.7 mile to Route 114. Turn left onto Route 114, go 4.8 miles, and turn left onto George Hill Road. Take George Hill Road 2.2 miles to the boat access, at the junction with Bog Road.

Grafton Pond
Grafton, NH

MAPS

New Hampshire Atlas: Map 34

USGS Quadrangle: Enfield Center

INFORMATION

Area: 235 acres

Prominent fish species: Smallmouth bass and pickerel

Contact information: Society for the Protection of New Hampshire Forests—603-224-9945

Grafton Pond stands out as one of the finest paddling destinations in New Hampshire. The Society for the Protection of New Hampshire Forests, one of the most effective organizations involved in land preservation, protects a large portion of the surrounding land. A few houses perch along the western tip, but these do not distract too much from the lake's remoteness probably because one easily can paddle out of view. Though small, the lake seems much larger, owing to the many deep inlets, hidden marshy areas, and rocky islands, which provide ideal underwater habitat for the many smallmouth bass that inhabit the pond. One could spend a few days exploring all the nooks and crannies of this lake and hiking some of the surrounding old logging roads.

A natural lake, enlarged and deepened with a dam, the pond has a maximum depth of 66 feet with quite clear water. Along the generally rocky, heavily wooded shoreline, conifers seem to dominate (balsam fir, red spruce, white pine, and hemlock), while farther from shore, red maple, white birch, and other hardwoods seem more common. Geologists will enjoy the granite outcroppings found throughout most of the lake, some of which sport sizable mica crystals, while bird watchers may

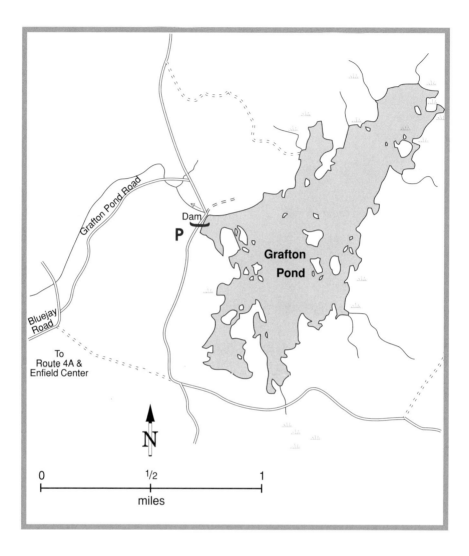

want to stay closer to the shallow, marshy areas. Islands and peninsulas jutting out into the lake provide wonderful grassy picnic sites.

Grafton Pond abounds with wildlife. Usually, a few pairs of loons nest here. With many relatively safe islands for nesting (away from raccoons and other predators) and a plentiful food supply, Grafton affords a great spot for them. During a late-April visit, we also saw quite a few wood ducks, osprey, and an assortment of more-common lake and pond birds: black ducks, mallards, great blue herons, kingfishers, and

Grafton Pond's deep coves and numerous islands offer plenty of opportunity for bird watching.

others. Quite a few beaver lodges occur along the northern shore, and one should keep an eye out for otter and mink.

A prohibition on motors larger than six horsepower keeps the pond relatively quiet and more enjoyable for the dedicated angler or paddler.

GETTING THERE
From Enfield Center, take Route 4A south for 2.2 miles and turn left onto Bluejay Road. After 0.9 mile, bear right at the fork onto Grafton Pond Road. Go another 0.9 mile, turn right, and you will reach the access in 0.2 mile.

The Bay/Blackwater River
Andover and Salisbury, NH

MAPS

New Hampshire Atlas: Map 35

USGS Quadrangle: Andover

INFORMATION

Length: 5 miles

Prominent fish species: Brook, brown, and rainbow trout

This wide, marshy section of the Blackwater River harbors lots of wildlife. The mating calls of frogs and toads in the spring lend a primeval feel to this wonderful place. Silver maple dots the shrubby shoreline, while pickerelweed and pondweed cover much of the water's surface. If you paddle upstream and go under the bridge, you will find some truly huge silver maple with bifurcated trunks. The winged samaras of the silver maple, the largest of the maple seedpods, serve as an important food source for squirrels and other wildlife.

Though a few houses occupy the shore, not much in the way of human presence impinges on this waterland, which provides an important breeding ground for mallards, black ducks, and wood ducks. If you paddle here in the early morning or evening, expect to see beaver swimming about.

GETTING THERE

From Andover, travel east on Routes 4/11. When Route 11 goes north, follow Route 4 east. Go 1.8 miles and turn right onto easy-to-miss Bay Road. The boat access is 0.7 mile down Bay Road on the right.

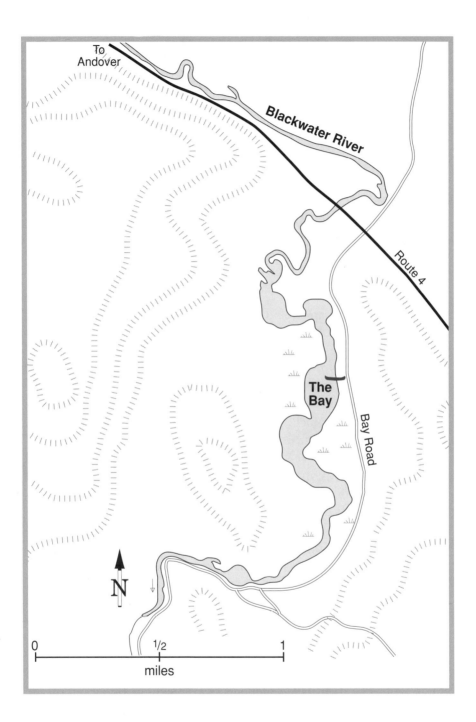

To
Andover

Blackwater River

Route 4

The
Bay

Bay Road

N

0   1/2   1
miles

Danbury Bog
Danbury, NH

MAPS

    New Hampshire Atlas: Map 35

    USGS Quadrangles: Andover and Danbury

INFORMATION

    Length: 2 miles

    Prominent fish species: Pickerel and perch

With mist burning off the water as we paddled out early one morning, we listened to deer snort from the reeds as they sloshed off through the marsh. We had hoped to see moose, but neither time that we paddled here did we have any luck. We had to content ourselves with the deer, a profusion of painted turtles, countless wood ducks, and myriad other wildlife and plant life. We saw black ducks, blue-winged teal, and all of the usual marsh birds, including a bittern out in full view, several great blue herons, goldfinches, and three swallow species.

If you want to get away from the personal watercraft and water-skiers that frequent the larger lakes in central New Hampshire, head over to Danbury Bog Wildlife Management Area, where aquatic vegetation rules the water. Though pickerelweed and yellow pond lily dominate, expect to find water shield, pondweed, sedge, and dozens of other aquatic species growing in profusion, all cleverly designed to keep out boats with motors. This area does not see much traffic; during the two times we paddled here, we saw only one canoe and one rowboat.

This extraordinary, wonderful spot lies just north of Ragged Mountain, and you can paddle up into the foothills, portaging over a couple of beaver dams. We watched a beaver slam its broad tail on the

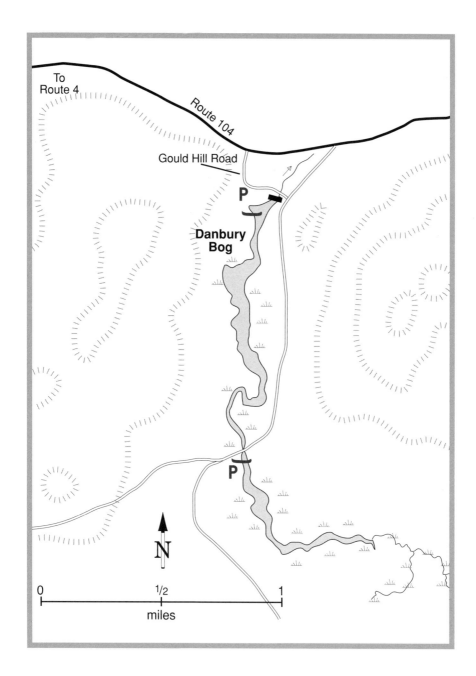

To
Route 4

Route 104

Gould Hill Road

P

Danbury Bog

P

0   1/2   1
miles

N

When the wind blows on the region's big lakes, try paddling the more placid waters of Danbury Bog.

water as it dove out of sight and saw muskrats harvest grass. Watch out for rocks poking up from the dark water as you paddle through the limited open channel of this vast wetland. One could spend a great deal of time exploring this marsh, identifying the birds, mammals, and aquatic plants and the shrubs along the shoreline. We found the best wildlife viewing to be at dawn and in the late afternoon.

Getting There

In Danbury, from the junction of Routes 4 and 104, go east on Route 104 for 1.0 mile and turn right onto Gould Hill Road. The boat access is 0.3 mile down Gould Hill Road on the right. An alternative put-in point is where the road bisects the bog; it is about 1.1 miles from the Gould Hill Road access point.

Wickwas Lake
Meredith, NH

MAPS

New Hampshire Atlas: Map 35

USGS Quadrangle: Winnisquam Lake

INFORMATION

Area: 328 acres

Prominent fish species: Largemouth bass, smallmouth bass, crappie, perch, and pickerel

In spite of development around parts of the shoreline and some motor-boat traffic, Wickwas Lake still offers some of the best canoeing in the Lakes Region of New Hampshire. Lots of shoreline variation, a number of beautiful islands, several marshy inlets, and a reputation for excellent bass fishing make Wickwas an excellent choice, except on the busiest summer weekends. It offers enough room for a full day of relaxed exploring. We chose to include this lake over nearby Pemigewasset because Wickwas suffers less road noise and sees fewer motorboats.

White pine, hemlock, and various hardwood species cover the heavily wooded shores. Most of the development occurs along the southern arm of the lake near the public landing, though the northern shore along Route 104 also has a few dozen houses. The eastern section, especially the deep inlet behind the large island, provides the most remote paddling. We could just barely paddle around the marshy eastern side of the island the two times that we paddled here, once in late May and once in late August in a high-water year. With a lot more pond vegetation or a slightly lower water level, that channel would not be navigable. On the other side of the island, a stand of tall red pine

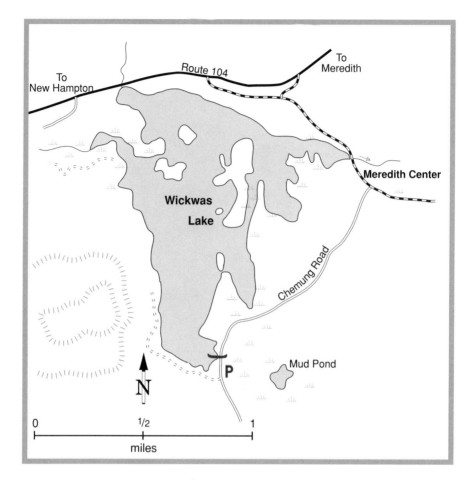

harbors a pleasant picnic spot on a large granite slab that extends into the lake.

Though we saw no bass anglers, we did see kingfishers and loons fishing. We know that smallmouth bass inhabit these waters because we saw a dead one, more than a foot long, by the boat access. Another notable sighting: the water celery, growing in some fairly deep water, had very long thin stems.

GETTING THERE

From I-93, Exit 23, take Route 104 east for 4.9 miles and turn right onto Meredith Center Road. Go about 1.0 mile and turn right onto Chemung Road. The access is 1.1 miles farther on the right, with parking on both sides of the road.

Suncook River
Barnstead, NH

MAPS

New Hampshire Atlas: Map 36

USGS Quadrangle: Pittsfield

INFORMATION

Area: 672 acres

Prominent fish species: Largemouth bass, smallmouth bass, pickerel, white perch, and rainbow trout

Camping: All state park campground reservations—603-271-3628 or www.nhparks.state.nh.us; Bear Brook State Park—603-485-9874; Pawtuckaway State Park—603-895-3031

The boat access is actually on Big Creek, which flows into the Suncook River. Plan to spend most of your time in the upper regions of the Suncook River (eastern end), including Big Creek, because once you paddle downstream to Old Route 28, houses line the shore and boat traffic picks up. Of course, if you want the exercise, paddling all the way down to the dam in Barnstead, which impounds this section of the Suncook, and back will give you plenty. We suggest that you avoid busy summer weekends. At any time during the summer, we prefer to stick to the upper reach with its many protected bays, inlets, and channels around islands.

This impoundment is one of the few areas we have paddled that includes large amounts of floating heart, *Nymphoides cordata*, a diminutive member of the gentian family. Its small heart-shaped leaves, about an inch across, are borne singly on long tendrils. Most aquatic plants are relegated to water shallower than about four feet;

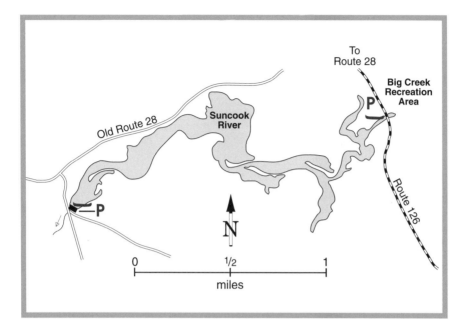

floating heart normally grows in much deeper water. Each stem can bear a few small white flowers in midsummer.

What struck us most about this area is the interesting mix of habitats: flowing and still water, protected bays and open water, mature forests and shrubby islands, marshes and deeper water. One could spend hours identifying the alder, viburnum, elderberry, other shrubs, and both floating and emergent aquatic plants.

GETTING THERE

From Pittsfield, take Route 28 north to Route 126. Take Route 126 south for 0.6 mile to the Big Creek Recreation Area on the right. Turn in next to the police station.

Manning Lake
Gilmanton, NH

MAPS

New Hampshire Atlas: Map 36

USGS Quadrangle: Gilmanton Iron Works

INFORMATION

Area: 202 acres

Prominent fish species: Largemouth bass, smallmouth bass, pickerel, perch, and brook trout

Manning Lake, a few miles south, as the crow flies, of Lake Winnipesaukee in central New Hampshire, stands out because of its crystal-clear water and the sandy bottom along much of the shoreline. The presence of numerous freshwater mussels provides evidence of the water's purity. About a dozen houses dot the lake's shore, but we did not have to share the water with any other boats on an otherwise busy Memorial Day weekend.

Nestled between Guinea Ridge to the south and the much taller Belknap Mountains to the north, Manning Lake enjoys a spectacular setting. Unlike the vast majority of lakes in Vermont and New Hampshire, Manning is totally natural. White pine, hemlock, red oak, basswood, red maple, highbush blueberry, and witch hazel—a fascinating low-growing tree that blooms in the late fall—grow along the shore. Large granite boulders dot some stretches of shoreline, though vegetation comes right down to the water's edge around most of the shore. The sandy bottom drops off quite rapidly in some areas, reaching a maximum depth of 56 feet.

You can paddle leisurely around the perimeter of Manning Lake, also known as Guinea Pond, in a couple of hours. Of course, you

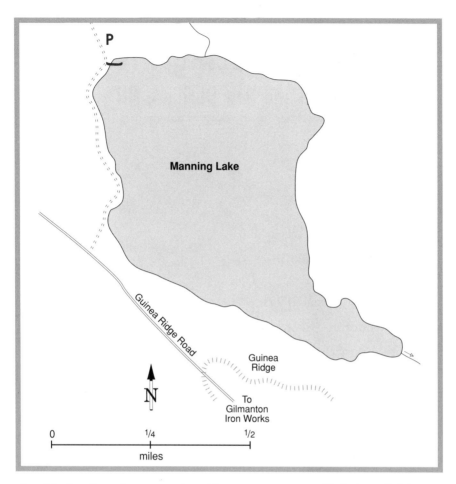

should plan for a lot more time if you want to try a little bass fishing or enjoy some swimming. In the early morning or late evening, you should see a beaver or two, and perhaps an otter.

Getting There

From Alton, take Route 140 west. In Gilmanton Iron Works, turn right onto Crystal Lake Road (5.4 miles from Route 11); take a fairly immediate left fork. Go 3.2 miles, passing the heavily built-up western shore of Crystal Lake. At the fork, veer left onto Guinea Ridge Road, go about 1.9 miles, and turn right onto Manning Lake Road. The put-in is 0.5 mile down Manning Lake Road.

Marsh Pond and Merrymeeting River
Alton and New Durham, NH

MAPS

New Hampshire Atlas: Map 37

USGS Quadrangle: Alton

INFORMATION

Marsh Pond area: 389 acres

Merrymeeting River length: 5 miles

Prominent fish species: Largemouth bass and pickerel

The Merrymeeting State Wildlife Management Area on the Merrymeeting River offers superb quietwater paddling. Busy Route 11 bisects the U-shaped section described here. We enjoyed paddling both sections, though the western part feels wilder—if you can ignore the Route 11 road noise. One could spend hours paddling this waterway, absorbed in the marsh's biologically rich wonders.

On the eastern side, deciduous trees and some scattered white pine form a backdrop, while narrow-leaved cattail, bulrush, pickerelweed, waterlily, sweet gale, sheep laurel, and many other shrubs populate the shoreline. Aquatic plants choke the water with vegetation. Watch for the typical marsh denizens, including beaver, muskrat, bullfrogs, wood and black ducks, great blue herons, red-winged blackbirds, song sparrows, yellow warblers, and eastern kingbirds.

We found tree swallows nesting colonially in a martin house, apparently unaware that tree swallows do not nest colonially. Instead, they chase other tree swallows away. To encourage bluebird nesting,

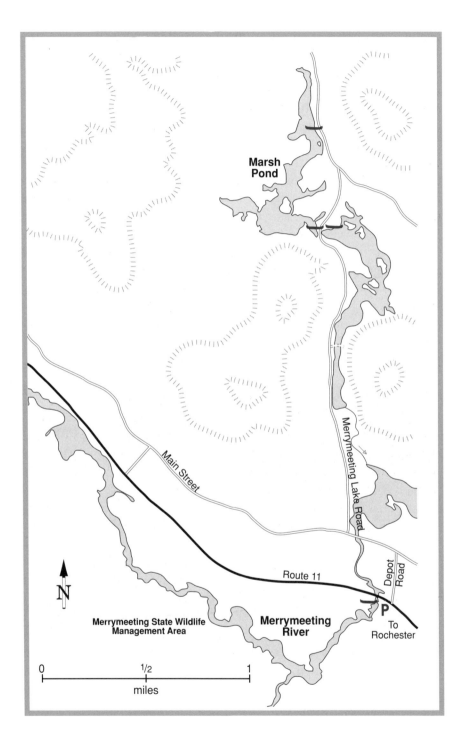

Marsh
Pond

Merrymeeting Lake Road

Main Street

N

Route 11

Depot
Road

P

To
Rochester

Merrymeeting State Wildlife
Management Area

Merrymeeting
River

0   1/2   1
        miles

people often put nesting boxes up in pairs. The more-aggressive tree swallows occupy the first box and then chase away other tree swallows, leaving the companion box free for bluebirds, which the swallows ignore. Apparently, these tree swallows have not heard of this theory. An alternate hypothesis: the sheer volume of available insects in this productive marsh may overwhelm their aggressive territorial tendencies.

Development increases as you approach the southern end; we would not paddle past the small access bridge across the narrows. On the north side of Merrymeeting Lake Road, only a couple of houses impinge on the wild character of Marsh Pond; we prefer paddling here to paddling on the south side of the road. This extensive marsh boasts tons of aquatic vegetation and islands thick with tamarack.

The section to the west of Route 11 wends its way through seas of aquatic vegetation for more than five sinuous miles, by far the best section to paddle, though it suffers from some Route 11 road noise. Pickerelweed guards the narrow channel through the wide expanse of marsh. The shoreline, off in the distance, begins with low brush followed by white pine. All of the usual pond vegetation occurs here in profusion, along with the usual marsh birds, including loads of ducks.

Beautiful swamp rose, *Rosa palustris*, grows along the shores of many marshes in the Northeast.

The sun sets through the pines of the Merrymeeting River Wildlife Management Area.

As we paddled back to the access with the sun setting over the marsh, a beaver slapped the water with its broad tail, as if to send us on our way so the nighttime creatures could hold sway.

Getting There

To get to Marsh Pond and the eastern section of Merrymeeting River from the Spaulding Turnpike in Rochester, take Exit 15 to Route 11, which goes northwest. After Old Route 11 crosses Route 11, turn right onto Depot Road in another 1.1 miles (Ridge Road goes left at this junction). At the T in 0.4 mile, turn left onto Main Street, go 0.5 mile, and turn right onto Merrymeeting Lake Road. The access point is in 1.6 miles at the bridge that separates Marsh Pond from this dammed-up section of the river.

To get to the western section, go back to Depot Road, take it to Route 11, turn right (northwest), and go 0.4 mile on Route 11 to the access on the left.

Salmon Falls River
Milton, NH

MAPS
New Hampshire Atlas: Map 37

USGS Quadrangle: Great East Lake, ME/NH

INFORMATION
Length: 2 miles

Prominent fish species: Smallmouth bass

This river forms the boundary between lower Maine and New Hampshire. For most of its considerable length, it is but a small stream; however, in Milton Mills, a dam causes the river to widen to paddlable proportions.

Although this section of the river runs for only about two miles, if you paddle here it will seem much longer. The channel meanders seemingly aimlessly through endless acres of aquatic vegetation, with some really nice patches of floating heart, with its diminutive waterlily-like leaves. The huge amount of underwater structure supports healthy fish populations, with—we are told—some huge smallmouth bass lurking under the lily pads.

If you enjoy exploring pond life amongst the lily pads, pickerel-weed, arrowhead, sedge, and rush, paddle here. In places, vegetation masks the main channel; what looks like a widened channel turns out to be a dead end, while the real channel snakes through a dense stand of pickerelweed.

The second time that we paddled here, we had to carry over a new beaver dam about a mile from the access point. In addition to seeing a new beaver lodge, we saw a muskrat, many ducks, a kingfisher, hundreds

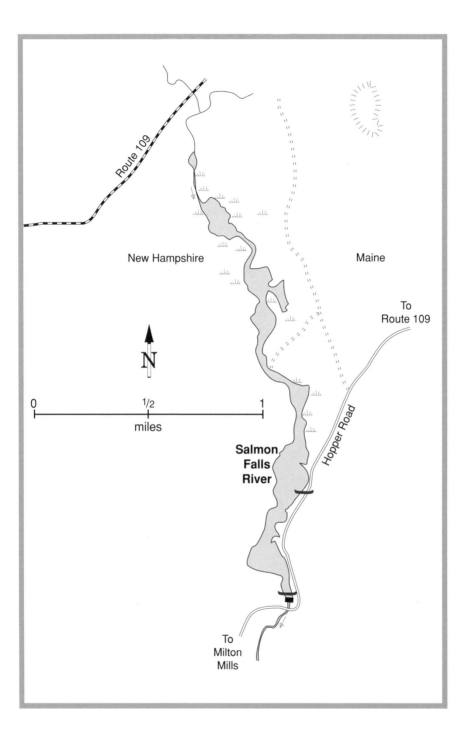

Route 109

New Hampshire

Maine

To
Route 109

N

0   1/2   1
miles

**Salmon
Falls
River**

Hopper Road

To
Milton
Mills

of red-winged blackbirds, and many dragonflies and damselflies. In the upper reaches, lots of tamarack grow out of sphagnum hummocks.

There are two put-in points, one at the dam site and the other 0.5 mile upstream. The dam site has more parking, but if you put in at the upper site, you will avoid paddling literally through the backyards of two houses. Once past these, the evidence of human civilization is slight until you reach the upper stretch of this small reservoir. A second reason for putting in upstream is that barely submerged rocks choke the lower section. Go slowly there.

GETTING THERE

From Milton Mills, with the U.S. Post Office on your right and the Milton Mills Village Store on your left, drive straight uphill. Go 0.3 mile, turn right onto Hopper Road, and continue 0.5 mile to the access, just over the bridge on the left. The second access, which avoids the backyards and submerged boulders, is another 0.5 mile.

Alternatively, from Sanford, Maine, take Routes 4A/109 through Springvale. When Routes 11 and 109 split, take Route 109, the left fork, go 3.6 miles, and turn left onto Old Route 9, which cuts diagonally across Route 109. After 0.2 mile, take the left fork onto Hopper Road. The access is on the right in another 3.1 miles.

Clark Pond
Canaan, NH

MAPS

New Hampshire Atlas: Map 38

USGS Quadrangle: Canaan

INFORMATION

Area: 97 acres

Prominent fish species: Smallmouth bass, pickerel, and yellow perch

Though Clark Pond gets a fair amount of traffic from anglers and has a few summer cottages along its shores, paddling on this long, narrow pond provides ample rewards. We most enjoyed the end farthest from the boat access, especially where the inlet from Little Clark Pond enters. You can paddle back in and portage over beaver dams. In early July, along with all of the typical bog plants, we found lots of rose pogonia orchid and cranberry in bloom.

The hillsides surrounding the pond harbor mostly deciduous trees, along with the occasional tall white pine. Sweet gale grows thickly along the shores, particularly in swampy areas. We found lots of *equisetum*, pickerelweed, pondweed, water shield, bur-reed, sundew, narrow-leafed cattail, and fragrant waterlily at the northwest end. Two loons competed with the less successful anglers when we paddled here.

GETTING THERE

From Route 4 in Canaan, turn north onto Canaan Street, go 3.4 miles, and turn right onto River Road. After 2.0 miles, turn left onto Clark Pond Road. In 1.3 miles go right at the fork; the boat access is in another 0.4 mile.

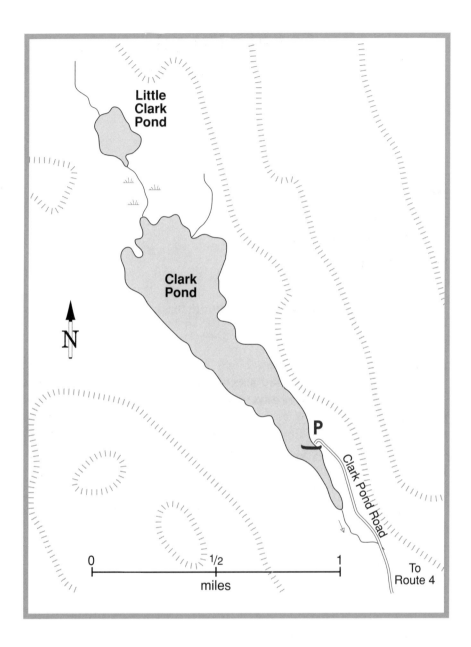

Little
Clark
Pond

Clark
Pond

N

P

Clark Pond Road

0   1/2   1
        miles

To
Route 4

Lake Armington and Lake Tarleton

Piermont and Warren, NH

MAPS

New Hampshire Atlas: Maps 38 and 42

USGS Quadrangle: Warren

INFORMATION

Lake Armington area: 142 acres

Lake Tarleton area: 315 acres

Prominent fish species: Lake Armington—smallmouth bass, pickerel, brown trout, and rainbow trout; Lake Tarleton—smallmouth bass, pickerel, brown trout, lake trout, and rainbow trout

Contact information: The Trust for Public Lands—617-367-6200; www.tpl.org

Though you will not paddle alone here, except perhaps in the off-season, the scenery makes Lake Tarleton and Lake Armington well worth a visit. The Appalachian Trail passes over the peaks just east of here, and those mountains provide a scenic backdrop for both lakes. Though Lake Armington has some development along its shores, the land surrounding Lake Tarleton has been added recently to the White Mountain National Forest through the farsighted efforts of The Trust for Public Lands and the New Hampshire Charitable Trust. These organizations have helped protect more than 5,300 acres around the lake.

The main difference between Lakes Armington and Tarleton is size. Lake Armington's smaller size, coupled with having Piermont Mountain due west, makes it much less susceptible to wind. Though we prefer to paddle Lake Armington because of its more intimate size and the fact that

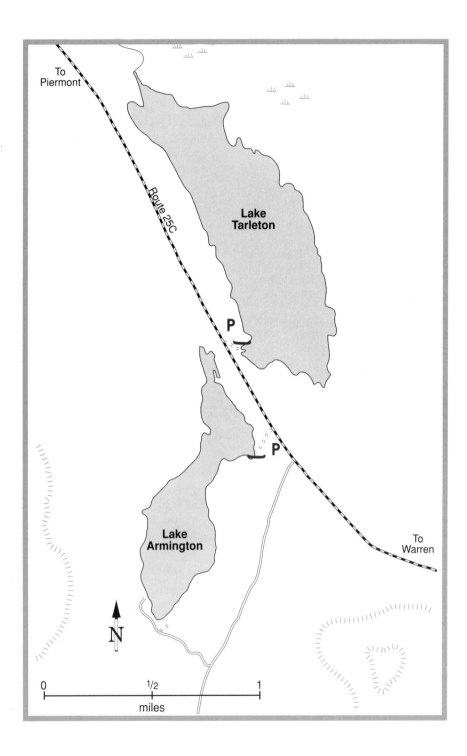

To
Piermont

Route 25C

Lake
Tarleton

P

P

Lake
Armington

To
Warren

N

0   1/2   1
miles

The Appalachian Trail passes over the mountaintops in the national forest east of Lake Tarleton.

personal watercraft are banned, anglers may want to take advantage of the exceptional smallmouth bass and trout fishing on Tarleton.

The water's clarity and the rich and varied hillsides, with mixed stands of spruce, white pine, hemlock, and white birch, make these lakes particularly inviting. Colorful sheep laurel blooms in June, songbirds forage on elderberries in late summer, loons dive for fish, and cedar waxwings fly overhead. Beaver activity seemed greater on Lake Armington, and we saw more ducks with young—perhaps because of lighter boat traffic.

GETTING THERE

From the west, from Piermont at the junction of Routes 10, 25, and 25C, take Route 25C 8.5 miles east toward Warren to the Lake Tarleton access on the left. The Lake Armington Road boat access is another 0.4 mile east on the right.

From the south or east, from Warren take Route 25C west. The Lake Armington Road access is on the left at the Piermont/Warren town line; the Lake Tarleton access is 0.4 mile farther west on the right.

Robartwood Pond and Campton Bog
Campton, NH

MAPS
New Hampshire Atlas: Map 39

USGS Quadrangle: Plymouth

INFORMATION
Length: 3 miles

Prominent fish species: Brook trout

This extraordinary pond, just off I-93, lies at the southern foot of the White Mountain National Forest. Peaks that rise more than a 1,000 feet above the pond border it immediately to the north and west. Many channels, some kept open by beaver, wend their way back from the dam on this long, narrow pond. Near the back of the pond, we surprised a beaver paddling around in the middle of the day, a sure sign that this pond gets little boat traffic. A relatively high beaver dam on the west end supports a large expanse of water—Campton Bog—also worth exploring.

Some black spruce and red maple have encroached on the boggy high ground crowded with shrubs. Look for round-leafed sundew on the sphagnum mats, and take note of the small leaves and flowers of the yellow pond lily. As we paddled the length of this weed-choked pond, our attention focused on the pondweed, water shield, fragrant waterlily, iris, sweet gale and lots more. A bald eagle feeding along the shore surprised us as it took flight.

With a flock of cedar waxwings wheeling overhead, tree and barn swallows skimming the water's surface, and wood thrushes calling from

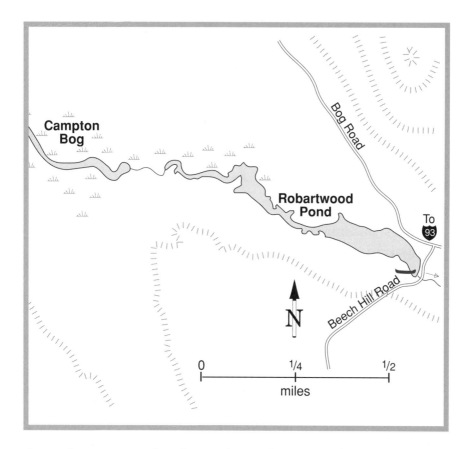

the understory, we found ourselves reluctant to leave this aquatic wonderland. As we paddled back to the access, we wondered what was next—maybe a moose? Though the bog provides excellent moose habitat, we contented ourselves with the wonderful scenery, myriad aquatic plants, a beaver that slapped the water with its tail as it dove out of sight, and the majestic bald eagle.

GETTING THERE

From I-93, Exit 27, go west on Bog Road for 2.4 miles and turn left onto Beech Hill Road. The access is 0.2 mile ahead on the right. Do not block the fire hydrant access.

White Oak Pond
Holderness, NH

MAPS
   New Hampshire Atlas: Map 39
   USGS Quadrangle: Holderness
INFORMATION
   Area: 291 acres

   Prominent fish species: Pickerel and yellow perch

Of the small Lakes Region ponds, White Oak remains one of our favorites. For starters, the state prohibits outboard motors larger than 7.5 horsepower. The few houses along the shore have small docks with canoes on racks, rather than huge docks jutting out into the lake with behemoth powerboats tied up waiting to be released. The lake seems tranquil and relaxed. On a Memorial Day weekend we saw only one other boat, and it was a solo canoe.

About a dozen quite unobtrusive houses dot the shoreline, primarily along the northeastern shore and the western end. Several privately owned islands, including a quite large one, provide extra shoreline to explore. The heavily wooded shoreline harbors white pine, red oak, red maple, and a few stands of hemlock. After quite a bit of looking, we actually found a sickly white-oak specimen; this is pretty far north for white oak. We also found a variety of fern around the lake: huge stands of royal and cinnamon ferns along the shore, with dense carpets of various wood ferns farther up the banks.

At times of high water, one can paddle quite far up the inlet creek on the pond's marshy eastern end, winding through the cattails, old beaver lodges, mossy hummocks, and thick marsh—ideal habitat for all

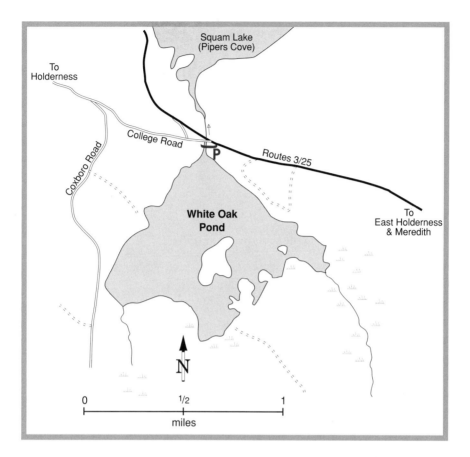

sorts of birds. We paddled about a half-mile up this inlet, surrounded by a peacefulness broken only by the singing of warblers, marsh wrens, and red-winged blackbirds. Out on the main lake we watched a pair of loons—from a fair distance, so as not to disturb them.

GETTING THERE

From the bridge in Holderness, go east on Routes 25/3 for 1.8 miles to the access on the right.

From Meredith, where Routes 25 and 3 join, travel west on Routes 25/3 to the boat access on the left, just after the White Oak Motel, where College Road splits off. The access is 2.9 miles from the junction of Routes 3/25 with Route 25B.

Squam Lake
Center Harbor, Holderness, Moultonborough, and Sandwich, NH

MAPS

New Hampshire Atlas: Maps 39 and 40

USGS Quadrangles: Center Harbor, Center Sandwich, Holderness, and Squam Mountains

INFORMATION

Area: 6,765 acres

Prominent fish species: Largemouth bass, smallmouth bass, perch, pickerel, landlocked salmon, lake trout, and rainbow trout

Camping, parking, boat rental, and *Squam Lake Chart*: Squam Lake Association—603-968-7336; www.squamlakes.org

Science education: The Squam Lake Natural Science Center on Route 113 in Holderness is a great place to visit, especially with children—603-968-7194; www.slnsc.org.

Squam Lake, one of New Hampshire's real treasures, remains one of our favorite lakes for an extended visit. This large, highly varied lake boasts dozens of islands, deep coves, and marshy inlets to explore. One could easily paddle every day for a week and still not explore the entirety of its 60-mile shoreline and all of the islands. Clean, crystal-clear water and sandy white beaches make for ideal swimming. Squam Lake, the setting for the film *On Golden Pond*, has its drawbacks, however. A fair amount of development crowds the shoreline and many of the islands. While the dreaded personal watercraft are banned, heavy motorboat traffic can make paddling unenjoyable, and even dangerous, during the

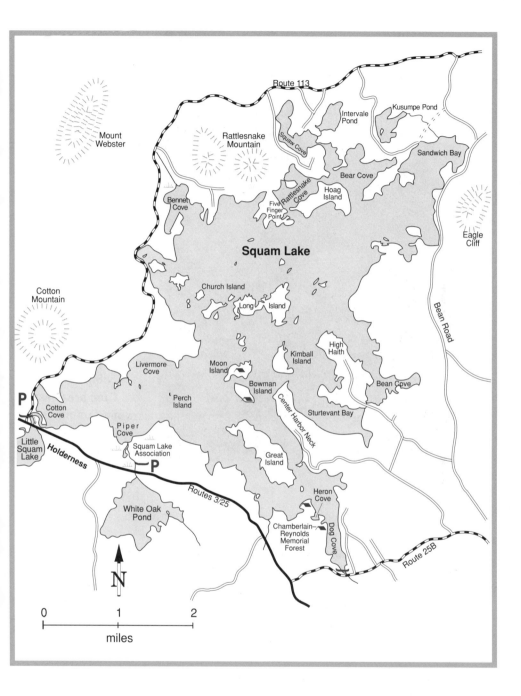

Mount
Webster

Rattlesnake
Mountain

Route 113

Squaw Cove

Intervale
Pond

Kusumpe Pond

Sandwich Bay

Bear Cove

Hoag
Island

Bennet
Cove

Rattlesnake
Cove

Five
Finger
Point

Eagle
Cliff

Squam Lake

Cotton
Mountain

Church Island

Long   Island

Bean Road

High
Haith

Kimball
Island

Livermore
Cove

Moon
Island

Bowman
Island

Bean Cove

Perch
Island

Center Harbor Neck

Sturtevant Bay

P

Cotton
Cove

Piper
Cove

Little
Squam
Lake

Holderness

Squam Lake
Association

P

Great
Island

Routes 3/25

Heron
Cove

White Oak
Pond

Chamberlain–
Reynolds
Memorial
Forest

Dog Cove

Route 25B

N

0   1   2

miles

Sally Andrews flipping bannock for breakfast while camping on Moon Island in Squam Lake.

summer months. If you decide to do a moonlight paddle, carry a bright flashlight to warn away oncoming motorboats.

Squam Lake also suffers from strong winds that can come up quickly and generate waves large enough to swamp an open boat. The wake from a big motorboat can amplify the wind-formed waves, compounding the problem. To reach some of the islands, including Moon and Bowman, you have to cross a mile or more of open water. Use great caution on Squam, and paddle elsewhere during adverse weather conditions.

In addition to the gorgeous setting and the myriad coves and shorelines to explore, Squam Lake boasts a huge loon population.

You can view most of Squam Lake from West Rattlesnake Mountain. The trail starts from Five Fingers Point near the northern end of the lake.

When you click on the Squam Lake Association website, you will hear loons calling. Biologists and volunteers have recorded loon numbers since 1975, when 26 adult loons fledged six chicks. The population built slowly and reached 60 by 2000. By demarcating nest sites with pylons, providing artificial islands for nest sites, and making some coves off-limits to boats, this large population may be sustainable. Another positive step occurred when the New Hampshire Department of Fish and Game banned lead sinkers, effective January 1, 2000; ingested lead sinkers killed a bald eagle at Lake Umbagog and, according to the Tufts University Wildlife Veterinary Clinic, lead poisoning causes more than 50 percent of loon mortality on its breeding grounds.

Among the usual mixed hardwoods, white pine, red pine, and hemlock that lace the heavily wooded shores and islands, you will see a few unusual species, such as black gum (*Nyssa sylvatica*), whose leaves turn a brilliant crimson early in the fall, and some huge, ancient specimens of more-common trees. Beautiful stands of mountain laurel grace some islands and peninsulas. In the marshy coves look for buttonbush, with its unusual round white flowers.

Because individuals own most of the islands and surrounding land, you may want to concentrate your exploring in three primary areas with natural areas open to the public: Five Fingers Point, Chamberlain-Reynolds Memorial Forest, and Moon and Bowman Islands. Though just as beautiful as these public-use areas, the private areas—remarkably—mostly remain free of No Trespassing signs. If we refrain from abusing private land, perhaps those shoreline trees can remain free of such signs. Of course, we should not abuse the public-access areas either; the owners could easily restrict use if littering, damage to vegetation, or violation of established rules becomes a problem.

On the northern shore of the lake, the University of New Hampshire owns Five Fingers Point, which offers deep coves, sandy beaches, marshy inlets, and forest trails to explore. From here you can hike up the two steep knolls—the Rattlesnakes—that overlook the lake. The exposed rock outcropping on West Rattlesnake affords a superb view of the lake. (For an alternate trail, see below.)

Rattlesnake and Squaw Coves, to the east and north of Five Fingers Point, enjoy protection from wind and represent the only parts of Squam Lake off-limits to water-skiing. Picnicking is allowed on portions of Hoag Island, though not overnight camping or fires.

The New England Forestry Foundation owns the 157-acre Chamberlain-Reynolds Memorial Forest, adjacent to Dog Cove at the southern part of the lake and managed by the Squam Lake Association. An extensive network of trails courses though this area, including a raised boardwalk through the swamp. The area, alive with birds, also supports some hemlocks and pines over two feet in diameter and more than 300 years old. A dock juts out on each side of nearby Heron Cove; a very nice, though heavily used, beach is located just around the peninsula from Heron Cove.

The Squam Lake Association maintains several camping sites—both small sites (six-person) and group sites (twelve-person)—on the lake: five near the southernmost tip of the lake in the Chamberlain-Reynolds Memorial Forest, two on Moon Island, and four on Bowman Island. The camping fee is for the site, not per person, and reservations must be made in advance. Fees ranged from $32 to $100 in 2000, depending on type of site and day of the week, and may be divided among a large group.

A boggy cove on Squam Lake harbors numerous species of aquatic plants.

Heron Cove contains the most isolated campsite, situated on a point of land above the cove, nestled beneath tall hemlocks and white pines, carpeted with soft pine needles, and ringed with mountain laurel and blueberry bushes. It includes a composting toilet, fire ring, small dock, and room for several tents. Because of the surrounding marshy area, you can reach the campsite only by boat.

Moon and Bowman Islands support the most exciting camping spots for the serious paddler. The islands, purchased by the Squam Lake Association in 1986 and 1994, harbor several tent sites. Short walks lead to a number of beautiful beaches—which Alex's daughters, age one and four, enjoyed for many hours during a four-day stay while doing research for the first edition. Though paddling across open water can be hazardous, Moon and Bowman Islands are wonderful places for kids.

If you plan to do much paddling here, buy a copy of the *Squam Lake Chart*, published on waterproof material by the Squam Lake Association and available at a number of area stores, as well as through the association. The one-page map in this book lacks sufficient detail for a lake this size.

GETTING THERE

Science Center access. The Squam Lake Association (SLA) provides three access points. One is opposite the Science Center of New Hampshire on Route 113, just north of the junction with Route 3 in Holderness; SLA deeded this access to the state. Parking is allowed for 24 hours maximum.

Dog Cove access. From the junction of Routes 3/25 and Route 25B, go 0.9 mile on Route 25B to the hard-to-see access to Dog Cove on the left. Park on either side of the road and carry your boat down a short trail to the water. This hand-carry access can get muddy at low water levels.

Piper Cove access. From the Squam River bridge (at the junction of Routes 3/25 with Route 113) in Holderness, go east 1.6 miles on Routes 3/25 to the SLA headquarters on Piper Cove. The parking fee in 2000 was $5.

Alternate trail to the Rattlesnakes. From its intersection with Routes 3/25, drive 5.5 miles north on Route 113 to the parking area on the left. To find the trailhead, cross the road and walk 100 feet back toward Holderness. The hike up to West Rattlesnake lookout is about 1.0 mile and takes roughly half an hour.

Garland Pond
Moultonborough, NH

MAPS

New Hampshire Atlas: Map 40

USGS Quadrangles: Center Harbor and Center Sandwich

INFORMATION

Area: 110 acres

Prominent fish species: Smallmouth bass, pickerel, and yellow perch

When wind whips up the waves on nearby Squam Lake, try Garland Pond instead. Because few people know of its existence and because the state has banned gasoline motors here, Garland Pond retains a wild, untrammeled feeling. Beautiful hillsides surround it, and the only house blends unobtrusively into the western hillside. Some road noise intrudes from Route 25, but that pretty much disappears as you paddle into the pond's northern reaches.

A diverse mix of deciduous trees dominates the hillsides and hovers over the shrubby shoreline. The usual pond vegetation provides ample places to hide for the many wood ducks that breed here. They scurried off into the brushy vegetation upon our approach. We watched a muskrat harvest yellow pond-lily fronds as we listened to wood thrushes calling from the hillsides. To explore the area fully, you will have to portage over several beaver dams. A great blue heron rookery must be nearby, as we spotted many of these stately birds patrolling the marsh for fish, snakes, frogs, and more. As we listened to the yellowthroats calling from the sweet gale in the northern boggy area, a garter snake slithered into the water, and iridescent green damselflies

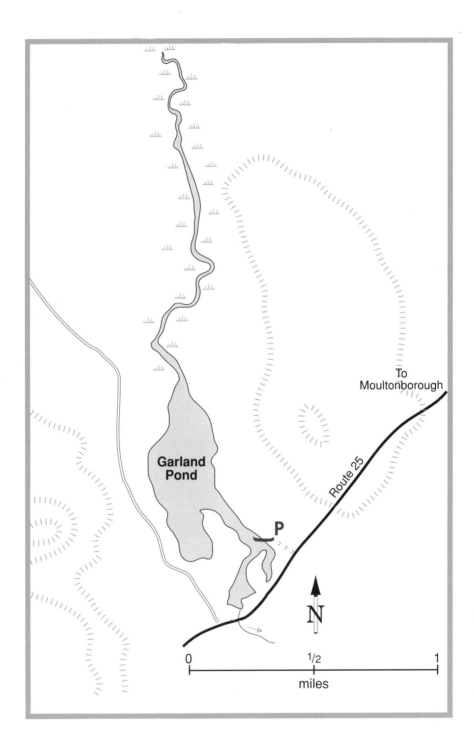

Garland
Pond

P

To
Moultonborough

Route 25

N

0   1/2   1
miles

A small beaver dam impedes progress when paddling on Garland Pond's inlet stream.

with black wingtips lit on the tips of vegetation protruding from the water's surface.

GETTING THERE

From the junction of Routes 25 and 109 in Moultonborough, head southeast on Route 25. Garland Pond Road is on the right in 0.6 mile. It is easy to miss, as it looks like a private driveway. Park in the little parking area in 0.2 mile; when we paddled here, driving farther was impossible because of a ditch across the road.

Copps Pond
Tuftonboro, NH

MAPS
New Hampshire Atlas: Map 40

USGS Quadrangle: Melvin Village

INFORMATION
Area: 180 acres

Prominent fish species: Pickerel and brook trout

In this region of New Hampshire, with many deep, clear lakes dotted with vacation homes, Copps Pond provides a pleasant alternative, especially on a windy day when you want a smaller, more protected spot. With no boat ramp on the pond and huge mats of floating vegetation, you shouldn't have to contend with motorboats. A highway department building and storage sheds on the northern side, along Route 109A, are the only development on the pond.

Really more of a marsh than an open body of water, Copps Pond provides a great spot for bird watching and plant identification. By mid-July, vegetation covers about 80 percent of this small pond's surface, with at least three different species of waterlily (water shield, fragrant waterlily, and yellow pond lily), pickerelweed, sedge, rush, and cattail. We also saw beautiful (and relatively rare) rose pogonia orchid and sundew on floating sphagnum mats. A number of wood duck nesting boxes surround the pond, which provides superb habitat for numerous species of waterfowl.

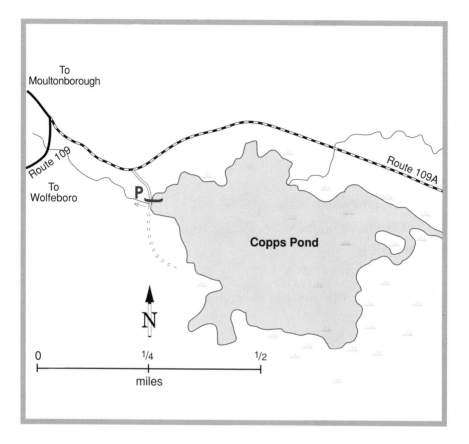

Getting there

From Moultonborough, take Route 109 south through Melvin village. Take Route 109A to the left when it splits off; continue for 0.2 mile on Route 109A and turn right onto a dirt road, which leads to the access.

Chocorua Lake
Tamworth, NH

MAPS

New Hampshire Atlas: Maps 40 and 41

USGS Quadrangle: Silver Lake

INFORMATION

Area: 222 acres

Prominent fish species: Smallmouth bass, pickerel, perch, brook trout, and brown trout

Camping: All state-park campground reservations—603-271-3628 or www.nhparks.state.nh.us; White Lake State Park—603-323-7350

Chocorua Lake, a pleasant spot for a morning or afternoon paddle, nestles beneath Mount Chocorua, one of New England's most picturesque and most photographed mountains. The 222-acre lake remains off-limits to motors, so you will only have to contend with road noise from Route 16, which runs along the eastern side of the lake. At the southern end you can paddle under a little bridge to get into adjoining Little Lake, smaller and more protected, but with more development than the larger lake.

Bird watchers should explore the several marshy areas on Chocorua and the more extensive marshy areas and two beaver lodges on Little Lake. Conservation land, open to the public, covers the entire eastern and northern sides of the lake. You can park and put in anywhere along old Route 16, which provides plenty of room for picnicking. You will find a great picnic area with big granite-slab tables and wooden benches built into the large pine trees near the passage between the two lakes. Huge white pine, red pine, and red oak add a wonderful backdrop

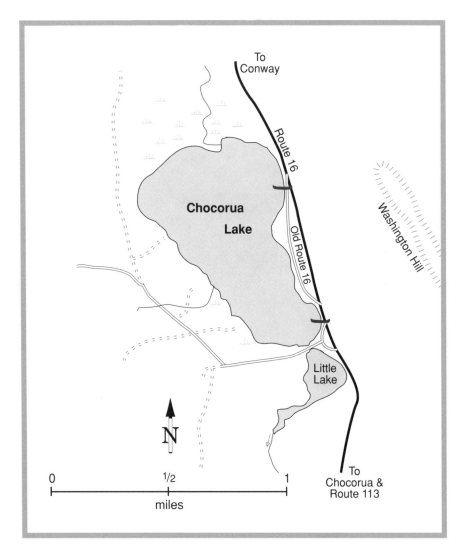

To
Conway

Route 16

Chocorua
Lake

Old Route 16

Washington Hill

Little
Lake

N

0   1/2   1
miles

To
Chocorua &
Route 113

to the entire eastern side of the lake. Brook trout fishing is supposed to be quite good at the lake's inlet and outlet.

Beware of strong winds that descend from the mountains to the northwest, creating hazardous conditions. Watch for clouds building near the craggy peak of Mount Chocorua, possibly a sign of gale-strength winds to follow. The second time here, we got drenched.

A small bridge separates Little Lake from Chocorua Lake. You can see Mount Chocorua from almost anywhere on the two lakes.

GETTING THERE

In Chocorua, at the junction of Routes 16 and 113, take Route 16 north for a few miles. Look for the lake off to the left; take a sharp left onto Old Route 16 (one-way south) to the boat access.

Cooks Pond and Cooks River
Madison, NH

MAPS

New Hampshire Atlas: Map 41

USGS Quadrangle: Ossipee Lake

INFORMATION

Length: 1.5 miles

Prominent fish species: Smallmouth bass and pickerel

Camping: All state-park campground reservations—603-271-3628 or www.nhparks.state.nh.us; White Lake State Park—603-323-7350

Driving up Route 41 toward Silver Lake, note the red pine along the road, particularly on the right (east) as you pass by the West Branch Pine Barrens, protected by The Nature Conservancy. The extensive stands of pine and shrubby understory bear a striking resemblance to the long-leaf pine forests of the rural south. As you drive down Lead Mine Road you can see at road cuts the sand and gravel soil that supports this vegetation regime.

Paddling out from the access onto Cooks Pond, note that shoreline pine gives way to mostly deciduous trees on the hillsides. Dense stands of shrubs dominate the boggy shore; we noted quite a bit of sheep laurel. Three houses hover above the pond's shore, the only development in evidence between the road and Silver Lake, about a mile downstream. Don't expect to paddle too quickly down the winding channel through the pickerelweed to Silver Lake; we had to negotiate a newly constructed beaver dam that raised the water level about a foot and a half.

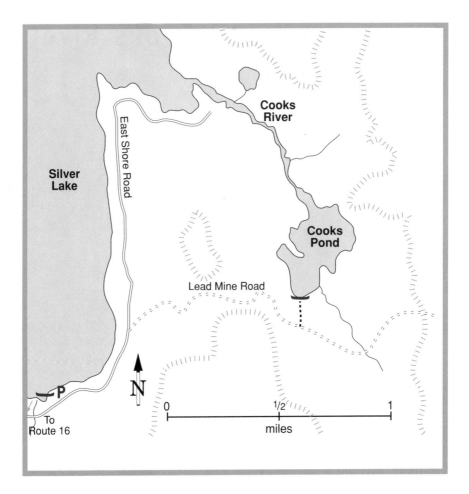

Along the shallow waterway, a broad expanse of marsh provides habitat for everything from frogs to moose; we saw tracks of the latter in many places along the banks. Aquatic vegetation—pickerelweed, pondweed, water celery, and more—gives way to cattails, reeds, and grasses along the shore. Note the very-short-needled black spruce, red maple, and dead trees on the sphagnum hummocks, along with pitcher plant and sundew. The few, small sugar maples along the left shore must get pruned frequently by beaver.

Round-leafed sundews, *Drosera rotundifolia*, grow in profusion on the sphagnum mats of Cooks Pond.

Passing through the winding channel as you near Silver Lake, Mount Chocorua and surrounding peaks pop into view, making this a magical place to paddle.

GETTING THERE

From West Ossipee at the junction of Routes 16 and 41, take Route 41 north for 2.2 miles and turn right onto East Shore Road. Pass by the Silver Lake access on the left after 0.8 mile. Turn right onto Lead Mine Road in another 0.4 mile (1.2 miles from Route 41). The easy-to-miss access trail is on the left at the bottom of a dip, 0.8 mile down Lead Mine Road. The put-in is about 100 yards down the trail to the pond.

When it is not too windy, you can also paddle up from the Silver Lake access along the lake's east shore for about a mile to Cooks River.

Conway Lake
Conway and Eaton, NH

MAPS

New Hampshire Atlas: Map 41

USGS Quadrangle: Conway

INFORMATION

Area: 1,298 acres

Prominent fish species: Smallmouth bass, pickerel, landlocked salmon, and rainbow trout

Camping: All state-park campground reservations—603-271-3628 or www.nhparks.state.nh.us; White Lake State Park—603-323-7350

This large lake, with its varied, lightly developed shoreline, marshy coves, and pine-covered islands, is set in a gorgeous backdrop just southeast of the White Mountains and offers excellent paddling. On a breezy day, particularly with wind from the south or west, one should stick to the southern end, which forks into two long and relatively narrow fingers. The smaller, southwestern finger remains undeveloped, and just a few houses impinge on the larger, more easterly inlet. Both provide marshy shelter for herons, ducks, beaver, and other wildlife.

We watched a deer drink at the water's edge and startled a great horned owl early one August morning at the southwestern tip. In the wider inlet a pair of loons joined us, and judging from fresh tracks in the mud near the southern boat access, we just missed seeing a moose. While paddling here on a windless June day, we photographed floating heart—one of the few aquatic plants that roots successfully in water deeper than four feet—water celery, and yellow pond lily. We also reveled in the beauty of the distant mountains.

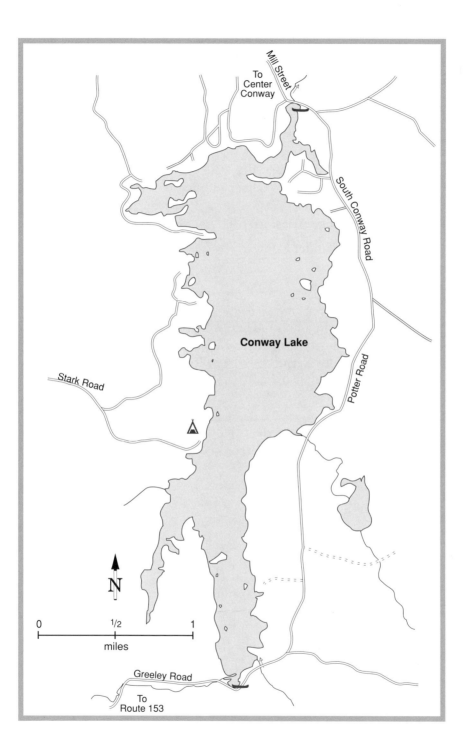

Mill Street

To
Center
Conway

South Conway Road

Conway Lake

Stark Road

Potter Road

N

0   1/2   1
miles

Greeley Road

To
Route 153

The western side of the lake most of the way up to the northern end has numerous deep marshy coves to explore and very little development, except around the one road near the southern fork and at the northern end. Be aware that the quite wide northern half of the lake can suffer from strong winds that come up quickly. While some coves provide wind protection, you can reach them only by paddling out on the open lake.

For a pleasant walk, take the trail from the parking area at the northern access; it includes signs describing several generations of water-powered mills that existed here. Near the ruins of the most recent mill building, you can still see metal hoops from the old wooden sluice, or penstock, scattered in the creek.

GETTING THERE

To reach the southern access from Conway, take Route 153 south. Watch for Greeley Road on the left, which leads directly to the access. Greeley Road turns off right about 1.0 mile north of Eaton Center.

To reach the northern access from Route 302 in Center Conway, take Mill Street south for 0.8 mile to the access on the right; parking is on the left.

Long Pond
Benton, NH

MAPS

New Hampshire Atlas: Map 42

USGS Quadrangle: East Haverhill

INFORMATION

Area: 124 acres

Prominent fish species: Brook trout

Camping: For regulations on primitive camping, contact the White Mountain National Forest—603-528-8755

Surrounded by the White Mountains and completely free from development, Long Pond remains one of our favorite bodies of water in the two-state region. Though relatively small, the pond feels much larger, owing to its long profile, highly varied shoreline, and several islands. One could sit for hours just absorbing the peacefulness and beauty.

The access and a small picnic area are located at the northern end. While Alex and his five-year-old daughter had breakfast here on a crisp September morning (after camping at Russell Pond, a half-hour away), they watched an otter cavorting 50 yards away. Paddling around the pond, you will see a couple of beaver lodges. The best time to see beaver, otter, and mink is early in the morning.

The northern half of the pond has a dozen or so islands to explore, and the marshy coves—particularly at the southern end—provide rich wildlife habitat. Tall trees dominate the shoreline; spires of balsam fir and spruce mix with occasional red maple and yellow and white birch. A dense growth of viburnum, alder, and other shrubs

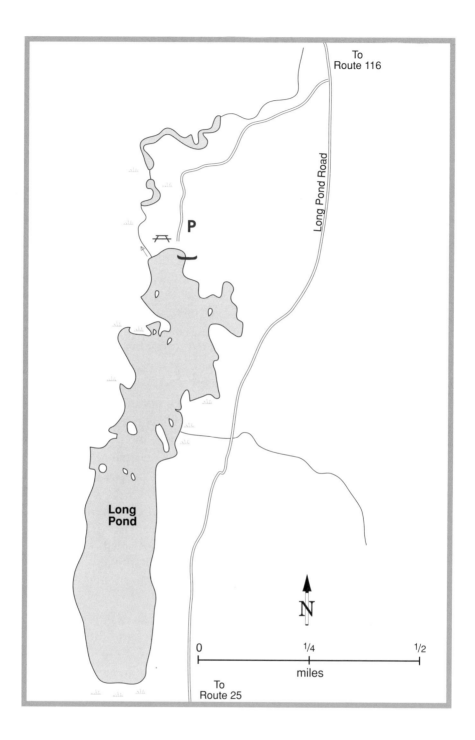

makes shore access quite difficult, but some rocky areas provide spots to disembark for a picnic lunch.

While you cannot camp on the islands in Long Pond, the national forest permits primitive camping in the surrounding area. If you park here during the day (no overnight parking), you need to display a recreational pass; there is a pay station at the boat access.

GETTING THERE

From I-93, Exit 32, in Lincoln, drive west on Route 112, joining Route 116 in about 11 miles. A mile farther, follow Route 116 as it splits off left. After 1.6 miles, turn left onto Long Pond Road (sign for Long Pond). After 2.5 miles turn right, following the sign for Long Pond; you will reach a picnic area in 0.5 mile.

From I-91, Exit 17, take Route 302 east through Woodsville. Turn right onto Route 112 east. Take a sharp right turn onto Route 116 south; continue as above.

From Route 25, follow a paved road north from Glencliff, then turn left onto unpaved Long Pond Road 1.0 mile north of Route 25. Go 4.1 miles and turn left onto the access road.

Upper Kimball Lake
Chatham, NH

MAPS

New Hampshire Atlas: Map 45

USGS Quadrangle: North Conway East

INFORMATION

Area: 136 acres

Prominent fish species: Smallmouth bass, pickerel, and perch

Right next to the Maine border, in the southeastern corner of New Hampshire's White Mountains, lies Upper Kimball Lake, a small and narrow body of water that receives little traffic. A number of houses, set back from the water, impinge somewhat on the northern section, but the southern end and inlet, which winds through a boggy marsh rich in bird life and interesting flora, make the pond well worth paddling.

One can paddle into the inlet at least a half-mile through thick stands of pickerelweed, waterlily, sedge, reed, cattail, and floating mats of sphagnum, dotted with sundew, so named because of glistening secretions on its small reddish-green fronds that attract tiny insects to their doom. Cranberry, sweet gale, various heaths, alder, and buttonbush have established footholds in the gradually filling fen. On solid ground along the shoreline, red maple and white pine dominate.

Even in mid-August, the birds seemed to be everywhere: tree and barn swallows danced over the water, red-winged blackbirds and cedar waxwings flitted among the pickerelweed blooms, sparrows hopped around old beaver lodges, and warblers dined on insects in the maple trees. Bring your binoculars and field guides for a great day of exploration!

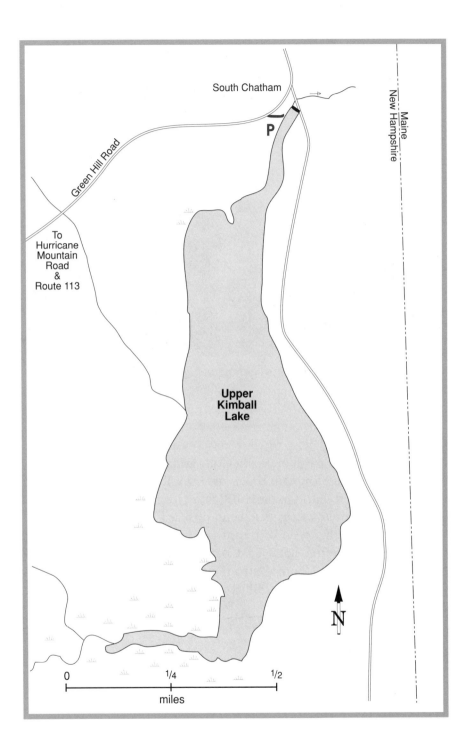

Buttonbush, *Cephalanthus occidentalis*, grows along shores and even in the water.

Getting There

From Intervale, just north of North Conway, take scenic, steep, narrow, winding Hurricane Mountain Road east from Route 16 for 6.1 miles to the T, and turn left onto Green Hill Road. Go another 2.0 miles to the access on the right at a sharp left-hand turn at the bottom of a hill.

From the south, and if you want to avoid the horrendous factory outlet and mall traffic between Conway and North Conway, take Route 113 east from Conway through Center Conway to East Conway, then turn left on Green Hill Road next to the Maine border.

Mountain Pond
Chatham, NH

MAPS

New Hampshire Atlas: Map 45

USGS Quadrangle: Chatham

INFORMATION

Area: 124 acres

Prominent fish species: Brook trout

Camping: For regulations on primitive camping in the White Mountain National Forest—603-528-8755

Because of its remoteness, getting to Mountain Pond requires some effort. Following a long drive up a winding, mostly unpaved road, you still have a carry of about a third of a mile to the pond. Further, vehicles parking at the access must display a federal recreation pass. But, if you appreciate out-of-the-way places—beautiful even on a drizzly, foggy day—your efforts will be amply rewarded. The pond, at an elevation of about 1,500 feet, nestles among the hills just over a dozen miles from Mount Washington, the Northeast's tallest mountain.

On the northern side of this totally natural pond, along the perimeter trail, an Adirondack shelter provides a haven for those looking for secluded lake-side camping, especially before Memorial Day and after Labor Day. You can also pitch a tent anywhere in this part of the White Mountain National Forest.

White pine, spruce, balsam fir, and white birch line the shores of Mountain Pond, along with a dense undergrowth of blueberry and other shrubs. Because of thick understory growth, few places allow you to pull the boat up and get out easily. Paddling around this small pond, you will find a beaver lodge and a small marshy area at the outlet on the

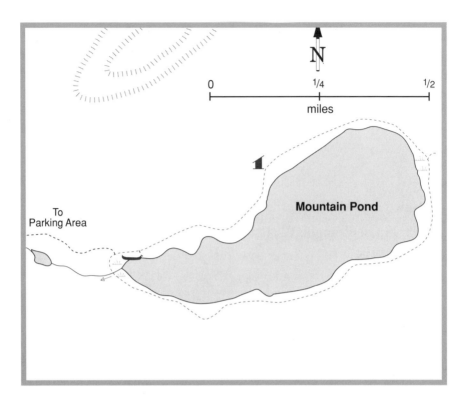

western end, where you might see a great blue heron or a few ducks. Loons inhabit the pond, but we did not see young on our visits here. Be careful not to disturb nesting loons.

GETTING THERE

From North Conway, take Route 16 north. Turn right onto Route 16A, go 1.9 miles, and turn right onto Town Hall Road, immediately after the bridge over the East Branch of the Saco River. After 2.5 miles, the steep, winding road turns to dirt (take the left fork). The parking area is 6.5 miles from Route 16A.

The put-in is approximately 0.3 mile (about 15 minutes) along a wide, though potentially soggy, trail. At the loop trail (marked by a sign) turn left, and within 100 yards or so you will see a trail to the right leading down to a nice put-in point. The Adirondack shelter is another 0.3 mile along the loop trail.

Black Flies and Mosquitoes:
Scourges of the North

Anyone who spends any time at all paddling or hiking the North Country knows these insects all too well. They detract from outdoor fun throughout the summer and make most of June virtually off-limits to outdoor recreation in northern parts of the Northeast. So what are these little beasts that hover in annoying clouds around your head as you portage your canoe or attempt to tie a fly on your line? Though it will not take away any of the pain or itch, understanding these insects may help us accept them as part of the ecosystem we enjoy.

BLACK FLIES

Black flies belong to the family Simuliidae, and most species of concern to us belong to the genus *Simulium*. Scientists have identified more than 1,500 species of black flies worldwide, including 300 in North America. Only 10 to 15 percent of black fly species suck blood from humans or domestic animals.

In parts of northern North America, black flies cause considerable livestock losses—mostly due to weight loss, since cattle do not eat well when tormented by flies, but sometimes they actually kill cattle. In parts of Alberta, Canada, cattle mortality rates from blood loss induced by black flies range from 1 to 4 percent. Researchers have collected as many as 10,000 feeding black flies from a single cow. Black fly problems in North America, however, pale compared to problems in Africa and Central America, where the aptly named species *Simulium damnosum* has infected an estimated 20 million people with onchocerciasis, or river blindness (a disease caused by roundworms transmitted by the fly).

Black flies begin their life cycle in streams and rivers. Adult females deposit eggs in the water, and maturing larvae attach themselves to rocks, plants, and other surfaces in the current. Two tiny, fanlike structures sweep food particles into their mouths. Black fly larvae can become so dense that they form a slippery, mosslike mat on rocks. A several-hundred-foot stretch of a narrow stream can support more than a million larvae. In a river, the population can be in the multibillions per mile.

After a period of days or weeks (depending on the species and available food), each larva builds a pupal case in which it metamorphoses into an adult black fly. When ready to emerge, it splits the pupal case and rides to the water's surface in a bubble of oxygen that had collected in the case.

Adult black flies have one primary goal: to make more black flies. Female black flies seek the nourishing blood meal that they need to lay eggs. Only females bite (actually more of a puncture-and-suck routine than a true bite); males sip nectar from flowers and search for mates. Black flies rely heavily on eyesight to find prey, so they are active almost exclusively during the daylight. Some black flies fly more than 50 miles in search of blood meals.

No black fly species preys exclusively on humans. We are too new on the evolutionary chain to be a specific host to black flies, which arose during the Jurassic period 180 million years ago. An estimated 30 to 45 black fly species in North America feed on humans. There is one species (*Simulium euryadminiculum*) that feeds only on loons.

Mosquitoes

The other major insect nemesis of paddlers is the ubiquitous mosquito. Mosquitoes, members of the Culicidae family, number more than 3,400 species worldwide, including 170 in North America. Three-quarters of the mosquito species in the U.S. and Canada belong to three genera: *Aedes* (78 species), *Culex* (29 species), and *Anopheles* (16 species).

As with black flies, mosquito larvae live an aquatic life. Unlike black flies, though, most mosquitoes have adapted to still water. Whether on a quiet bog or on the Great Bay salt marsh, you can usually find mosquito larvae wriggling about during the spring and early summer months. In a wet spring, you can find lots of them. They eat algae and other organic matter that they filter out of the water with brushlike appendages. Larvae molt several times as they grow and develop into pupae. Both larvae and pupae breathe through air tubes at the water's surface.

Adult mosquitoes have short life spans. Most females live about a month, while males live only about a week. The high-pitched buzz of mosquitoes comes from beating their wings at about 1,000 beats per second. Females generate a higher-pitched whine than males, which helps the males locate mates. Males can be recognized with a hand lens by their much bushier antennae, used to locate females.

Both male and female mosquitoes feed on plant nectar as their primary energy source, but females of most species also require a blood meal to fuel egg production. The habit of female mosquitoes to feed on blood—and especially our blood—has given this insect its deservedly nasty reputation.

As with black flies, a mosquito does not really bite. Rather, she stabs through the victim's skin with six sharp stylets that form the center of the proboscis. Saliva flows into the puncture to keep the blood from coagulating. The reaction most people have to mosquito bites—itching and swelling—is an allergic reaction to the saliva. Upon repeated exposure to mosquito bites, one gradually builds up resistance.

While really just a nuisance in the Northeast, mosquitoes cause death and illness in the tropics. Disease-carrying mosquitoes cause more human deaths than any other animal. They carry more than 100 different diseases, including malaria, yellow fever, encephalitis, filariasis, and dengue. The most destructive of these, malaria, kills about 1 million people a year, mostly children, and as many as 200 million people worldwide carry the disease.

Southern latitudes have far greater mosquito-species diversity (as many as 150 different species can be found in a square mile in some parts of the tropics), but the numbers of individuals generally increase farther north. In the Arctic, with fewer than a dozen species, adults can be so thick they literally blacken the skies. In one experiment, several rugged (and, we suspect, intellectually challenged) Canadian researchers bared their torsos, arms, and legs to Arctic mosquitoes and reported as many as 9,000 bites per minute! At this rate, an unprotected person could lose half of his or her blood in two hours.

So, you see, we really do not have it so bad in New Hampshire and Vermont. Most of our mosquitoes do not carry deadly diseases (though there are occasional cases of mosquito-borne encephalitis and recent outbreaks of west Nile virus), and even in the Connecticut Lakes region in June, we have found it rare to get more than a thousand bites a minute.

BLACK FLY AND MOSQUITO CONTROL

Humans have tried many different control strategies. For mosquito control, we drained thousands of square miles of salt marsh during the 1930s and 1940s by building long, straight drainage ditches—many are still visible. (As much as half of the wetland area in the U.S. has been lost during the last 200 years—partly for mosquito control and partly for development and agriculture.) Along with eliminating habitat, we have used thousands of tons of pesticides in the battle, mostly against mosquitoes. DDT was the chemical of choice for decades because of its supposed safety to the environment—a claim that proved tragically untrue. Since the banning of DDT and other deadly chlorinated-hydrocarbon pesticides in 1973, osprey, bald eagle, peregrine falcon, and other important bird species have begun to make a comeback in the Northeast.

Today, most attention focuses on biological control of these insects. Biological control relies on natural enemies of the pest: viruses, protozoa, bacteria, fungi, and parasites. The most successful control found has been a bacterium discovered in 1977 from samples of sand collected in the Negev Desert. This is *Bacillus thuringiensis* variety *israelensis*, generally known as Bti. Gardeners use another variety of this bacterium for controlling cabbage loopers, corn borers, and other garden pests, and foresters use it for gypsy moth control. Bti bacteria produce protein crystals that react with other chemicals in the insects' stomachs, producing a poison that kills the larvae.

While Bti currently enjoys high success rates, hidden problems could arise, just as with DDT, especially as bioengineers incorporate the Bti gene into plants. This widespread and indiscriminate spreading of the Bti protein could easily lead to pest resistance. Entomologists and conservation biologists also worry that monarch butterflies, on their 1,000-mile-plus migrations to their Mexico wintering grounds, will suffer huge mortality rates from Bti-engineered corn.

PROTECTING YOURSELF FROM BITING INSECTS

One option: stay out of the woods—buy a good book on paddling and read about it. While a bit extreme, this might be a good choice in June when clouds of black flies and mosquitoes may stick in your mind as the most memorable part of an outing. Largely because of biting insects, our favorite times for canoeing in the North Country are in the autumn and in May—during that narrow window between ice-out and the black fly hatch.

During all but the height of the black fly season in June, however, these insects should not spoil your trip. Out on the water where breezes often blow, paddlers can often escape insects. Proper clothing forms the most important line of defense against both black flies and mosquitoes. During black fly season, wear long-sleeved, tight-knit shirts with elastic cuffs. Wear long pants with elastic cuffs, or tuck your pant legs into oversized socks. Black flies land on your clothing and search for openings, such as wrists, ankles, and necks. A mosquito-cloth head net works well, but with a collared shirt, black flies will usually find a route in. Cotton gloves can help too.

Mosquitoes can penetrate soft clothing better than black flies, so a more rugged material such as canvas works well for shirts and pants. Wearing two light shirts also works. Tight cuffs are not as important because mosquitoes usually fly directly to their dining table. With mosquito-cloth head nets, try to keep the mosquito cloth away from your skin—buy one with a metal band from which the cloth hangs. Make sure it has a drawstring or elastic; otherwise, mosquitoes inevitably find their way in.

Insect repellents generally repel mosquitoes better than black flies. DEET (N,N-diethylmetatoluamide) remains the chemical of choice for most folks in the North Country. Fortunately, one of our co-authors is a chemist and is able to pronounce this name. Unfortunately, he also knows enough about its chemical structure to be concerned about potential toxicity to humans. Most repellents outdoorspeople swear by have DEET as the primary active ingredient; some are almost 100 percent DEET. Because DEET works by evaporating into the nearby air to clog insects' odor receptors, you have to keep slathering it on. While we admit to keeping some high-test DEET around when the bugs get really bad, we recommend clothing as the primary defensive strategy. If you must use DEET, apply it to your clothes, rather than your person. There are other products on the market and innovative methods for repelling these insects. Some work better than others.

Is There Anything Good about Black Flies and Mosquitoes?

In reviewing the problems with black flies and mosquitoes, one wonders what might possibly be good about the little beasts. The answer lies in the role they play in aquatic ecosystems, where they provide a vital food source for a wide variety of animals. Many game fish rely on black fly and mosquito larvae for at least a part of their diets. One study found that black fly larvae comprise up to 25 percent of the brook trout diet. Even if black fly and mosquito larvae do not provide a direct food source for game fish and waterfowl, the larvae form a vital part of the food chain upon which these animals rely. If we appreciate angling for brook trout, listening to the evening song of the loon, or watching the stately great blue heron, we should recognize that these species might not be here without black flies and mosquitoes.

Connecticut River— Northern Section

Haverill, Lyman, and Monroe, NH
Barnet, Newbury, and Waterford, VT

MAPS

New Hampshire Atlas: Maps 42 and 46

Vermont Atlas: Maps 42 and 43

USGS Quadrangles: Barnet, VT, and Lower Waterford, NH

INFORMATION

Woodsville/Wells River length: 6.5 miles

Comerford Reservoir length: 10 miles

Prominent fish species: Largemouth bass, smallmouth bass, northern pike, pickerel, perch, walleye, brook trout, brown trout, and rainbow trout

Though adventuresome paddlers periodically traverse the Connecticut River's entire 400-plus-mile length as it flows from the Canadian border in the Connecticut Lakes region of New Hampshire to Long Island Sound off Connecticut, most of that paddle occurs on impoundments. Only a tiny fraction of the total river miles consists of free-flowing water. We include two nice northern reaches of the river—the section below Woodsville, NH/Wells River, VT, and Comerford Reservoir.

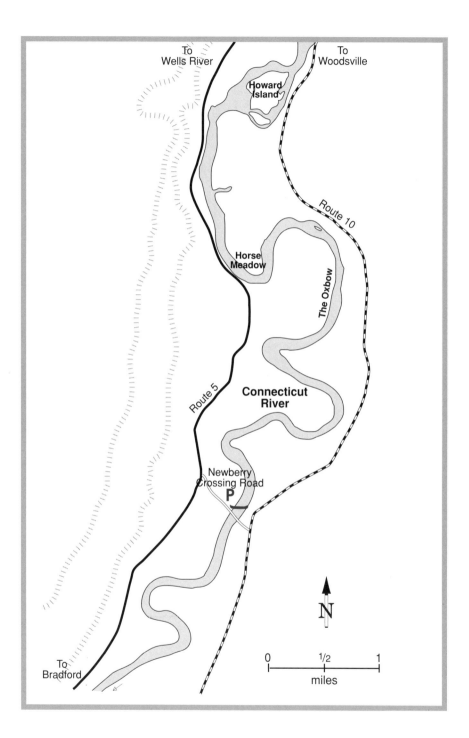

To
Wells River

To
Woodsville

Howard
Island

Route 10

Horse
Meadow

The Oxbow

Route 5

Connecticut
River

Newberry
Crossing Road

P

N

To
Bradford

0   1/2   1

miles

Andrew Hayes paddles a sea kayak on the Connecticut River. These sleek craft are a joy to paddle.

Woodsville, NH/Wells River, VT, Section. From the access, you can paddle upstream for a few miles through rolling farm country. We spotted cedar waxwings, black ducks, kingfishers, lots of spotted sandpipers and killdeer, and an osprey plying the waters for fish. Asters bloomed in profusion, and we paddled leisurely under the spreading canopy of ancient silver maple.

The real draw—and our primary reason for including this section—lies to the east: the string of White Mountain peaks that provide a backdrop to this meandering section of the Connecticut. These peaks, traversed by the Appalachian Trail, reach to over 4,000 feet—Kinsman Mountain at 4,358 feet; Mount Blue to the south at 4,529 feet; and way off in the distance Lafayette, Lincoln, and others in the Franconia Notch region that stretch to over 5,000 feet. We found it hard to keep our eyes on the water amid such splendor. Paddling around the Oxbow affords views from several angles.

Paddling north, the current gradually picks up, blocking further progress. The great thing, though, is that as you paddle back downstream you get another look at the mountains and another opportunity to waste more film.

Comerford Reservoir Section. Some of the larger Connecticut River reservoirs, such as nearby Moore Reservoir, provide vast expanses of water that act as magnets for water-skiers, personal watercraft, and wind, none of which are compatible with quietwater paddling. We include smaller Comerford Reservoir because of its location in a relatively narrow gorge and its more streamlike character. In the summer, winds generally blow either from the south or from the northwest; Comerford's generally northeast-to-southwest orientation provides a modicum of wind protection.

GETTING THERE

Woodsville, NH/Wells River, VT, Section. From I-91, Exit 16, turn right onto Route 25. Go 0.5 mile and turn north onto Route 5. Go north for 7.7 miles and turn right onto Newberry Crossing Road (sign for NH Route 10), leading to Haverill Bridge. The access is 0.4 mile on the left, just before the bridge.

Comerford Section. From I-93, take either Exit 43 or 44, and head west on Routes 18/135 toward Vermont. When Routes 18 and 135 split, take Route 18 to the right. Take an immediate right off Route 18 into the large parking area, go to the end, and turn under the Connecticut River bridge to reach the access. According to the DeLorme atlas, another access is located on the Vermont side, just east of East Barnet; we did not investigate this access point.

Androscoggin River and Pontook Reservoir
Dummer, NH

MAPS

New Hampshire Atlas: Map 50

USGS Quadrangles: Dummer Ponds and Tea Kettle Ridge

INFORMATION

Pontook Reservoir area: 280 acres

Prominent fish species: Pontook Reservoir—largemouth bass and pickerel; Androscoggin River—smallmouth bass, landlocked salmon, brook trout, brown trout, and rainbow trout

Though Pontook Reservoir on the Androscoggin River spans Route 16, we heartily recommend this as a paddling destination. As you drive north along the Androscoggin from Berlin, note the boom piers in the water. The following comes verbatim from a plaque along the river:

> The small man-made islands in the river were used to secure a chain of boom logs, which divided the Androscoggin River during the colorful and dramatic annual log drives. When the Brown Paper Company and the International Paper Company shared the river to float their logs from the forests far upriver to the mills at Berlin, the logs were stamped on the ends with a marking hammer to identify their ownership, and they were sorted at a sorting gap further upriver. The log drives ended in 1963. The old piers continue to serve as a reminder of North Country heritage.

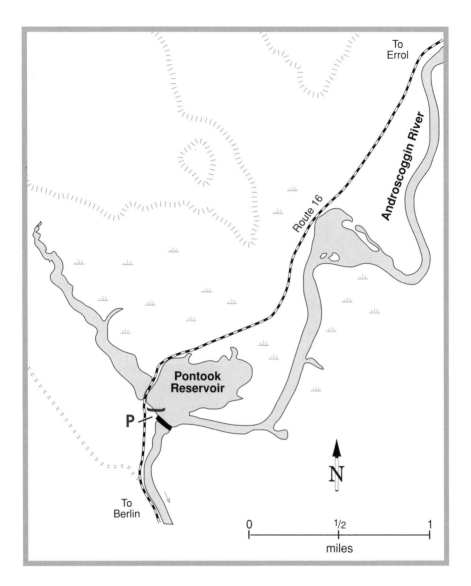

To
Errol

Androscoggin River

Route 16

Pontook
Reservoir

P

To
Berlin

N

0   1/2   1

miles

We watched three mature moose at the reservoir in June, two bulls with large racks and a cow. Myriad other wildlife typical of the northern forest appears here as well. We saw white-winged crossbills, white-throated sparrows, hermit and wood thrushes, a pair of loons with two chicks, and an osprey. In the spring of 2000, a pair of bald eagles began building a nest here, evidence of the species' ongoing recovery in New England.

The northern boreal forest crowds the shores of Pontook Reservoir on the Androscoggin River.

On the river side of Route 16, we paddled about two miles upstream from the dam before we ran into current that helped us turn back. *Please note: below the dam is for expert paddlers only.* Beaver had pruned back the alder along the shore. Lichen-festooned balsam fir provided a solid visual wall between the reservoir and the forest, and we wondered if the lack of deciduous trees, except for the occasional red maple, resulted from long-term beaver activity.

On the west side of Route 16, a group of painted turtles sunned on a log, and we enjoyed the beauty of purple iris stands in bloom. Horsetail crowded the end of the shallow reservoir, and sweet gale and a few birches interrupted the balsam fir domination in this low-lying boggy environment. Paddling to the back of the pond not only puts distance between you and the lightly traveled road, but it also gets you into the heart of prime moose habitat.

GETTING THERE

From Berlin, go north on Route 16 for about 19 miles along the Androscoggin River. From the junction of Routes 16 and 110B in Milan, the boat access is 5.7 miles north on the right. The reservoir spans the road.

Lake Umbagog
Errol, New Hampshire

MAPS

New Hampshire Atlas: Map 51

Maine Atlas: Maps 17 and 18

USGS Quadrangles: LakeUmbagog South and LakeUmbagog North

INFORMATION

Area: 7,850 acres

Prominent fish species: Smallmouth bass, pickerel, northern pike, yellow perch, and brook trout

Contact information: Lake Umbagog National Wildlife Refuge—603-482-3415

Camping: All state-park campground reservations—603-271-3628 or www.nhparks.state.nh.us; Lake Umbagog Campground—603-482-0934. They rent canoes and will tow you—for a fee—to your campsite. Access from the southern end requires paddling across a sizable stretch of open water; we prefer reserving a site near the mouth of the Androscoggin or Magalloway Rivers to minimize paddling over open water.

With the tremendous variety of wildlife and the number of ducks nesting here, we should not be surprised that Lake Umbagog has become one of our newest national wildlife refuges. Established in November 1992 with the purchase by the federal government of the first tracts of land, the Lake Umbagog National Wildlife Refuge remains small, but the U.S. Fish and Wildlife Service intends to obtain

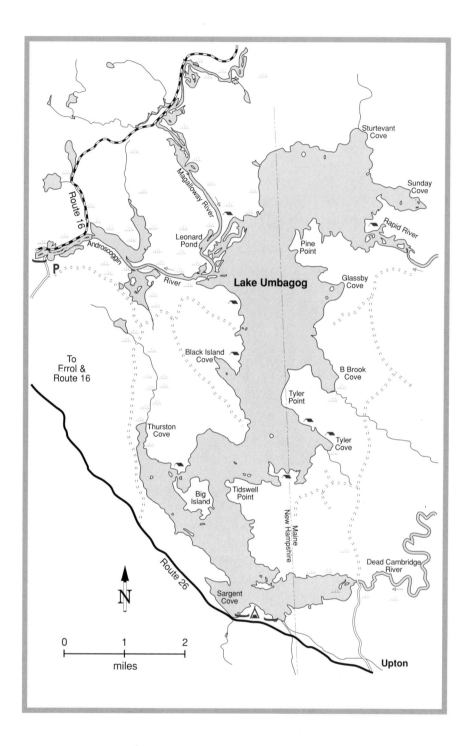

Sturtevant
Cove

Sunday
Cove

Magalloway River

Rapid River

Route 16

Pine
Point

Leonard
Pond

Androscoggin

P

River

Lake Umbagog

Glassby
Cove

To
Frrol &
Route 16

Black Island
Cove

B Brook
Cove

Tyler
Point

Thurston
Cove

Tyler
Cove

Big
Island

Tidswell
Point

Maine
New Hampshire

Dead Cambridge
River

Route 26

N

Sargent
Cove

0   1   2
miles

Upton

Part of Lake Umbagog's highly varied shoreline on a quiet morning.

title or conservation easements that would increase the refuge to nearly 10,000 acres.

Umbagog, pronounced "um-BAY-gog," straddles the Maine–New Hampshire border, covering more than 12 square miles. Oriented generally north-south, with a highly varied shoreline that extends for more than 40 miles plus dozens of islands, this magnificent lake exudes wildness. Readily accessible to the backcountry paddler, Lake Umbagog Campground manages 30 wilderness sites around the lake. A few private cottages and camps dot parts of the lake, and motorboat traffic has increased in recent years, but we expect very little future development. We should all encourage New Hampshire and Maine to restrict motorboat use for the protection of moose and nesting ducks, loons, and bald eagles.

A very shallow lake—Umbagog means "shallow water"—with average depths of only about 15 feet, the many marshy areas provide ideal nesting habitat for such species as ring-necked, black, mallard, and wood ducks, and hooded and common mergansers. Wood ducks and

Early-morning fishing on Big Island, near the southern end of Lake Umbagog.

hooded mergansers (our two common cavity nesters) use the approximately 100 nesting boxes around the lake.

Leonard Pond, the largest marshy area, near the northwestern corner of the lake, sports an extensive, grassy marsh that has supported nesting bald eagles since 1989—no eagles nested in New Hampshire from 1949 to 1988—right where the Magalloway enters and the Androscoggin exits the lake. In 1989 the first chick died, but biologists placed in the nest a chick from a captive pair; the eagles adopted the foster chick and raised it successfully. In some years since, the pair nested successfully, in others years not. In the spring of 1994 during nesting, the male died from lead sinker ingestion. (On January 1, 2000, New Hampshire banned the use of lead sinkers weighing one ounce or less to protect loons and other waterfowl.) The female abandoned the lone egg but found a new mate. In the

A bull moose heads toward shore in a cove east of Tidswell Point. Moose appear frequently on the shores of Lake Umbagog.

summer of 1997, nesting failed, but in 1998 they raised two young successfully; 1998 also saw the first nesting attempt by a second eagle pair in the state, this one at Spoonwood Pond in southern New Hampshire. In 1999, the Umbagog pair raised another pair successfully. In 2000, though the Umbagog hatchlings died, probably because of cold, wet weather, the year marked a new first—four pairs of eagles began nesting in New Hampshire; besides the Umbagog and Spoonwood pairs, attempts were made on the Connecticut River near Hinsdale and at nearby Pontook Reservoir.

This mirrors what has happened nationally in the lower 48 states: from a low of 417 pairs in 1963, the population rebounded to 791 pairs in 1974; 1,188 pairs in 1981; 3,035 in 1990; 4,712 in 1995; and more than 6,000 in 2000. Because of the remarkable recovery of the population since the banning of DDT, which caused disastrous eggshell thinning, then-President Clinton announced in 1995 that the bald eagle's status would change from endangered to threatened.

Osprey, meanwhile, have had an even better time of it. In 1994, approximately 25 pairs nested in the vicinity of Umbagog, and they successfully reared 35 chicks. They continue to be common on Umbagog. Loons have had mixed success. A lot of loons summer on the lake—of 22 territorial pairs, 13 pairs actually nested, fledging a total of 11 chicks in 1994. However, in late July 1997, when we paddled here, biologists told us that few chicks had survived the late, cold spring. During May, June, and July, be particularly careful about nesting loons. Even a quiet paddler inadvertently getting too close to a nest can result in the adults abandoning it, and loons always nest very close to the water.

Our favorite places on Umbagog include Leonard Pond, the coves along the inlet of the Rapid River on the northeast, and the small coves and islands east of Tidswell Point. Big Island, purchased by the Society for the Protection of New Hampshire Forests in the 1980s, is also wonderful and includes six campsites. For camping with kids, sites on the north shore of Tyler Cove (#s 21, 22, and 23) stand out because of the protected sandy swimming beach at the cove's end.

We also enjoy paddling the slow-flowing, meandering Androscoggin and Magalloway Rivers. Paddling toward Umbagog on either river, a number of marshy ponds both to the right and left await your exploration. Keep an eye out for moose, otter, and mink.

Moose abound. Look for them standing belly deep in the Magalloway River, in ponds off to the left of the Androscoggin, or in any of the numerous coves on the lake. In the early-morning light, in a cove just east of Tidswell Point, we watched three moose browsing by the water's edge. At the far southeastern end—the most developed part of the lake—we got our closest look at a moose not 200 yards from a cottage near the mouth of the Dead Cambridge River. We have also watched them swim across open water in the early morning, moving along at a brisk pace.

The varied vegetation around Umbagog includes conifers that predominate in most areas: balsam fir, spruce, northern white cedar, hemlock, and white pine; in other areas deciduous trees, including yellow and paper birch, red maple, and an occasional red oak, predominate. We also saw a few relatively rare jack pine.

Potentially dangerous winds and waves can come up very quickly on this large lake, making open-boat paddling hazardous. Paddling around the lake during a two-day period in August, we got into heavy winds both afternoons, even though the water was like glass on each of those mornings. Wind blowing from the north or northwest across several miles of water can build up sizable waves!

Many fish inhabit the lake—as evidenced by the large osprey population. In mid-August we caught yellow perch, smallmouth bass, and lots of lake chub (a whitefish with large scales and a deeply forked tail) up to a few pounds. With the right bait, lures, or flies, one should not have too much trouble pulling a few tasty meals out of the lake.

GETTING THERE

To reach the Androscoggin River access from Errol, go south on Route 26 a short distance and turn left onto North Mountain Pond Road just 100 yards or so after crossing the bridge over the Androscoggin River. Look for a sign, Access to Public Water, at the turnoff. Follow the road about 1.0 mile to the access. From here, the main lake is about 3.0 miles up the river.

Another public access on the lake is at the southern end, off Route 26. Backcountry campsite users can put in at the Lake Umbagog Campground, 0.7 mile east of the public boat launch.

First Connecticut Lake and Lake Francis
Clarksville and Pittsburg, NH

MAPS

New Hampshire Atlas: Maps 52 and 53

USGS Quadrangles: Lake Francis, Magalloway Mountain, and Pittsburg

INFORMATION

First Connecticut Lake area: 2,807 acres

Lake Francis area: 2,051 acres

Prominent fish species: First Connecticut Lake—landlocked salmon, lake trout, and rainbow trout; Lake Francis—pickerel, landlocked salmon, brown trout, lake trout, and rainbow trout

Camping: All state-park campground reservations—603-271-3628 or www.nhparks.state.nh.us; Deer Mountain Campground (primitive camping) and Lake Francis State Park—603-538-6965

Rental cottages: North Country Chamber of Commerce—603-237-8939

First Connecticut Lake and Lake Francis, like the other Connecticut Lakes (see sections on Second and Third Lakes), are jewels of northern New Hampshire. Though some limited development has encroached on their shores, they still offer superb wilderness paddling. In the more remote inlets during all but the busiest seasons, moose and people may appear with about the same frequency. When we paddled here on a July Fourth weekend, few boats plied these waters. For the angler, these lakes offer excellent lake trout and salmon fishing.

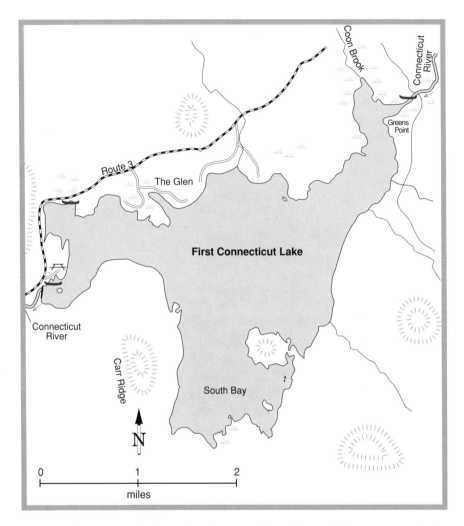

Be forewarned, though, that on these large lakes even a fairly gentle wind can generate sizable waves. Make it a rule to stick close to shore, and always wear your life vest. When the wind blows, visit one of the smaller ponds instead (see sections on East Inlet, Scott Bog, and Third Connecticut Lake). Unexpected winds coming out of the southeast were so strong as Alex paddled down the northern shore of First Lake that he found himself surfing on two-foot waves in his small solo canoe. The front third of the boat rose right out of the water as large waves passed under. Exciting perhaps, but potentially quite dangerous. Be careful!

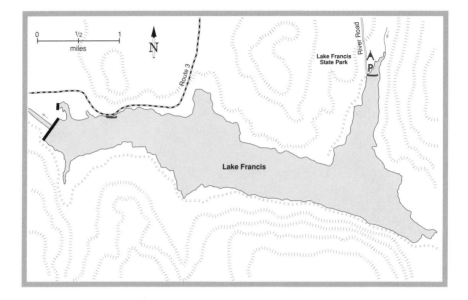

When the weather forecast promises calm conditions, a huge amount of shoreline awaits exploration on either of these lakes. With an uncertain weather forecast, stick close to the access points, where you have better access to Route 3 and civilization.

First Connecticut Lake. The northern tip of First Lake, including the Connecticut River and Coon Brook inlets, provides marshy habitat for moose, beaver, deer, and otter. You can paddle up Coon Brook a short distance through the marsh and alder thickets until rocks block your progress. You can really feel the remoteness on this part of the lake, surrounded by thickly wooded spruce-fir forests and listening to the eerie cry of the loon. On an early morning with mist rising from the lake, moose browsing on aquatic vegetation, and birds singing from the wooded shore, it feels like a different world.

The western arm of First Lake, though not seeming quite as remote, is also very beautiful. You could spend a half-day just paddling around this end from the put-in near the dam, never even venturing onto the largest section of the lake.

Lake Francis. This lake, particularly the eastern end, has a similar feel to that of First Lake. We prefer the put-in near Lake Francis State

Park because Route 3 travels close by the northern shore on the lake's west end, and traffic noise can be bothersome on busy weekends. The main part of Lake Francis, elongated in an east-west direction, can be treacherous when the wind blows from the west or northwest; under these conditions, paddle one of the smaller bodies of water in the region or stick to the protected west shore of the upper arm near the state park.

GETTING THERE

First Connecticut Lake. To reach the northeastern tip, where the Connecticut River flows in, go south on Route 3 from Deer Mountain Campground for 2.3 miles past the Second Connecticut Lake dam; turn left (southeast) onto a dirt road at the sign for Magalloway Mountain lookout. From the south, this turnoff is roughly 4.7 miles from the dam at First Lake (an alternate put-in site). Take this dirt road 1.1 miles to the timber bridge, the put-in point. There are some light rapids for the first couple 100 feet downstream from this bridge (you can carry along the shore if you wish); then the river opens up into a gradually widening arm of First Lake.

Lake Francis. There is a well-marked access on Route 3. A more remote access lies just beyond Lake Francis State Park; follow the signs to the park and continue a short way beyond the park to the access on the left.

Second Connecticut Lake
Pittsburg, NH

MAPS

New Hampshire Atlas: Map 53

USGS Quadrangle: Second Connecticut Lake

INFORMATION

Area: 1,286 acres

Prominent fish species: Smelt, landlocked salmon, brook trout, and lake trout

Camping: All state-park campground reservations—603-271-3628 or www.nhparks.state.nh.us; Deer Mountain Campground (primitive camping) and Lake Francis State Park—603-538-6965

Rental cottages: North Country Chamber of Commerce—603-237-8939

Second Connecticut Lake remains one of our favorite big lakes in Vermont and New Hampshire. Less than half as large as First Connecticut, it suffers much less from development. Though more manageable for the paddler, winds can arise quickly and generate sizable waves; if the winds blow, choose one of the nearby smaller bodies of water instead (see sections on East Inlet, Scott Bog, and Third Connecticut Lake). And, as always on large lakes, wear your personal flotation device.

The 11 miles of highly varied shoreline—with deep spruce-fir forests all around—offer almost endless opportunities for exploration. At dawn and dusk you may see moose grazing on pond vegetation in the various marshy inlets, along with otter, mink, great blue heron, various ducks, and several pairs of loons. Fishing for lake trout and salmon can be excellent.

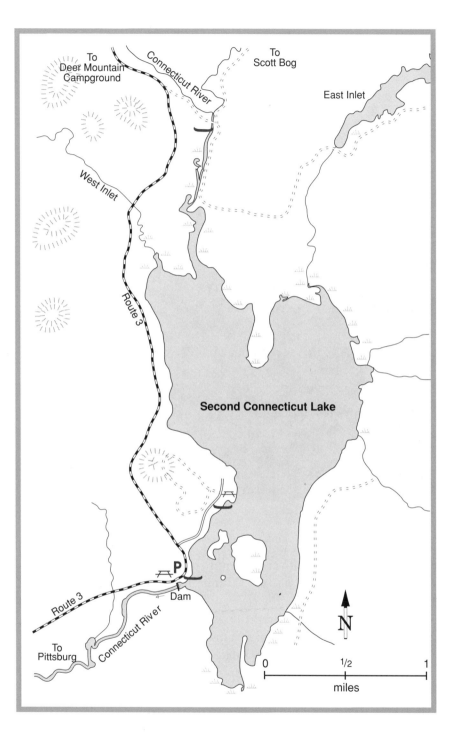

To
Deer Mountain
Campground

Connecticut River

To
Scott Bog

East Inlet

West Inlet

Route 3

Second Connecticut Lake

P

Dam

Route 3

To
Pittsburg

Connecticut River

N

0   1/2   1
miles

Purple iris, *Iris versicolor,* blooms along the edges of many marshes in the Northeast.

A great place to put in for a day of paddling is at the northern tip where the Connecticut River (still more of a creek here) passes beneath a timber bridge on a dirt road, 1.0 mile from Deer Mountain Campground. Scott Creek joins the river just above the bridge. Paddle south on the gently flowing and gradually widening channel for about a mile until it opens into the main lake. This entire northern end of the lake, including the river and West Inlet, offers fantastic paddling: thick, grassy marshes full of inlets to explore and dark green spruce and fir trees rising in sharp spires behind them. The water is clean, though slightly reddish brown from natural tannins. We especially liked the bent-over leaves of a slightly purplish water celery that graced the surface.

Paddling down the river on one trip, as we neared the open lake, we spotted a bald eagle perched along the edge, and a bittern shot up from the shoreside grasses. White-throated sparrows called from the brush as we investigated the large patches of purple iris in bloom.

Paddling around the eastern, undeveloped side of the lake, you will pass a number of other similar inlets, each with its own secrets to reveal. Among the rocky and marshy shoreline sections, you will also find a few sandy beaches. Two fairly large islands and one small one add interest to the southern end of the lake. As with all islands on remote lakes, be careful not to disturb nesting loons.

GETTING THERE

To reach the Connecticut River access, go south on Route 3 for 0.6 mile from Deer Mountain Campground, turn left onto an unmarked gravel road, and go 0.4 mile to a timber bridge, the put-in point. The main boat launch for the lake is on the west shore just north of the islands, reachable from a well-marked access road off Route 3. You can also launch from the picnic area at the dam farther south, although this requires a somewhat longer carry.

East Inlet
Pittsburg, NH

MAPS

New Hampshire Atlas: Map 53

USGS Quadrangle: Second Connecticut Lake

INFORMATION

Area: 45 acres

Prominent fish species: Brook trout

Camping: All state-park campground reservations—603-271-3628 or www.nhparks.state.nh.us; Deer Mountain Campground (primitive camping) and Lake Francis State Park—603-538-6965

Conservation: New Hampshire Nature Conservancy—603-224-5853

A moose grazed belly-deep on the far shore of East Inlet when we drove in on one trip; on another trip, a young bull moose cavorted in the shallows about a half-mile up on the left. In neither case did the moose seem overly concerned by our presence. Tree swallows skimmed the surface, and families of black and wood ducks scurried for protective cover among the reeds at water's edge. Several great blue herons fished the shallows, while trout dimpled the surface all around. Paddling next to the shore, we could study the remarkable pitcher plants in full bloom, their odd reddish flowers on straight stems bowing over as if looking at the sphagnum beneath.

East Inlet is within the Norton Pool and Moose Pasture Natural Area, preserved by the New Hampshire Nature Conservancy. Located in the northern tip of the state near the better-known Connecticut Lakes, East Inlet has to be one of the most beautiful bodies of water we

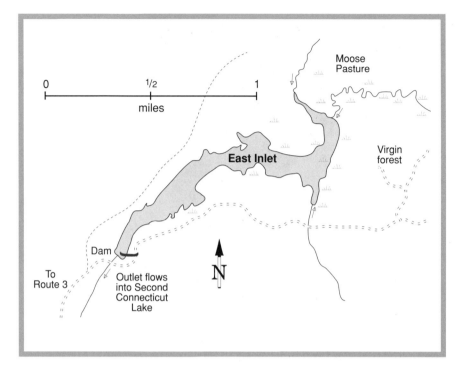

have paddled. It is small—just 45 acres of open water in a long, sinewy channel set within several 100 acres of marsh—but truly wild and pristine. Water celery dominates the surface. Ancient, rotting stumps peer out from the brackish water, and huge fields of reed and sedge sway in the breeze. Farther away from the water on solid ground, deep green spires of spruce and fir make up the northern boreal forest. Paddling this extraordinary place sure beats fighting the waves on the larger lakes in this area; in addition, gasoline motors are prohibited.

At the far end of the open water and across the alder swamp is a section of virgin spruce-fir forest, one of the only remaining stands of such forest in New England. You can reach it by canoe and foot, but you will get your feet plenty wet. A better way to get there is by road. Paddling northeast from the dam, the wide channel continues for a mile or so, eventually turning to marsh as the inlet stream winds a serpentine pathway through a thick alder swamp. Tamarack joins the spruce and fir along the shores at this end. For more paddling room, go left through this marshy section, called Moose Pasture, where separating

A young bull moose, *Alces alces*, seemingly oblivious to our presence, feeds in the shallows of East Inlet.

the real channel from an isolated oxbow is quite a challenge. With some diligence, and if you ignore the bugs, you can paddle quite a distance up the inlet stream.

Paddling here has an air of excitement to it, since you never know what might be around the next bend: beaver, a family of ducks, moose. The farther up this inlet you paddle, the smaller the channel becomes, with the ever-present alders reaching out into the creek from both sides. Eventually the alders completely block your passage.

Getting There

Go south on Route 3 from Deer Mountain Campground for 0.6 mile, and turn left (east) onto an unmarked dirt road. Cross a timber bridge at 0.4 mile and turn right, following the northern tip of Second Connecticut Lake before veering away. (See also the map of Second Connecticut Lake.) Follow this road approximately 1.6 miles to the dam at East Inlet.

To investigate the stand of virgin forest, continue driving past the East Inlet dam for 2.5 miles, then take the left fork. From there it is a rather difficult hike past the ruins of an old bridge. The old-growth forest will be on your left (to the west).

Scott Bog
Pittsburg, NH

MAPS
  New Hampshire Atlas: Map 53
  USGS Quadrangle: Second Connecticut Lake

INFORMATION
  Area: 100 acres

  Prominent fish species: Brook trout

  Camping: All state-park campground reservations—603-271-3628 or www.nhparks.state.nh.us; Deer Mountain Campground (primitive camping) and Lake Francis State Park—603-538-6965

Way in the northern tip of New Hampshire, along with the well-known Connecticut Lakes, a few out-of-the-way bodies of water are highly worth exploring. On difficult-to-find Scott Bog, located between Second and Third Connecticut Lakes, with no motors allowed, you will not see too many other visitors—at least of the human variety. One privately owned cabin stands on the east side of the lake, leased from Champion Paper, which owns most of the surrounding land.

Spruce-fir forests surround Scott Bog, a beautiful, shallow northern fen, with floating sphagnum mats, yellow pond lily, water celery, pitcher plant, bur-reed, alder, and tamarack. The smells of the Northern Forest seemed to seep into our senses here. A beaver dam clogs the northern end, along with many sun-whitened snags of old trees, left over from dam construction. When we paddled here the second time, in the evening, three beaver swam about, slapping the water with their tails.

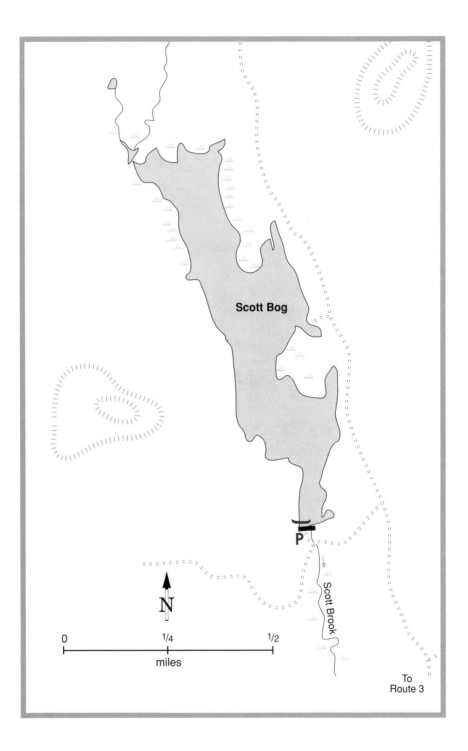

Scott Bog

Scott Brook

To
Route 3

N

0   1/4   1/2

miles

A wood duck nesting box stands against a northern boreal forest backdrop on Scott Bog.

If high winds keep you off the larger Connecticut Lakes, Scott Bog, just a short drive from Deer Mountain Campground, is a good alternative. The marshy shores, full of wildlife, make ideal moose habitat. In the early-morning hours, moose may join you in Scott Bog and along the roads leading into the bog.

GETTING THERE

From Deer Mountain Campground, go south on Route 3 for 0.6 mile and turn left (east) onto an unmarked dirt road. Cross a timber bridge after 0.4 mile; turn left and continue 2.1 miles to a fork. Take the left fork for 0.4 mile and turn left (there should be a sign here pointing to the access). After crossing the outlet stream in another 0.2 mile, turn right down to the access. Note that some sections of these roads can suffer from ruts and boulders, especially near the bog. (See also the map of Second Connecticut Lake.)

Third Connecticut Lake
Pittsburg, NH

MAPS

New Hampshire Atlas: Map 53

USGS Quadrangle: Second Connecticut Lake

INFORMATION

Area: 278 acres

Prominent fish species: Lake trout, brook trout, and rainbow trout

Camping: All state-park campground reservations—603-271-3628 or www.nhparks.state.nh.us; Deer Mountain Campground (primitive camping) and Lake Francis State Park—603-538-6965

Rental cottages: North Country Chamber of Commerce—603-237-8939

Third Connecticut Lake lies less than a mile from the Canadian border, near the northern tip of New Hampshire. Close to the headwaters of the Connecticut River (that distinction belongs to tiny Fourth Connecticut Lake), Third Lake nestles beautifully into the deep boreal forest of Coos County. With an entirely undeveloped shoreline, this 100-foot-deep lake provides good lake-trout fishing. Rainbow and brook trout are also found here.

Unlike the larger and better-known Second and First Connecticut Lakes, Third Lake's gravel shoreline has little variety, with few inlets to explore. From the access on Route 3, you can scan nearly the entire lake perimeter. If motorboats cruise by, the remote feeling disappears easily. Nonetheless, visit Third Lake for fishing or for no other reason than to get out on the northwestern shore and step across the Connecticut "River"—just a couple feet wide here—where

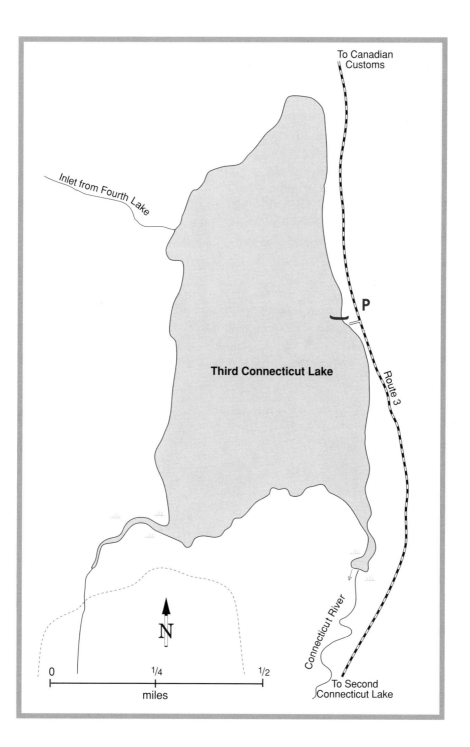

To Canadian Customs

Inlet from Fourth Lake

P

Route 3

Third Connecticut Lake

Connecticut River

N

0   1/4   1/2

miles

To Second Connecticut Lake

it trickles into the lake. At the northern tip, you can also take advantage of a nice, sandy swimming beach.

If you want a real surprise, drive north on Route 3 from Third Connecticut Lake into Canada. As you cross the border, a sudden and dramatic change takes place. You leave the deep boreal wilderness forest of spruce and fir and enter into open farmland. You have to experience it to believe it.

At the U.S. Customs office, you can pick up a hiking map and walk into so-called Fourth Connecticut Lake. The walk takes you along the U.S.-Canada border, then down to the little pond where the mighty Connecticut River (New England's longest and most important river) begins its 410-mile journey to Long Island Sound.

GETTING THERE
From the Connecticut Lakes region, go north on Route 3 for 4.2 miles past the Deer Mountain Campground to the access on the left. Driving along Route 3, watch out for moose—and for cars stopped in the middle of the road as the occupants watch moose!

Snapping Turtle
Hidden Dweller of the Pond

The snapping turtle is the most common species of turtle in New Hampshire and Vermont—even more common than the painted turtle. In fact, it inhabits almost every beaver pond, millpond, lake, marsh, and slow-moving stream in the Northeast. Hundreds may live in some bodies of water, but you would not know it. Even if you spend quite a bit of time paddling, you rarely see these large turtles. Unlike their sun-loving cousin, the painted turtle, snappers prefer pond-bottom depths and rarely bask in the sun.

You can easily recognize snapping turtles, *Chelydra serpentina*, if you come across them, especially out of water.

Their long, spiny-ridged tails and very large heads relative to body size give them away. The young have distinct ridges on the top shell (carapace), though on larger adults the shell may have worn smooth. On the underside, the small bottom shell (plastron) has a crosslike shape.

Mature snapping turtles grow quite large. The carapace can reach a length of 20 inches (which means an overall length, nose to tail, of over three feet). A large turtle can weigh more than 60 pounds. No other turtle in the Northeast approaches this size.

When paddling clear, shallow water, we occasionally see snappers underwater. On a few occasions we have seen them on the bank above a pond or slow-moving river—probably en route to a nearby body of water, or perhaps a female out of water to lay a clutch of eggs. Snappers may travel great distances in search of suitable nesting sites—one marked individual traveled 16 kilometers round-trip. Our usual glimpse of snappers, though, is just the triangular nose sticking out of the water ahead of us as we paddle along.

Many people fear snapping turtles—and we admit to a bit of concern when two large snappers chased one another just inches beneath our canoe in a shallow pond—but they really pose no harm as long as they remain in the water. Even in the unlikely event that a snapper bites a swimmer's toe underwater, it quickly lets go, realizing that the quarry is more than it can handle. In the water, the shy snapper avoids any human contact. Watch out for snappers on land, though. They lash out with lightning speed if they feel threatened. A large snapper, with its massive jaw muscles and razor-sharp beak, exerts more than 400 pounds per square inch of force with its bite—enough to sever a finger easily.

They have existed for at least 80 million years, and scientists believe them to be the oldest reptiles in North America. Like all turtles, their rib cage and vertebrae have evolved into a bony carapace and plastron. With most turtles, this shell provides armored protection, but the snapper's small plastron offers almost no protection to its underside. The small plastron also makes snapping turtles vulnerable to leeches, and they sometimes leave the water to rid themselves of this parasite.

Most turtles hibernate for long periods during winter, but snapping turtles are relatively resistant to cold. We sometimes see them swimming beneath the ice in the middle of winter, though in northern New England they typically hibernate in the bottom mud for some time during the dead of winter. When idle underwater, snappers do not need to surface for air. Special surfaces in their rear cloacal cavity extract dissolved oxygen from the water, much like gills. When active, though, they need more oxygen and must surface for air—providing the quiet paddler an opportunity to catch a glimpse of one.

Omnivores and opportunists, snapping turtles dine on a wide range of animal and plant material, including fish, frogs, salamanders, occasional ducklings and loon chicks, dead animals, and aquatic plants. Snappers can kill anything their size or smaller, but they seem to prefer the easy meal. They have a superb sense of smell, which they use to scavenge for dead animals. Interestingly, this trait on occasion has been used to find human drowning victims. The snapping turtle literature recounts one story of a Native American who assisted in finding and retrieving drowning victims using a snapping turtle on a long leash. When released into the water, the turtle would unerringly head right for the decomposing corpse, latch onto it with its strong jaws, and its handler would slowly reel it in—corpse and all.

Mature females leave the water in late spring or early summer to lay eggs. They dig a hole and typically deposit from 20 to 30 (rarely, up to 80) eggs the size and shape of ping-pong balls, then covers the hole. Some females lay eggs in two or more holes; they often will dig several false holes to mislead predators, which take a heavy toll on snapping turtle clutches. The eggs usually hatch in the fall, some 70 to 100 days after laying (depending on temperature), and the inch-long hatchlings make a beeline for the water—often as raccoons, birds, and other predators gobble them up.

As with many turtles, nest temperature may determine the sex of young snappers. Several studies found that at very cool or very warm temperatures, the embryos all developed into females, while intermediate temperatures produced males. In most nests, the temperature regime varies with location, so both males and females develop.

Snapper populations remain quite secure in the Northeast—unlike those of most other turtles. They seem to tolerate current levels of environmental pollution and to live even in highly polluted marshy areas in cities. Some regard snapper meat highly, resulting in heavy trapping in certain areas. If you come across a snapping turtle out of water, avoid the temptation to deliver it to the nearest body of water—chances are pretty good that it knows where to head to lay its eggs and does not need assistance in this endeavor.

Sadawga Pond
Whitingham, VT

MAPS
  Vermont Atlas: Map 21

  USGS Quadrangles: Jacksonville and Readsboro

INFORMATION
  Area: 194 acres

  Prominent fish species: Largemouth bass, pickerel, and yellow perch

  Primitive camping: For locations and maps, contact the Manchester Ranger District, Green Mountain National Forest—802-362-2307.

Sadawga Pond, located just above the Massachusetts border in Whitingham, Vermont, has an unusual feature: a floating island. Sphagnum moss and other fen vegetation cover the sizable island—about 25 acres—which provides firm enough footing for some tamarack as tall as 20 feet. According to a 1952 article in *Vermont Life*, this is one of only two honest-to-goodness floating islands in the world (Switzerland has the other). While clearly an exaggeration—floating mats of peat occur commonly in New England—Sadawga's floating island is probably the most dramatic you will see.

  Apparently it formed in the early 1800s when dams raised the level of the existing small pond. The original pond must have been a kettle hole that gradually closed in from the sides, with much of the pond edge floating (as in quaking bogs). When the water level rose, a root mass

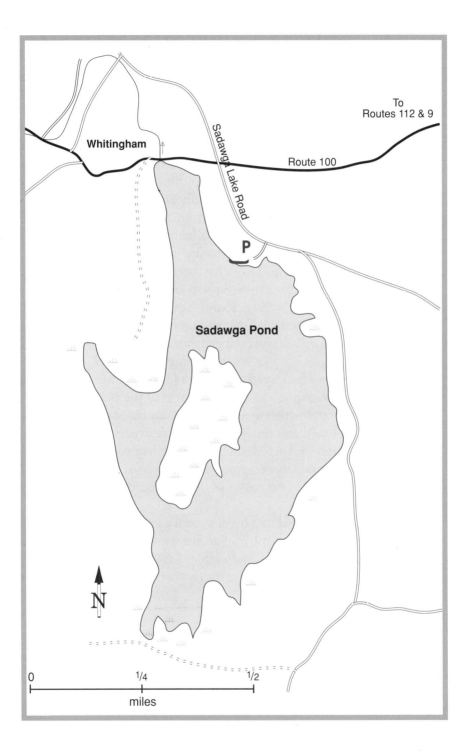

To
Routes 112 & 9

Whitingham

Sadawga Lake Road

Route 100

P

Sadawga Pond

N

0   1/4   1/2
miles

portion broke free and floated to the surface. Although the island—really several connected islands—floats, it does not sail around the lake like a raft. Roots now tether it to the ground beneath the pond. In shifting winds, the island pivots a little, usually the extent of its movement.

Sadawga's floating island has at times caused headaches for the lake-side residents on the northern and eastern shoreline. In 1926, a large section broke off in a storm and for several years floated around the pond, periodically lodging in front of cottages, disrupting access to the water. That continues to happen from time to time, though rarely. The main island appears to be more solidly anchored to the bottom of the pond. Resist the temptation to land on the island. Your footsteps could damage the fragile fen ecosystem, and it would be dangerous if you fell through the cushiony mat into the deep water below.

In more recent years, Sadawga has been the subject of a mystery. Local residents found an overturned rowboat and believed its occupant had drowned. But they never found the body, despite extensive searches. Some have speculated that the disappearance was staged.

The name Sadawga derives either from the Mohawk Indian word meaning "swiftly flowing water" or, according to local lore, from an old Indian by that name who stayed in the area long after his people left—the more likely explanation, given the stillness of the pond.

Except for the northern and eastern ends, Sadawga remains relatively undeveloped and the houses unobtrusive. Extensive marshy areas line the shore, and a few shallow inlets beg to be explored. As on the floating island, sweet gale, cranberry, various heaths, and diminutive sundew grow on tussocks of sphagnum moss on much of the fenlike shoreline.

We saw lots of wood ducks here, as well as a large congregation of Canada geese in mid-September. Farther away from the water, the heavily wooded land supports red maple, hemlock, and beech, along with a few large serviceberry trees, some with trunks as large as eight inches in diameter.

GETTING THERE

From Wilmington take Route 100 south; Sadawga Lake Road is off Route 100, 3.3 miles west of the junction with Route 112.

From Whitingham Center take Route 100 east for a few hundred feet, turn right onto Sadawga Lake Road, and go 0.2 mile to the access.

Somerset Reservoir
Somerset and Stratton, VT

MAPS

Vermont Atlas: Map 21

USGS Quadrangles: Mount Snow and Stratton Mountain

INFORMATION

Area: 1,597 acres

Prominent fish species: Smallmouth bass, pickerel, yellow perch, and brook trout

Primitive camping: Contact the Manchester Ranger District, Green Mountain National Forest—802-362-2307

For the paddler looking for some real exercise in beautiful surroundings, try a day on Somerset Reservoir in southern Vermont. Rolling mountains—including Mount Snow, its northern face visible from most of the lake—bound this long, narrow lake on the upper reaches of the Deerfield River. Though surrounded by Green Mountain National Forest, the reservoir and immediate shoreline were owned by New England Power Company, but it sold its interest to Pacific Gas and Electric (PG&E) in 1998. Two years later, in May 2000, the Vermont Land Trust purchased development rights for 15,736 acres along the Deerfield Valley, including around Somerset.

A second major change came about in January 1996. A group of southern Vermont residents, led by co-author Alex Wilson, convinced the state Water Resources Board to ban personal watercraft and water-skiing and to restrict speeds to 10 MPH. Given the Water Resources Board's propensity to allow high-impact uses on large bodies of water, we should all rejoice over this remarkable regulation.

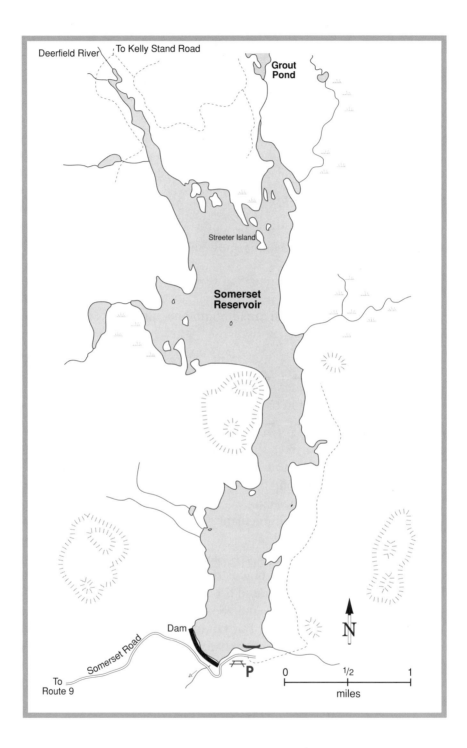

Deerfield River

To Kelly Stand Road

Grout Pond

Streeter Island

Somerset Reservoir

Dam

Somerset Road

To Route 9

N

P

0   1/2   1

miles

The lake extends roughly five miles from the dam to the northernmost point, the East Branch of the Deerfield River inlet. Another arm extends farther to the east, fed by the Grout Pond outlet. A number of nice islands dot the lake's northern extension, including Streeter Island, maintained as a picnic area. To explore the whole 16-mile perimeter requires a full day. If you tend to stop frequently to enjoy the wildlife—we watched a mink drag a pumpkinseed sunfish, almost as large as the mink, along the shore—you may have trouble getting all the way around in a day. The heavily wooded shoreline lends itself well to relaxed exploring and wildlife observation. The mixed deciduous and coniferous woods abound with warblers, woodpeckers, and other birds. Somerset is the southernmost Vermont lake with nesting loons.

PG&E controls the Somerset Reservoir level for hydropower generation (the water flows into the Searsburg Dam penstock, which you pass on the road in). Though it maintains the water level through loon nesting season (May through July), after July the level can drop significantly, making the reservoir less attractive to the paddler. Note that winds can arise quickly on this long body of water—with surrounding mountains acting as a north-to-south funnel—generating very serious whitecaps. On breezy days, stick to smaller bodies of water in the area, such as Grout, Branch, and Sadawga Ponds.

GETTING THERE

From Wilmington, go west on Route 9 for about 6.0 miles and turn right onto Somerset Road. Stay right at the fork; it is about 9.0 miles to the access.

You can also reach the lake by portaging in 0.8 mile from the Grout Pond Recreation Area on marked trails.

Grout Pond and Branch Pond

Stratton and Sunderland, VT

MAPS

> **Vermont Atlas:** Maps 21 and 25

> **USGS Quadrangles:** Stratton Mountain and Sunderland

INFORMATION

> **Grout Pond area:** 86 acres

> **Branch Pond area:** 43 acres

> **Prominent fish species:** Smallmouth bass, pickerel, and yellow perch

> **Primitive camping:** Contact the Manchester Ranger District, Green Mountain National Forest—802-362-2307

These two small ponds, located within the Green Mountain National Forest in southern Vermont, offer delightful paddling. The Forest Service allows primitive camping in most of the national forest, including (in 2000) around both of these ponds. A small, developed recreation area is situated close to the Grout Pond boat access. Numerous hiking trails crisscross the area, including one that extends around Grout Pond; one that leads to the northern end of Somerset Reservoir; and our favorite, the trail from Branch Pond to Bourn Pond. The Appalachian and Long Trails also pass through the area.

Grout Pond. We return to this wonderful spot year after year. Though small, the pond offers plenty of space for a relaxed day of paddling, without the distraction of motorboats, personal watercraft, or water-skiers. Two shelters on the northeastern shore and a half-dozen tent sites with fireplaces and picnic tables lay scattered around the

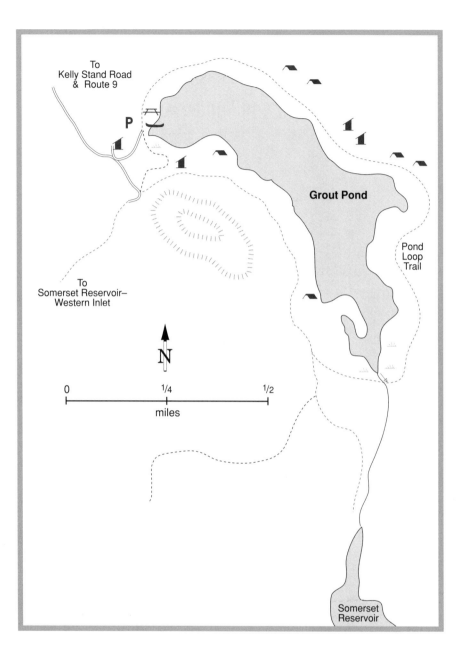

To
Kelly Stand Road
& Route 9

P

Grout Pond

Pond
Loop
Trail

To
Somerset Reservoir–
Western Inlet

N

0   1/4   1/2
miles

Somerset
Reservoir

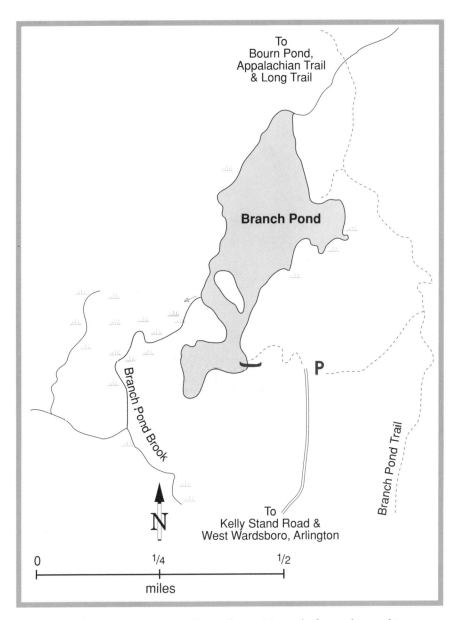

To
Bourn Pond,
Appalachian Trail
& Long Trail

Branch Pond

Branch Pond Brook

P

Branch Pond Trail

N

To
Kelly Stand Road &
West Wardsboro, Arlington

0   1/4   1/2

miles

pond. You have to carry your boat about 50 yards from the parking area to the launching area.

Grout Pond provides an ideal spot to acquaint young children with canoe-camping. With a trail all the way around the lake and a quick paddle from even the farthest campsite, you can get to civilization

An early-morning paddle on Grout Pond, with the mist rising from the water.

quickly if you want. The primitive camping, however, provides a much different experience from public or private campgrounds with close-together campsites, RVs, TVs, satellite dishes, and the like. Kids will enjoy the sandy swimming beach at the northwestern access point, along with plenty of places to fish for yellow perch, sunfish, and bass. You can usually see beaver if you paddle the lake in the late evening or early morning—Alex's daughters got their first good look at these industrious animals here.

We often come to Grout Pond in the autumn for our last camping trip of the year. The pond, gorgeous in its full autumn regalia of reds and yellows, offers an especially breathtaking shoreline of red maples against a brilliant blue, bug-free, autumn sky.

Branch Pond. Branch Pond sits nestled high in the 15,680-acre Lye Brook Wilderness. Worthy of inclusion here for its pristine beauty and unusual vegetation, the pond offers a wonderful morning or afternoon of leisurely paddling. Look for moose here, along with the many unusual plants of a northern fen, including carnivorous sundews and pitcher plants growing on tussocks of sphagnum moss. Along the shore you will see tamarack, a northern species and our only conifer to lose its needles in winter. The clear water and varied shoreline offer opportunities for some exploring, though lake-side vegetation restricts access somewhat. Be very careful walking on the sphagnum-moss tussocks; your footsteps can damage the fragile plants.

Several primitive campsites dot the shores of Branch Pond, and the Forest Service permits camping anywhere, for now, in this part of the Green Mountain National Forest. The fragile ecosystem around Branch Pond, however, needs careful treatment when camping.

GETTING THERE

Access to both ponds is from Kelly Stand Road (also called West Wardsboro–Arlington Road); from Grout Pond to the west, the road is not plowed in winter.

Grout Pond. From West Wardsboro, turn west onto Kelly Stand Road from Route 100 (approximately 14 miles north of Route 9 or 9.0 miles south of Route 30). About 6.0 miles from West Wardsboro, turn left on the well-marked access road and go 1.0 mile to Grout Pond.

Branch Pond. Continue on Kelly Stand Road about 4.5 miles beyond the turnoff for Grout Pond. Turn right and go 2.5 miles to the end. The carry down to Branch Pond is about 0.3 mile, with the trail leading through deep spruce-fir woods full of trillium and lots of other spring wildflowers.

Retreat Meadows, Herricks Cove, and Connecticut River—Southern Section

Brattleboro, Rockingham, and Vernon, VT
Charlestown, Chesterfield, Hinsdale, and Walpole, NH

MAPS

Vermont Atlas: Maps 23 and 27

New Hampshire Atlas: Maps 18 and 25

USGS Quadrangles: Bellows Falls and Brattleboro

INFORMATION

Retreat Meadows length: 7 miles

Herricks Cove length: 6 miles

Prominent fish species: Largemouth bass, smallmouth bass, pickerel, northern pike, perch, walleye, brook trout, brown trout, and rainbow trout

It surprises many to learn that the vast majority of the Connecticut River's 400-plus-mile length—from the Canadian border to Long Island Sound—backs up behind dams. Unfortunately, only a tiny fraction of the river consists of free-flowing water. The lower reaches of the Connecticut River offer fine paddling in the impoundments behind Bellows Falls and Vernon Dam.

Bellows Falls/North Walpole Area. Herricks Cove and several other marshy coves along the Connecticut River above Bellows Falls offer a very pleasant day of paddling through extraordinary marshes, favorite areas of bird watchers, especially during spring and fall migration. From the boat access and picnic area at Herricks Cove, you can explore the broad Williams River delta that forms this cove, or paddle either upriver or down to four other coves well worth visiting.

On the western edge of Herricks Cove, the current becomes quite noticeable and the bottom sandy—not bad for swimming on a hot day. You reach the Route 5 bridge about two-thirds of a mile from the cove's mouth, and the much taller I-91 bridge, several hundred yards farther. Paddling amid the many islands, we saw muskrat and lots of evidence of beaver. Songbirds filled the alder, dogwood, and willow, and an osprey wheeled overhead, searching for fish.

North of Herricks Cove you will find Roundys Cove on the western shore (in Vermont) and Great Meadow on the eastern shore (in New Hampshire). One could spend a great deal of time exploring here!

South of Herricks Cove, if you follow the western shore of the river and look closely along the railroad bed, you will find extensive marble mine tailings and polished marble pieces that must have been dumped into the river at some point. We found some beautiful pieces— which provided ballast for Alex's ill-balanced solo canoe on a windy day. Samples ranged from pure-white to rich-green conglomerates, to pink and gray.

Farther south, about two miles from the boat access, you reach the access to Albees Cove on the western shore. We found, behind a beaver lodge, one very narrow, winding channel into the cove, probably impenetrable once vegetation grows up (we visited in mid-May). Just beyond this entrance, another, much wider channel allows access, and below the island the cove is fully accessible—though shallow water may limit access during low-water times. The adventurous might want to paddle under the very low, concrete railroad bridge to the western section of Albees Cove. By mid-May, fragrant waterlily and assorted other aquatic vegetation grow thick. Depending on water depth and vegetation, you can paddle north until the marsh closes in.

On the New Hampshire side just south of Herricks Cove, you will find several entrances into Meanys Cove, really more of a channel

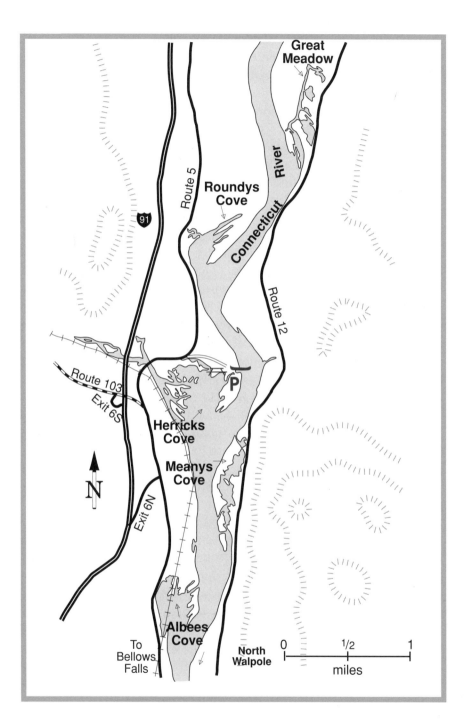

Great
Meadow

Roundys
Cove

Connecticut River

Route 5

Route 12

91

Route 103

Exit 6S

Herricks
Cove

N

Meanys
Cove

Exit 6N

P

Albees
Cove

To
Bellows
Falls

North
Walpole

0   1/2   1

miles

through the cattail swamp, thick with aquatic vegetation. We saw lots of fish amid the waterlily pads.

Just to the south of the boat access and parking area is a wonderful picnic area that you can walk to or reach by boat.

Brattleboro/Hinsdale Area. The Retreat Meadows, named for the Brattleboro Retreat, one of the oldest private mental hospitals in the United States (founded in the mid-1800s), offers a great place to spend a day of paddling within a stone's throw of downtown Brattleboro. Now largely transformed into a substance abuse and outpatient mental health facility, the retreat's large residential buildings can be seen along the south shore of the Meadows.

The West River flows through the Meadows before it intersects the Connecticut, offering a quiet place to paddle, especially when winds blow up and down the Connecticut. The marsh harbors the typical wetland bird species and some unusual visitors at times, such as the lesser black-backed gull. In the Retreat Meadows proper, look for muskrat and beaver (especially near dusk) as you explore the winding channels and islands of this extensive cattail marsh. In the early spring we have often seen wood ducks and hooded mergansers here. You can paddle up the West River, passing under the I-91 bridge far above, until the current becomes too strong about a half-mile upstream.

You can sneak out onto the Connecticut to take in the beauty of Wantastiquet Mountain on the New Hampshire side and paddle downstream, away from the bustle of Brattleboro, exploring inlets, islands, and channels. On your way, just before entering the Connecticut, you will pass Vermont Canoe Touring Center (802-257-5008), where you can rent canoes and kayaks.

Bald eagles recently have attempted nesting in this area. Sometimes in the winter, they perch out over the water just above and below the Vernon dam, fishing the waters kept open by Vermont Yankee Nuclear Power Plant's thermal pollution and scavenging fish killed by the water churning through the dam's turbines. We once watched a mature eagle divebomb a couple of mergansers for about five minutes. Each time the mergansers tried to fly, the eagle swooped down on them; when they resurfaced after a dive, the relentless eagle dove on them again. Eventually, the mergansers flew upriver with the eagle in hot pursuit.

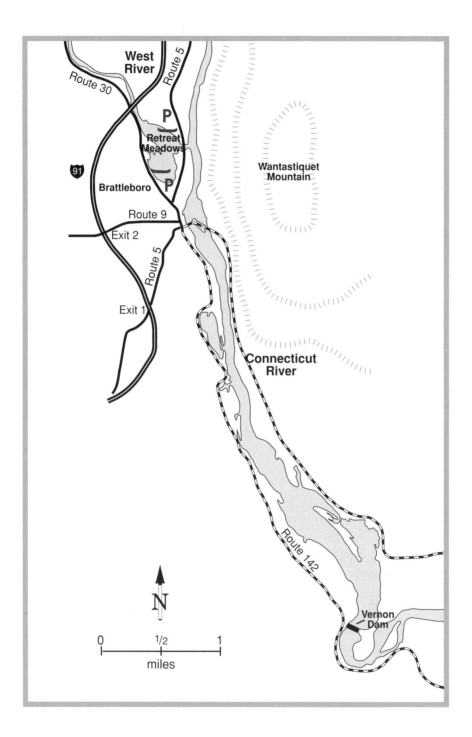

West
River

Route 5

Route 30

P

Retreat
Meadows

91

P

Wantastiquet
Mountain

Brattleboro

Route 9

Exit 2

Route 5

Exit 1

Connecticut
River

Route 142

N

0   1/2   1
miles

Vernon
Dam

GETTING THERE

Herricks Cove. From I-91 northbound take Exit 6, turn left onto Route 5 north, and go 1.3 miles to the access on the right at the NEPCO picnic area. From I-91 southbound take Exit 6 onto Route 103 south and go to the junction with Route 5. Turn left onto Route 5 north and go 0.8 mile to the sign for the NEPCO picnic area.

Retreat Meadows. From Brattleboro go north on Route 30 for about 0.4 mile past the flashing yellow caution light at the Brattleboro Retreat; look for the water off to the right. Park along the road. Alternatively, you can put in by the Marina restaurant. Go north on Putney Road (Route 5); immediately after crossing the West River bridge, turn left at the Marina restaurant sign. Unload your boat by the Marina, then drive back to the parking area up above.

Gale Meadows Pond
Winhall, VT

MAPS

Vermont Atlas: Map 25

USGS Quadrangles: Londonderry and Peru

INFORMATION

Area: 195 acres

Prominent fish species: Largemouth bass, pickerel, yellow perch, and brown trout

Located just north of Bondville, Gale Meadows Pond provides an ideal spot for a relaxed day of fishing, bird watching, or simply exploring. This shallow pond offers a varied shoreline. Marshes hug parts of the shore, particularly the southern end, where reed, sedge, alder, and cattail provide habitat for beaver; you will see lots of evidence of them. Large stands of fern—ostrich, sensitive, cinnamon, and royal—spill over the banks. At both the southern and northern ends, the sun-whitened stumps left over from the pond's damming provide nesting holes for hundreds of tree swallows; several wood duck nesting boxes provide more nesting space. Aquatic vegetation and submerged logs may impede paddling in these parts.

The northern end seems much more fenlike, with tamarack and floating sphagnum islands. Except for the swampy areas, mixed conifer and deciduous trees line most of the heavily wooded shoreline. There is one farmhouse on the western shore, and another house sits back from the water at the southern tip, but this is no recent development. In the early 1960s, a group of area landowners protected the pond and surrounding area from development; the Vermont Department of Fish and Wildlife manages it. In late 1991, the Vermont Water Resources

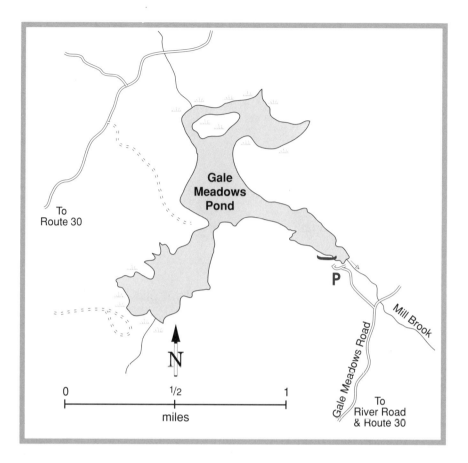

Board established a 5 MPH speed limit on Gale Meadows Pond, which makes the pond excellent for quietwater paddling and fishing.

GETTING THERE

From Bondville and Route 30, turn north onto River Road. After 0.8 mile take a left fork onto Gale Meadows Road, go another 0.9 mile, and take another left fork, just before the bridge over Mill Brook. This road dead-ends at the access.

Lowell Lake
Londonderry, VT

MAPS

    Vermont Atlas: Map 26

    USGS Quadrangle: Londonderry

INFORMATION

    Area: 102 acres

    Prominent fish species: Largemouth bass, pickerel, and yellow perch

Lowell Lake, a real gem in southern Vermont, covers about half of Lowell Lake State Park. Created in 1981, the state substantially expanded and officially dedicated the park in 1996, when the Vermont Land Trust helped acquire an additional 154 acres from the White family. The park includes most of the shoreline and several islands.

Tall hills to the north and south provide a scenic backdrop to this shallow, weedy pond. Small islands make the pond seem larger, and some huge, tall trees lend a certain majesty. When we paddled here in late September, several other canoes and kayaks plied the waters, pushing through the thick surface vegetation of this productive water body. Hiking trails also course through the woods along the shoreline.

Water shield dominates the surface, though other marshland plants poke up here and there through thick subsurface vegetation, much of which consists of masses of bladderwort. Buttonbush, leatherleaf, and other shrubs line the shores. Make sure that you fully explore the marshland on the pond's north side, paddling in and out of the islands along the cattail swamp, through the fragrant waterlily and water shield. The huge beaver lodges impressed us, though we saw little fresh beaver activity.

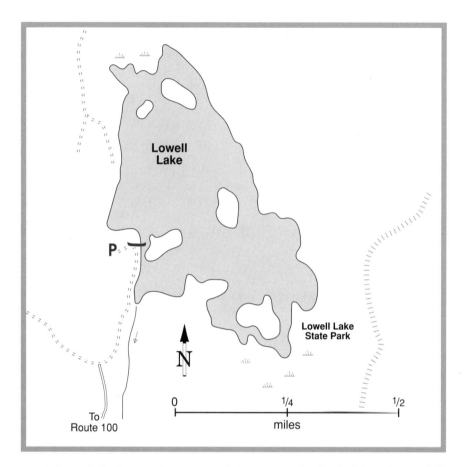

Toward dusk on a late-June visit, we watched a bald eagle, in full adult plumage, survey its surroundings from a tall white pine at the lake's northern end. Later in the season, we paddled here on a warm, sunny day, and as we watched a gathering of Canada geese, they and the early-turning red maple on the far shore told us that fall would come soon. We knew that we would be back to paddle the entire thing, to explore the pond as it awakens in the spring.

GETTING THERE

From Londonderry at the junction of Routes 11 and 100, take Route 11 east for 3.0 miles and turn left onto Lowell Lake Road. At the T in the road in 0.7 mile, take the right, less-traveled fork. The parking area is another 0.2 mile.

The Beaver
Resident Wetlands Engineer

The beaver, *Castor canadensis,* is one of the most fascinating and remarkable animals found in New England's lakes, ponds, and streams. Unlike many other animals, beaver actively modify their environment. The sole representative of the family Castoridae, this 30- to 100-pound rodent—the largest rodent in North America—descends directly from a bear-sized ancestor that lived a million years ago.

Quietwater paddlers frequently see beaver dams and lodges, especially on more-out-of-the-way lakes and ponds. This tireless, industrious mammal uses branches pruned from stream-side trees or downed timber to construct dams and lodges. Beaver now work mostly under the cover of darkness, especially in areas suffering from large amounts of human traffic. In the wilds, however, where few humans tread, beaver work away in broad daylight. We mention in our lake, pond, and stream descriptions where we have seen beaver active during the day.

Beaver build dams to raise a stream or pond's water level, providing the resident colony with access to trees growing farther away. The deeper water also allows beaver to cache branches underwater for winter retrieval, even when thick layers of ice cover their winter stores. They also dig small canals through marsh and meadow to transport branches from distant trees. Just as we find paddling easier than carrying a boat, beaver prefer swimming with a branch—taking advantage of water's buoyancy—than carrying it overland. If you have the good fortune to see a beaver swimming with a larger branch, or if you stop to inspect a winter store, check to see whether the animal has pruned off the leafy twigs to reduce drag.

Studies show that the sound of flowing water guides beaver in their dam-building—they jam sticks into the dam where they hear the gurgle of water. In one experiment, researchers played a tape of gurgling water; beaver responded by jamming sticks into locations from which the sound emanated, even though no water actually flowed there. Beaver dams can be very large, over 10 feet high and hundreds of feet long. The largest dam ever recorded, near the present town of Berlin, New Hampshire, spanned 4,000 feet and created a lake with 40 lodges!

Beaver dams benefit many other species, providing important habitat for waterfowl, fish, moose, muskrat, and other animals. Plus, the dams provide flood control, minimize erosion along stream banks, increase aquifer recharge, and improve water quality, both by allowing silt to settle out and by providing biological filtration through aquatic plants. We credit beaver with creating much of America's best farmland by damming watercourses, thus allowing nutrient-rich silt to accumulate over many years. As the ponds fill in, meadows form.

The beaver lodge includes an underwater entrance and usually two different platform levels: a main floor about four inches above the water level, and a sleeping shelf another two inches higher.

Beaver may construct the lodge in the center of a pond, totally surrounded by water, but more commonly site it on the edge. Before the onset of winter, beaver cover much of the lodge with mud—which they carry on their broad tails while swimming—which freezes to provide an almost impenetrable fortress. The river otter—the only predator that can get in—can swim through the underwater entrance. Beaver leave the peak more permeable for ventilation.

Near the lodge, in deep water, beaver store up a winter's worth of branches in an underwater food cache. They jam branches butt-first into the pond-bottom mud to keep them under the ice and then swim out of their lodges to bring back the stored branches to eat. While they prefer alder and willow, they also love the cambium layer—just beneath the bark—of such hardwoods as yellow birch, white ash, and black cherry. During the spring and summer months, beaver eat primarily pond vegetation, shrubs, herbaceous plants along the shore, and even algae. We have watched them munching voraciously on yellow pond-lily stems.

Beaver have adapted remarkably well to their unique aquatic lifestyle. They have two layers of fur: long silky guard hairs and a dense woolly underfur. By regularly grooming this fur with a special comblike split toenail and keeping it oiled, water seldom totally wets through to the beaver's skin. Their noses and ears have special valves that keep them shut when underwater, and special folds of skin in the mouth enable beaver to gnaw underwater and carry branches in their teeth without getting water down their throats. Their back feet have fully webbed toes to provide propulsion underwater, and their tails provide important rudder control, which helps them swim in a straight line when dragging a large branch. Their respiratory and circulatory systems have adapted to underwater swimming, enabling a beaver to stay underwater for up to 15 minutes and to swim up to a half-mile. Similar adaptations evolved independently in whales, seals, loons, and other air-breathing divers—though snapping turtles rely on a very different mechanism for staying underwater (see the chapter on snapping turtles). Finally, as with other rodents, their teeth grow constantly and remain sharp through use.

Castor oil, that medicinal cure-all of yesteryear, comes from special perineal scent glands. Beaver use the oily yellow liquid to waterproof their fur and to communicate. Along the banks of ponds and lakes, you may see mud mounds scented with this castoreum; it has a strong but not unpleasant smell and, in fact, forms a base ingredient in some expensive perfumes.

Beaver generally mate for life and maintain an extended family structure. Young stay with their parents for two years, so both yearlings and the current year's kits live with the two parents in the lodge. Females usually bear two—sometimes three—kits between April and June. Born fully furred with their eyes open, they can walk and swim almost immediately, though they rarely leave the lodge until at least a month of age. The yearlings and both parents assist in bringing food to the kits as well as with dam and lodge construction.

The demand for beaver pelts, more than any other factor, was responsible for the early exploration of North America. Trappers nearly exterminated them by the late 1800s, but last-minute legislative protection in the 1890s saved them from extinction. In New Hampshire, the state released six beaver in the late 1920s as part of a restocking program. Then began what certainly might be the most successful endangered species reintroduction program. By 1955, beaver had repopulated the entire state.

Although we have removed most of their natural predators—wolves, cougars, and bobcats—beaver populations have not rebounded to historic highs, mainly due to habitat loss and their engineering activities that often conflict with humans.

As you paddle along the shoreline of lakes or quiet rivers, keep an eye out for tell-tale signs of beaver, including gnaw marks on trees, distinctive conical stumps of cut trees, canals leading off into the marsh, alder branches trimmed back along narrow passages, and well-worn paths leading away from the water's edge where the hardworking mammals have dragged more distant branches to the water. Exploring a quiet beaver pond by canoe or kayak—carrying over the dam if necessary—often provides a substantial reward because it allows access to pristine ponds and marshes.

We see beaver most often in the late evening or early morning. Paddle quietly toward a beaver lodge around dusk. Wait patiently, and you are likely to see the animals emerge for evening feeding and perhaps construction work on a dam or lodge. When a beaver senses danger it slaps the water with its tail and dives with a loud *ker-chunk*! Try not to invade their personal space; observe them from a respectful distance. We hope that you will find it as exhilarating as we do to emerge from a tight bend in a marshy stream and come across a beaver pruning back the alders, or to drift silently toward a beaver at dusk, watching it go about its various activities.

Lake Champlain— Southern End
Addison, Benson, Bridport, Orwell, Shoreham, and West Haven, VT

MAPS

Vermont Atlas: Maps 28 and 32

USGS Quadrangles: Crown Point, Port Henry, Putnam, Ticonderoga, and Whitehall, NY; Benson, Bridport, and Orwell, VT

INFORMATION

Length: 35 miles, paddled south to north

Prominent fish species: Largemouth bass, smallmouth bass, pickerel, yellow perch, northern pike, landlocked salmon, walleye, brown trout, rainbow trout, and lake trout

Camping: Chipman Point Marina—802-948-2288

Most of Lake Champlain is too large to tackle in an open boat, but the narrower southern end is often an enjoyable exception—though even here wind sometimes produces dangerous paddling conditions, and the wakes from large boats coming up the Champlain Canal can easily swamp an open boat. Near the southern tip of the lake, about a mile north of the Poultney River inlet, The Nature Conservancy maintains an access point on the Helen W. Buckner Preserve at its Bald Mountain property.

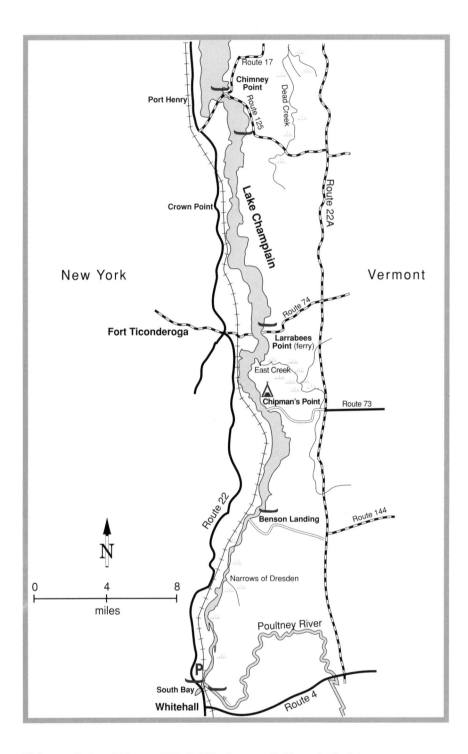

Loading up the canoe at the narrow south end of Lake Champlain. The bike is for the return trip to the car.

The extreme southern tip of Lake Champlain up to Benson Landing is very narrow. Silver maple and old willow line the marshy banks, extending their branches out over the fairly murky water. A railroad follows the New York bank of the river, but otherwise little development impinges on the water. Innumerable birds inhabit the banks and trees. Painted turtles slide into the water from partially submerged logs as you pass by. Numerous backwaters and inlets invite exploration. Filled with thick vegetation, including cattail, sedge, and arrowhead, unfortunately these coves also contain Eurasian milfoil and water chestnut, two introduced aquatic plants that choke out native vegetation.

Halfway up to Benson Landing, you pass through the Narrows of Dresden, a beautiful section of lake bounded by tall cliffs with cedar, hemlock, and white birch clinging to rock crevices and hanging down to the water's edge. Though the lake's narrowness seems comforting, watch for wakes. Large cabin cruisers pass through on the way from the

Great Lakes to Florida, via the Champlain Canal, which extends south from the Poultney River. A 40-foot cabin cruiser, as we found out, creates a very large wake. In a lake only 100 or 200 yards wide, you will get the full impact, which can be a three-foot wave—enough to swamp an open boat if you do not deal with it correctly. Point the boat into the approaching wave, or escape into a protected cove or behind an island when possible. We found ourselves constantly looking over our shoulders and planning an escape route.

A nice long, 18-mile round trip takes you to where the lake opens up, about a mile south of Benson Landing. If you continue north, big water, with mile-wide stretches, allows even moderate winds (10 to 15 knots) to generate big waves. We experienced foot-and-a-half-high waves that lapped over the bow of our heavily laden canoe. Some fairly remote stretches of shoreline along here provide suitable camping spots, or you can continue north to the private campground at Chipman's Point. There is a good boat access at Benson Landing and a smaller one three miles up, in Orwell.

East Creek, which flows into the lake across from Fort Ticonderoga, offers a fantastic side trip. You can paddle four or five miles up this meandering brook (noted for its bass fishing) through cattail and sedge marshes and along deep deciduous woods and grassy dairy fields into the East Creek Wildlife Management Area. Shagbark hickory, white oak, and basswood, along with more-typical Vermont trees, line the way. The variety of habitat found along East Creek provides excellent bird watching. Unfortunately, you cannot paddle all the way to a road access—a large, beautiful falls dropping steeply over a sloping rock face blocks your way. Some of the largest silver maple we have seen grow along the North Branch. The one we had lunch under looked at least 24 feet in circumference!

Back out on Lake Champlain, a relatively short paddle takes you to Larrabees Point, where the ferry crosses; the boat access off Route 73, south of the ferry, makes a good access point for a trip to East Creek. From Larrabees Point north, the lake gradually widens; we recommend not going beyond the bridge at Chimney Point, another 14 miles or so above Larrabees Point, because the lake is too big to be enjoyed. (See sections on Little Otter Creek, Missisquoi, Jewett and Stevens Brooks, and Rock River farther north for other paddling locations on Lake Champlain.)

The adventurous might want to try what we did on this section of the lake. We took a bicycle along in the canoe, and after two full days of paddling, John got the short straw, bicycled back to the car (Route 22 is a little more direct), and drove back to pick up the canoe and Alex, his well-rested canoeing partner.

A trip on Lake Champlain, even on the more manageable southern section, takes more planning than most of the other trips covered in this book. For more detailed information, use USGS topographic maps or the *Vermont Atlas*.

GETTING THERE

The map included here has a scale too large for finding the access. Use detailed road maps or topographic maps of both the Vermont and New York sides. We found the best way to go is through Whitehall, NY.

From the junction of Routes 4 and 22 in Whitehall, go north on Route 22 for 0.5 mile to Sanders Street, turn right, and cross the bridge over the Champlain Canal. Turn left onto Williams Street, go north for 0.7 mile, and turn left onto Route 10. After 0.6 mile when the paved road goes right, turn left onto a gravel road that crosses the Poultney River into Vermont. Turn left and follow the river for 1.8 miles to the marked pullout at The Nature Conservancy's Helen W. Buckner Preserve at Bald Mountain. The access is on the left, with limited parking for a few cars about 50 yards back down the road, on the other side.

A better, easier-to-find access is from South Bay in New York. Paddle out from South Bay under the railroad trestle and head left. From Whitehall, go north on Route 22, cross the bridge over South Bay, and take the second right, which leads to the boat access. The access is 2.8 miles from Whitehall. For information on paddling South Bay, see the *AMC Quiet Water Canoe Guide: New York*.

Use the *Vermont Atlas* or road maps to find the access points farther north along the lake.

Bomoseen Lake, Glen Lake, and Half Moon Pond
Castleton, Fair Haven, and Hubbardton, VT

MAPS

    Vermont Atlas: Map 28

    USGS Quadrangle: Bomoseen

INFORMATION

    Bomoseen Lake area: 2,360 acres

    Glen Lake area: 191 acres

    Half Moon Pond area: 23 acres

    Prominent fish species: Bomoseen Lake—smallmouth bass, largemouth bass, yellow perch, northern pike, brook trout, and brown trout; Glen Lake—smallmouth bass, largemouth bass, yellow perch, northern pike, and rainbow trout; Half Moon Pond— largemouth bass, yellow perch, and rainbow trout

    Camping: Bomoseen State Park—802-265-4242; Half Moon State Park—802-273-2848

Bomoseen Lake, Glen Lake, and Half Moon Pond nestle into the hills of western Vermont at the northern reaches of the Taconic Mountains. A number of nearby slate quarries still produce the slate shingles for which Vermont is known. You can get a feel for the area's sedimentary geology by exploring the exposed ledge and layered rock of the Glen Lake shoreline. Millions of years ago, clays that accumulated on the ocean floor compressed into shale. When the ocean floor uplifted to form the Taconic Mountains, heat and pressure metamorphosed the shale into much harder slate.

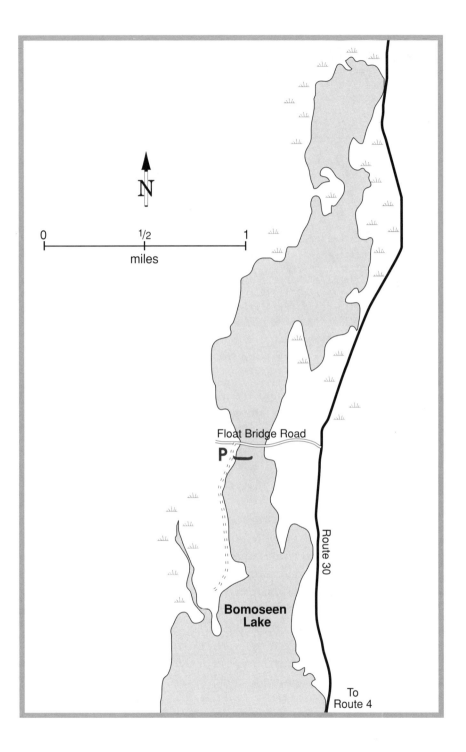

N

0   1/2   1

miles

Float Bridge Road

P

Route 30

**Bomoseen
Lake**

To
Route 4

The marshy, northern reaches of Bomoseen Lake harbor huge patches of fragrant waterlily, *Nymphaea odorata*.

Bomoseen Lake. Bomoseen is a large, popular lake, the largest lake wholly within the state. Anyone looking for peace and quiet, except in the off-season, should avoid the main part of the lake. We include the far northern and least-traveled section here, and we probably would avoid the lake altogether on busy summer weekends.

Why do we include Bomoseen in a quietwater canoe guide? For two reasons: because of enormous patches of fragrant waterlily, whose blossoms are the largest we have seen; we could not get over the size of these blossoms. We just paddled out into the middle and reveled in the splendor of these gorgeous plants. Second, because of the state parks and other protected lands, particularly to the west, wildlife abounds in this region. On a hot, busy Saturday in late June, we spied deer that had come down to the shore for a midday drink, saw several great blue herons stalking fish, and watched a wood duck feeding with its young.

From the boat access at the northern end of the lake, go under the bridge; not as many boats motor into the shallow, Eurasian-milfoil-choked north end. We prefer sticking mostly to the less-developed

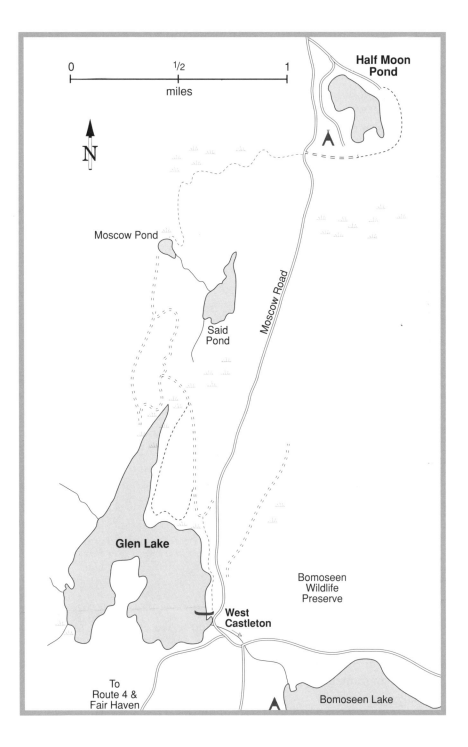

western shoreline. In addition to the large patches of fragrant waterlily, and the invasive milfoil, expect to see a couple of species of pondweed, yellow pond lily, water shield, and lots of turtles and frogs. We saw one small patch of the invasive water chestnut, which we ripped up and carted off, but we would not be surprised to find in a few years that it had turned into a real problem, as it has elsewhere in the Northeast.

Glen Lake. Compared with the summertime frenzy on Bomoseen, paddling is quite pleasant here. A 5 MPH speed limit keeps large boats away, and the state forbids use of personal watercraft. This midsize lake has only minimal development, with three or four houses at the southern end near the dam and put-in point. The shoreline, mostly wild and heavily wooded (principally hemlock, white pine, red maple, and white birch), gives way to water that boasts excellent fishing—supposedly, somebody once pulled a 30-pound northern out of Glen Lake.

From the outlet, the Glen Lake Trail extends around the eastern shoreline on public land, rounds the northern tip of the lake, and then travels up to Moscow and Half Moon Ponds. Though not readily accessible by trail, Said Pond, southwest of Moscow Pond, might be found with a topographical map. Another trail, the Slate History Trail, takes you through what is left of the West Castleton Railroad and Slate Company. A self-guiding pamphlet describes the area's slate history. You can get this pamphlet and trail maps at Half Moon or Bomoseen State Parks, just north and southeast, respectively, of Glen Lake.

Half Moon Pond. We include small Half Moon Pond because it offers some enjoyable paddling and harbors a very pleasant campground, although it does suffer from overuse, with more than 60 campsites and lean-tos around the pond. We found a beaver lodge at the northern end that you might want to check out in the evening or early morning, the most active time for beaver. Half Moon State Park also rents canoes.

GETTING THERE

Bomoseen Lake. To get to Bomoseen Lake from the junction of Routes 4 (Exit 4) and 30, go north 4.3 miles on Route 30 to Float Bridge Road. Turn left onto Float Bridge Road, cross the bridge, and take an immediate left onto the boat access for the northern part of the lake.

Glen Lake. To get to Glen Lake from the south, take the paved road that leads north from Fair Haven to West Castleton (from the east, get off Route 4 at Exit 3 and turn north onto this road, which turns into Glen Lake Drive). The access to Glen Lake is 4.3 miles north of Route 4 (cross over Route 4). From Half Moon State Park, take Moscow Road south 2.8 miles, bearing right in West Castleton, and look for the Glen Lake access on the right.

Half Moon Pond. To get to Half Moon Pond, go north from Glen Lake, or coming south on Route 30, turn right onto Hortonville Road; turn south onto Black Pond Road after a couple of miles.

Wallingford Pond
Wallingford, VT

MAPS

Vermont Atlas: Map 29

USGS Quadrangle: Wallingford

INFORMATION

Area: 86 acres

Prominent fish species: Smallmouth bass, pickerel, and yellow perch

Primitive camping: Contact the Manchester Ranger District, Green Mountain National Forest—802-362-2307

Situated completely within Green Mountain National Forest, remote Wallingford Pond does not suffer from development, except that the road in gets chewed up badly by four-wheel-drive trucks. We strongly recommend that you carry your boat in, rather than risk ruining your vehicle on this rutty road and damaging the ecosystem at the road's end.

Wallingford Pond seems much larger than its 86 acres, probably because of its clover-leaf shape, which divides the pond into three segments. A variety of trees—balsam fir, spruce, red maple, white birch, and yellow birch—populate the heavily wooded shoreline, along with thickly grown alder, making access to the shore difficult. Several marshy areas, especially at the inlet near the southern end, provide nesting and feeding habitat for waterfowl and the occasional moose. Other sections of shoreline seem more boglike, with sphagnum tussocks, heath, and sundew.

As you paddle into the southern arm of the pond, be careful of sharp rocks just below the surface in the connecting channel. Especially in late summer, with the low water levels, be careful to avoid damaging your boat. Five or six unmaintained primitive sites around the pond provide places to camp.

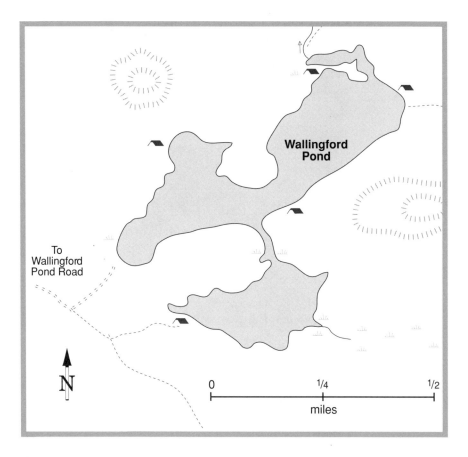

GETTING THERE

From Route 7 in Wallingford, take Route 140 east. Turn right at the sign for White Rocks Picnic Area, but stay on the main gravel road instead of turning into the picnic area. Go 2.0 miles, turn right onto Wallingford Pond Road, and go another 2.0 miles to the access.

The road into the pond should be limited to foot traffic. It takes about 30 minutes—longer if you stop to rest—to hike the mile into the pond. There is a gradual climb, followed by a gradual drop to the pond.

North Hartland Lake
Hartford and Hartland, VT

MAPS

Vermont Atlas: Map 31

USGS Quadrangles: Hartland, VT/NH; North Hartland, NH; and Quechee, VT

INFORMATION

Area: 215 acres

Prominent fish species: Largemouth bass, yellow perch, and rainbow trout

Camping: Quechee Gorge State Park—802-295-2990

Paddling entrance fee and hours: $2; 8:00 A.M.–8:00 P.M.

North Hartland Lake, a long, narrow reservoir, reaches back up to the Quechee Gorge, with its 165-foot walls carved out by the Ottauquechee River. This scenic area, surrounded by layered hillsides, offers great paddling, hiking (from the state park), camping, and fishing. Though you will not have to share the water with personal watercraft, you may find some high-speed boating on busy summer weekends.

In mid-May, the brushy shorelines appeared quite natural—with diverse shrubs close to shore and stately white pine standing guard from the hillsides. But the water level in the reservoir, particularly in early spring, can vary greatly, reaching 100 feet higher than the natural summer level. We wonder what the beaver do when water climbs well up the wooded hillsides.

Bird life abounds: We heard some very noisy great blue herons calling from the pines and wonder if a small rookery is located here. If

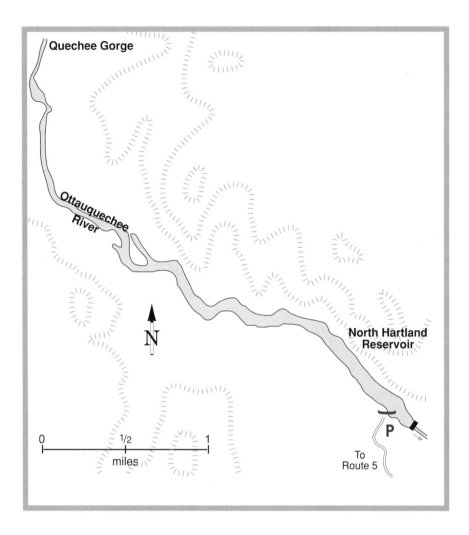

Quechee Gorge

Ottauquechee River

N

North Hartland Reservoir

0   1/2   1
miles

P

To Route 5

so, it would be unusual; they usually nest in dead trees in marshes. Dozens of spotted sandpipers patrolled the shores, bobbing their tails incessantly whenever they alighted. And we surprised a flock of turkeys on the hillside. These magnificent game birds, standing over three feet tall, once inhabited most forested parts of eastern North America, foraging on acorns, chestnuts, beechnuts, seeds, and insects. With the clearing of forests, loss of the American chestnut to chestnut blight, and unregulated hunting, the wild turkey disappeared over most of its

An eastern garter snake, *Thamnophis sirtalis*, swims in front of the boat.

range. Recently reintroduced in many areas, turkeys once again range over large tracts of Vermont and Hew Hampshire.

Getting There

Take Route 5 south from White River Junction. Just before reaching the I-91 bridge, turn right onto a paved road that goes by the Hartland Volunteer Fire Department. Go about 1.0 mile and turn right onto the lake access road.

East Creek, South Fork
Orwell, VT

MAPS
> **Vermont Atlas:** Map 32
>
> **USGS Quadrangle:** Orwell

INFORMATION
> **Area:** 120 acres
>
> **Prominent fish species:** Largemouth bass

The state has dammed the South Fork of East Creek in a few places, providing extraordinary waterfowl habitat in the low-lying farm country of the Champlain Valley. Farm runoff nutrifies the water, causing profuse aquatic plant growth that supports lots of fish and wildlife. However, this so-called nonpoint source pollution, so evident here, can have a profound effect on larger bodies of water, such as Lake Champlain, as it washes in from every little farm creek. Because the nutrifying source—primarily fertilizer—gets applied over such a wide area, keeping it out of bodies of water is a real challenge.

When we paddled here in early July, the water was already so choked with vegetation that we had a hard time finding any open water. Do not expect to zip through this water. Instead, take a leisurely paddle, wending your way around the islands of thick vegetation: pondweed, bur-reed, narrow-leafed arrowhead, narrow-leafed cattail, bulrush, reed, sedge, duckweed, smartweed, and purple loosestrife, to name a few.

Note the white waterlily with the huge green leaves, some of which span nearly a foot. Fragrant waterlily occurs as two subspecies: *Nymphaea odorata* subspecies *odorata* and subspecies *tuberosa*. Most guidebooks list these as separate species, but they recently have been

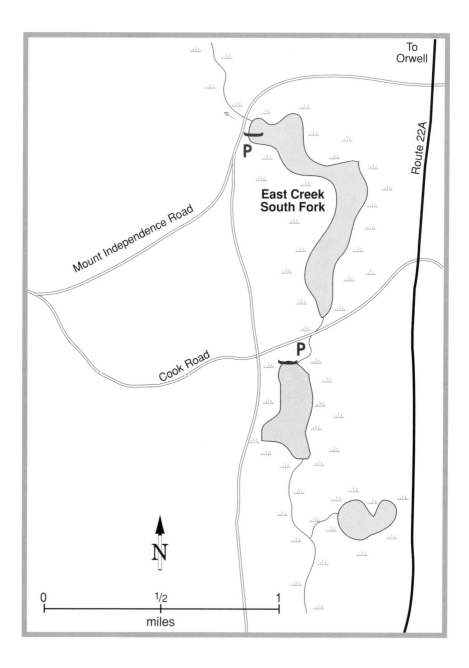

lumped into one species by taxonomists. The more common sub-species, *odorata*, normally has much smaller leaves, with both the leaves and the flower sepals tinged with purple. The less common *tuberosa* subspecies has large green leaves and green sepals. A dwarf white waterlily, *Nymphaea leibergii*, which is critically imperiled in the Northeast, also exists. We have seen this rare plant in only a bodies few of water. *N. leibergii* used to be lumped with the pygmy waterlily, *N. tetragona*, of the Northwest, so this is an example of taxonomists splitting two populations into distinct species.

Many pairs of Canada geese raise their broods here, along with several other species of ducks. Grebes, dozens of tree swallows, red-winged blackbirds, and many other species breed here.

The dense vegetation includes Eurasian milfoil and water chestnut. Note the warnings about picking up "hitchhikers" at the boat access. This does not refer to the two-legged variety, but instead includes three serious aquatic pests: Eurasian milfoil, water chestnut, and zebra mussels. All three can easily hitch rides on boat trailers, in bilges, and even on canoe and kayak hulls, to be deposited later in the next water-way. Lake Champlain already suffers from infestation of these, and the worry is that they will get transported to every other body of water in the vicinity. We pulled up all of the water chestnut that we found, about a bushel, and tossed it out on the bank to rot.

Biologists worry that these three alien species, introduced from Europe and Asia to the East Coast by humans, will eventually infect most bodies of water in the East and Midwest. They arrived without their natural predators, established themselves easily, and now crowd out native species.

GETTING THERE

In Orwell, from the junction of Routes 22A and 73, travel south on Route 22A for 0.6 mile and turn right onto Cook Road. The access is 0.6 mile down Cook Road on the left.

Richville Pond
Shoreham, VT

MAPS

Vermont Atlas: Map 32

USGS Quadrangle: Orwell

INFORMATION

Area: 124 acres

Prominent fish species: Largemouth bass, yellow perch, and northern pike

Just to the east of Lake Champlain lies Richville Pond, another of those winding, marshy bodies of water absolutely brimming with wildlife (see sections on Dead Creek; the southern portion of Lake Champlain that describes East Creek; and the separate East Creek, South Fork, entry).

Richville Pond's northern reach, a widened section of the Lemon Fair River, rarely exceeds 100 yards in width. East of the covered bridge, the pond narrows to a winding creek; by the end of June weed growth may restrict passage along this section. About a half-mile east of the covered bridge the creek forks, and you can take either channel (the smaller north fork is a little difficult to find). The distance from the northern fishing access to the covered bridge is a little less than two miles, and in the spring you can paddle on the creek at least a mile past the bridge.

The entire marshy shore grows thick with cattail, sedge, bulrush, arrowhead, wild onion, and fragrant waterlily. Unfortunately, Eurasian milfoil has choked out some of the native vegetation.

Paddling along through rich, rolling farmland and patchy stands of mixed hardwoods and white pine, songbirds make this bird-watcher's

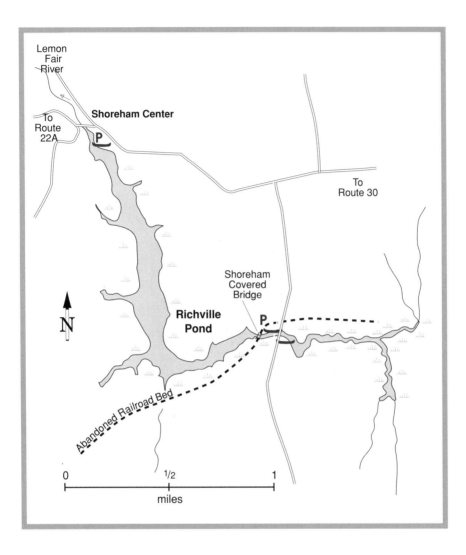

paradise come alive. We watched a white-tailed doe grazing in reeds as high as her back and listened to a symphony of songbirds all along the pond. Fishing is supposed to be excellent.

The origin of the name "Lemon Fair" has generated quite a bit of disagreement over the years. Some say it is a corruption of "lamentable affair." In 1824, Zedock Thompson recorded the story of an old woman who came across the stream and said it was truly a lamentable affair. Others attribute the lamentable affair to an Indian massacre or a

Picturesque Shoreham covered bridge over Richville Pond, one of only two covered railroad bridges remaining in Vermont.

drowning. Another says it is a pronunciation of the French *Les Monts Verts* (the green mountains), or most likely, according to Esther Swift in *Vermont Place Names*, it comes from the French name for the river, Limon Faire.

The 108-foot-long Shoreham bridge, which crosses the pond where it narrows toward the eastern end, represents one of only two covered railroad bridges remaining in Vermont. The tall, stately, well-maintained Howe truss bridge, built in 1897 but not used since 1951, holds a lot of interest for those into heavy-timber construction.

GETTING THERE

Richville Pond can be reached either from Route 22A or from Route 30. To reach the northern access, from the junction of Routes 22A and 74 west in Shoreham, go south for 0.4 mile and turn left onto Richville Road. The access is on the right just after crossing the Lemon Fair River (about 2.5 miles from Route 22A). To get to the Shoreham covered bridge access point, continue on for 0.7 mile, turn right, and go 0.7 mile down Shoreham Depot Road. A well-hidden access trail leads from the parking area down to the water.

From Whiting, turn west off Route 30 onto Shoreham-Whiting Road. Turn left onto Shoreham Depot Road in 2.9 miles. The northern access is another 0.7 mile west on Shoreham-Whiting Road.

Otter Creek
Cornwall, Leicester, Middlebury, Salisbury, Sudbury, and Whiting, VT

MAPS

Vermont Atlas: Maps 32 and 33

USGS Quadrangles: Brandon, Cornwall, East Middlebury, and Sudbury

INFORMATION

Length: 15 miles

Prominent fish species: Largemouth bass, smallmouth bass, pickerel, and northern pike

Otter Creek and the Battenkill River originate side by side on the slopes of the southern Green Mountains in Bennington County. From there the Battenkill, a famous trout stream, flows west into New York, while Otter Creek flows northward through a whole litany of towns: Dorset, Danby, Peru, Mount Tabor, Wallingford, Clarendon, Rutland, Pittsford, Brandon—the list seems to go on endlessly—Sudbury, Leicester, Whiting, Salisbury, Cornwall, Middlebury, Weybridge, New Haven, Addison, Waltham, Panton, and Vergennes before flowing into Lake Champlain at Ferrisburg. Is there a Vermont river that flows through more towns?

For much of its northward journey, Otter Creek flows through broad flood plains taken over by sometimes impenetrable marshes. Silver maple lines the bank as the creek meanders through open farm country. The river flows through the 15,000-acre northern white cedar swamps in Cornwall and Whiting, where the Vermont Nature

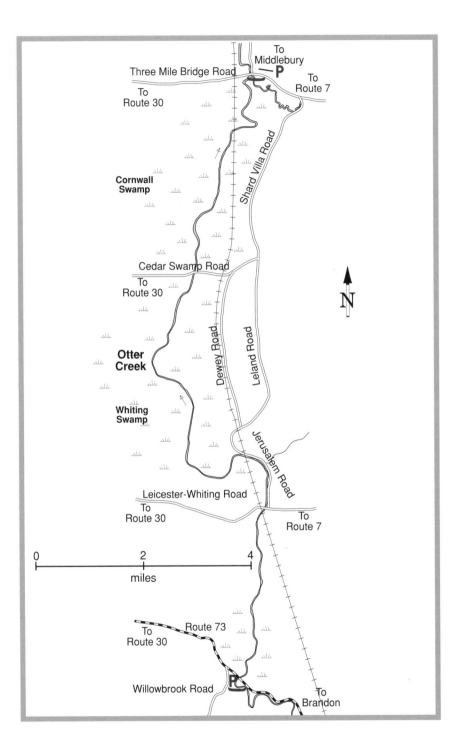

Three Mile Bridge Road

To Middlebury

P

To Route 7

To Route 30

Shard Villa Road

Cornwall Swamp

N

Cedar Swamp Road

To Route 30

Dewey Road

Leland Road

Otter Creek

Whiting Swamp

Jerusalem Road

Leicester-Whiting Road

To Route 30

To Route 7

0   2   4

miles

Route 73

To Route 30

P

Willowbrook Road

To Brandon

A variety of trees overhang the banks of Otter Creek.

Conservancy has protected miles of riverbank and more than 2,000 acres of bottomland.

We include much of the middle section here, between Brandon and Middlebury—the section that flows through Cornwall and Whiting Swamps. Beaver activity and floods cause logjams that can require short portages. We have paddled sections of Otter Creek in both directions, though during periods of high water you will need to make a one-way trip. We recommend paddling upstream from the Three Mile Bridge Road access through the Cornwall Swamp, followed by a leisurely paddle back to your vehicle.

Even though much of the river traverses open farm country, the generally wooded shores harbor lots of wildlife, including wood ducks, geese, flickers, crows, white-throated sparrows, downy woodpeckers, yellow-bellied sapsuckers, large numbers of grackles, and lots more.

GETTING THERE

From Route 7 in Middlebury, go south on Creek Road for 2.6 miles to the access at the T with Three Mile Bridge Road.

Silver Lake
Leicester, VT

MAPS

Vermont Atlas: Map 33

USGS Quadrangle: East Middlebury

INFORMATION

Area: 103 acres

Prominent fish species: Yellow perch, brown trout, and rainbow trout

Contact information: Camping—Branbury State Park, off Route 53 in Salisbury—802-247-5925; Maps—Silver Lake and Moosalamoo Hiking Trails, Middlebury Ranger District—802-388-4362

For the hearty paddler who likes less-traveled areas and does not mind a fairly long portage, Silver Lake is great. This small lake has a fairly regular shoreline with few coves or marshy areas to explore, but camped under the tall hemlocks and gazing across the lake on a quiet autumn morning, the exquisite setting more than makes up for the lake's limitations.

Fifteen campsites dot the Silver Lake Recreation Area. Two wells with hand pumps provide fresh water, and outhouses are located in both the picnic and camping areas. You can camp here year-round for free, but the water pump handles get removed before risk of freeze-up. Most of the campsites hover near the shore; a few really stunning sites nestle beneath towering hemlocks on a thick bed of needles, surrounded by huge rock outcroppings.

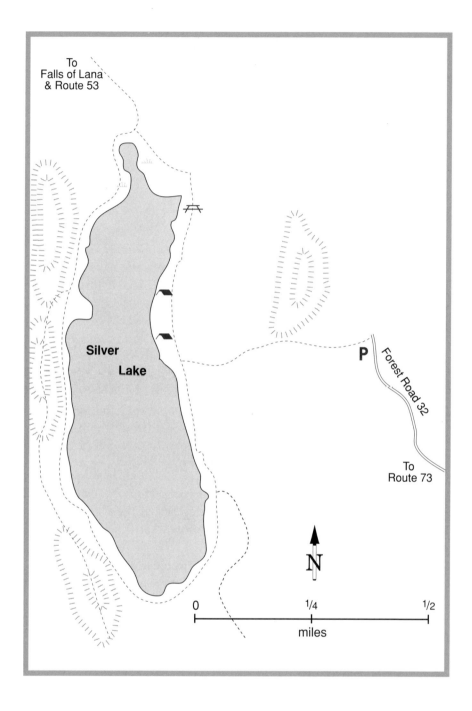

To
Falls of Lana
& Route 53

Silver
Lake

P

Forest Road 32

To
Route 73

N

0   1/4   1/2
miles

Besides the Silver Lake Loop Trail, a number of good trails exist in this part of Green Mountain National Forest. If you did not hike in via the Falls of Lana, be sure to check it out. General Wool camped here with his troops in 1850, and his party decided such an attractive place needed a better name than Sucker Brook Falls, so they named it Falls of Lana after their leader—*lana* is Spanish for "wool." Other hiking trails in the vicinity of Silver Lake include the Leicester Hollow, Chandler Ridge, and Goshen Trails.

GETTING THERE

There are two access routes to the lake. From the west, park just off Route 53 (5.3 miles north of the intersection with Route 73) and follow the trail 1.5 miles in, most of it steeply uphill, past the Falls of Lana to the lake. The trail leads to the northern end of the lake by the dam and picnic area; campsites are around to the left on the eastern shore.

For carrying a boat in, a much better access point is from the east side. Take Route 73 east from Route 53 for 1.7 miles and turn left (north) onto Forest Road 32. You will see a sign for Silver Lake at the turnoff. After 0.6 mile, FR 32 turns to the left across a creek. After 2.4 miles, turn left off Carlisle Hill Road onto Silver Lake Road (this is still FR 32). Go right at the fork after 0.7 mile and continue on for another 1.5 miles to the Silver Lake access (about 4.6 miles from Route 73). The carry into Silver Lake is 0.6 mile, most of it gently downhill. When you get to the Silver Lake Loop Trail, the campsites are a few hundred yards to the right.

Chittenden Reservoir and Lefferts Pond
Chittenden, VT

MAPS

    Vermont Atlas: Map 33

    USGS Quadrangle: Chittenden

INFORMATION

    Chittenden Reservoir area: 750 acres

    Lefferts Pond area: 55 acres

    Prominent fish species: Chittenden Reservoir—walleye, yellow perch, landlocked salmon, brook trout, brown trout, and rainbow trout

Chittenden Reservoir and Lefferts Pond nestle into the beautiful Green Mountains of central Vermont. The surrounding mountains—some of Vermont's tallest, stretching to well over 3,000 feet—provide a wild and remote feeling. Along the shores hardwoods predominate, including several species of birch and maple, though stands of hemlock, spruce, and balsam fir intersperse. On a peak autumn day, this area can be stunning. Plan for a little hiking in addition to paddling. A great trail starts at Lefferts Pond and extends around Chittenden Reservoir. Moss-covered boulders, thick banks of fern, bubbling brooks, and lots of wildlife provide for great hiking. We saw numerous moose tracks during our visits. The famous Long Trail, which traverses Vermont from Massachusetts to Canada, also runs close by.

    You might have some modest difficulty finding Chittenden Reservoir, but your effort will be rewarded, unless boat traffic picks up in the

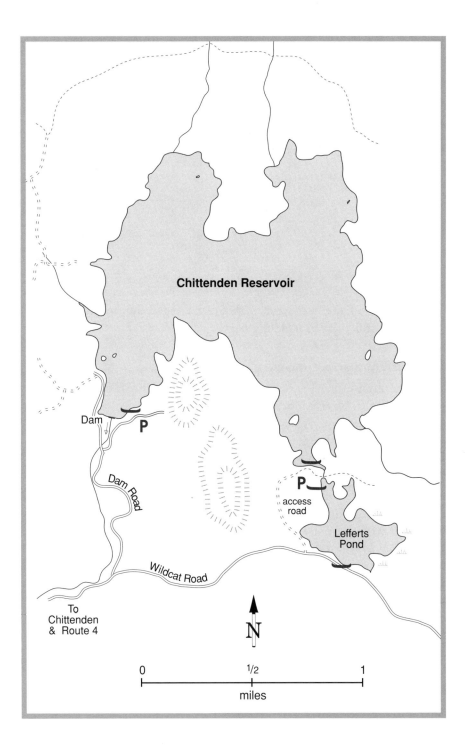

Chittenden Reservoir

Dam

P

Dam Road

P

access
road

Lefferts
Pond

Wildcat Road

To
Chittenden
& Route 4

N

0   1/2   1
miles

Scenic Lefferts Pond is covered with aquatic vegetation by midsummer, though we still enjoyed paddling here.

future. Exploring the numerous inlets and bays around the lake's perimeter could provide a full day or more of paddling. Central Vermont Public Service Corporation (CVPS), before it deeded over the surrounding land to the national forest, limited motorboats to 15 horsepower on Chittenden and banned personal watercraft and water-skiing; those signs were still up in the summer of 2000. However, the state Water Resources Board, which now regulates use of Chittenden, has decided that even though personal watercraft and water-skiing had not been allowed on Chittenden, they should be now. Go figure! This is another loss to quietwater paddlers, loons, and other wildlife; once conversions to more-consumptive uses take place, we will have a hard time winning them back.

Chittenden's large size means that wind can be a problem. On a breezy day stick close to the coves, or paddle on Lefferts Pond. Small and very shallow, Lefferts Pond, a real gem, teems with aquatic plants and wildlife. On an April morning not long after ice-out, we watched a river otter pull a six-or-seven-inch fish up on a rock and eat it. You can also expect to see muskrat and lots of waterfowl, including wood ducks, which often nest in boxes CVPS put up on both Lefferts and

Chittenden. When we paddled here in 2000, beaver had dammed up the outlet of Lefferts Pond, raising the level somewhat. A pair of loons also frequently nests on Chittenden or Lefferts, making this one of only a handful of lakes in Vermont that support nesting loons. (The loons' nesting success depends on people keeping their distance during nesting season.)

Lefferts Pond and the area immediately surrounding it is a Wildlife Management Area. The state does not permit gasoline-powered boats, and because the pond is shallow, aquatic vegetation restricts paddling during much of the season, particularly on the southern end. When we paddled here midsummer, water shield, with lesser amounts of pondweed, covered more than 90 percent of the surface. A thick stand of horsetail covers some of the southern border. Even so, the paddling and wildlife viewing were wonderful.

GETTING THERE

To get to the dam access on Chittenden Reservoir, where trailered boats put in, drive northeast from Rutland on Route 4 about 4.0 miles. In Mendon, turn left toward East Pittsford. At the T, turn right toward Chittenden. Where Mountain Top Road bears off left, stay right on Dam Road and go 2.0 miles to the dam. Turn right onto the gravel access road 0.7 mile past the dam.

To reach the eastern carry-in access on Chittenden and Lefferts Pond, bear right onto Wildcat Road about 1.1 miles after passing the Mountain Top Road turnoff. Turn left onto the access road 1.0 mile farther; the parking area is another 0.5 mile. Chittenden is on the left, but by walking a few hundred feet straight ahead, you can also put in on the northern cove of Lefferts Pond. You can also get onto Lefferts Pond by continuing on Wildcat Road past the access road. You will see the carry-in access on the left as the road passes Lefferts Pond.

Dead Creek
Addison and Panton, VT

MAPS

Vermont Atlas: Map 38

USGS Quadrangles: Port Henry, NY, and Westport, NY

INFORMATION

Area: 753 acres from Otter Creek through the Dead Creek Wildlife Management Area

Prominent fish species: Largemouth bass, smallmouth bass, northern pike, and yellow perch

Camping: Button Bay State Park—802-475-2377; D.A.R. State Park—802-759-2354

Flowing into Otter Creek a few miles from Lake Champlain, just west of Vergennes, several dammed sections of Dead Creek form a wonderful, spidery lake and marsh, with no development along the water. The most fertile farming country in Vermont surrounds the area.

Dead Creek seems somehow out of place in Vermont as it winds through rolling farmland, with silos visible across open fields of corn, and green pastures filled with grazing dairy cows. Except for the occasional stand of white pine, most of the trees along the banks consist of more-southern varieties, the most common being white oak and shagbark hickory; Vermont's Champlain Valley represents one of the northernmost extensions of their range.

The murky brown water—the result of farmland nutrification and rooting carp—meanders slowly along on a nearly imperceptible north-flowing current. The shallow stretches, thick with cattail, provide ideal habitat for various wading birds, nesting geese, herons, and ducks.

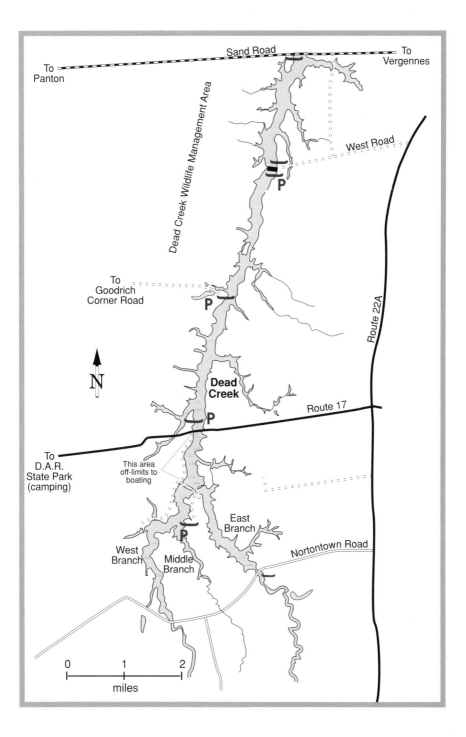

To Panton

Sand Road

To Vergennes

Dead Creek Wildlife Management Area

West Road

Route 22A

To Goodrich Corner Road

P

N

Dead Creek

Route 17

P

To D.A.R. State Park (camping)

This area off-limits to boating

P

East Branch

Nortontown Road

West Branch

Middle Branch

0   1   2
miles

We saw an immature bald eagle perched on a dead snag, along with an adult osprey, red-tailed hawks, and other raptors. We also saw several delicate and colorful (and nonpoisonous) northern water snakes swimming through the water with their heads sticking up to look around. During fall migration, this is one of the best places in New England to see snow geese.

Dead Creek provides a wonderful spot to lose yourself for a day or two, to leave behind the worries of society and listen to the melodious song of the marsh wren. Some of that peace and quiet disappears for a few weeks each fall, however, during waterfowl-hunting season. Unless you hunt, you would do well to keep away at this time.

GETTING THERE

There are six access points; all require a hand-carry to the water. The area is divided into three sections, separated by either a dam or a marsh that is off-limits to boating in order to protect waterfowl nesting habitat.

Northern Section. From Route 22A in Vergennes, take Sand Road toward Panton to the bridge over the dam. Put in on the south side of the bridge. You can also portage up over the bridge on West Road into the middle section.

Middle Section. Launch from West Road, off Route 22A (turn right 2.4 miles south of where Route 22A crosses Otter Creek). Note: this poorly maintained road may be difficult to travel during the spring. West Road dead-ends at Dead Creek. From here there is a very pleasant 3.0-mile paddle (more if you explore all the side inlets) down to a parking area on Route 17 (a second access point). Another access point on a better road is off Goodrich Corner Road on the west side.

Southern Section. Turn south onto the gravel road just west of the bridge on Route 17. After about 0.6 mile, take the left fork across a small wooden bridge to a parking area. Put in either on the East Branch or West Branch. Near the southern end of the East Branch, Nortontown Road crosses over, providing another access point (at a small pullout area just east of the bridge on the north side of the road).

Little Otter Creek
Ferrisburg, VT

MAPS

    Vermont Atlas: Map 38

    USGS Quadrangle: Westport, NY

INFORMATION

    Area: 735 acres

    Prominent fish species: Largemouth bass, smallmouth bass, northern pike, yellow perch, walleye, brook trout, brown trout, and rainbow trout

    Camping: Button Bay State Park—802-475-2377

We can only describe our time at Little Otter Creek Wildlife Management Area as spectacular. We spent most of our time paddling the area south of Hawkins Road because motorboats have no access there. The culverts under the road do not have enough headroom, so after paddling just a short distance to the right (south) from the boat access, we carried our boats up over the road and into the southern section.

You can paddle back up this south arm quite a distance; at a sharp right bend, it enters a very shallow wooded marsh with silver maple canopy, where we saw lots of beaver activity and many black ducks. Unfortunately, we also saw Eurasian milfoil and the beginnings of a water-chestnut invasion. This area may not be paddlable at low-water levels.

Given the profusion of wood duck nesting boxes, we expected to see wood ducks—but we never could have imagined how many we would see in this expansive marsh when we paddled here in late August. One flock of well over 100 wood ducks settled in to roost in the rushes

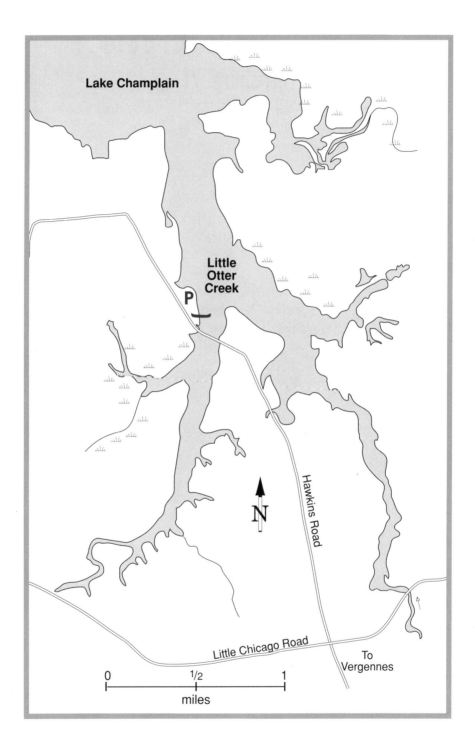

Lake Champlain

Little
Otter
Creek

P

N

Hawkins Road

Little Chicago Road

To
Vergennes

0   1/2   1
miles

right next to our boats, against the gorgeous backdrop of the setting sun. As they alighted, their unducklike cries magnified the feeling of primordial abundance. We also saw many black ducks and many other typical marsh birds, including several adult osprey and a couple of unoccupied nests in various locations within the more than 1,000 acres of the Wildlife Management Area.

We paddled over and among the myriad types of aquatic vegetation, particularly the white waterlilies. Two subspecies of fragrant waterlily exist in this region: *Nymphaea odorata* ssp. *odorata* and *Nymphaea odorata* ssp. *tuberosa*. Though guidebooks describe these as separate species, taxonomists have recently lumped them into one species. You can distinguish *tuberosa* from the more common *odorata* waterlilies: *tuberosa* lily pads have green undersides, the flowers have green sepals, and both are often quite large, while the usually smaller *odorata* lily pads have purple-tinged undersides and sepals.

Interestingly, after they have finished blooming, the flowers of fragrant waterlily get pulled underwater by a coiling action of the stems. This protects the seed head and permits the seeds to ripen over a period of three or four weeks. After the seeds ripen, the seed head, or aril, breaks free and floats to the surface. Here it gradually decomposes and releases its seeds to sink into the pond bottom.

We paddled the rest of the Little Otter Creek Wildlife Management Area, returning to the access after sunset, having seen extraordinary plants, birds, and scenery. Paddle here when the winds come up on Lake Champlain; the south branch, in particular, affords protection from the wind. In late August, not only are you likely to see wood ducks, but much of the aquatic vegetation will be in bloom— from buttonbush to water smartweed, from floating heart to pondweed, and from fragrant waterlily to yellow pond lily.

GETTING THERE

From the junction of Routes 22A and 7 in Vergennes, go north on Route 7 and turn left after 0.5 mile onto Botsford Road. In 0.9 mile take the left fork. Cross Little Chicago Road onto Hawkins Road and go 2.1 miles to the boat access on the right.

Winona Lake
Bristol, VT

MAPS

Vermont Atlas: Map 39

USGS Quadrangle: Bristol

INFORMATION

Area: 234 acres

Prominent fish species: Largemouth bass, yellow perch, pickerel, and northern pike

Winona Lake represents another relatively unknown place, a real treat to stumble across. Located about 40 minutes south of Burlington and nestled beneath the Hogback Mountains that rise from the eastern shore, the 234-acre lake enjoys a gorgeous setting. The state fishing access on gently flowing Pond Brook, which flows north out of the lake, provides a panoramic view of the lake to the south. As you paddle in you see absolutely no development on the lake—only a few farms to the south—although a half-dozen camps hide among thick stands of trees on the far (eastern) side.

Dense stands of swamp loosestrife (*Decodon verticillatus*)—not to be confused with invasive purple loosestrife (*Lythrum salicaria*), which has choked wetlands in recent years—dominate the marshy shoreline. Look for long, pointed, willowlike leaves in whorls of three growing out of arched, whitish stems and, in late summer, showy reddish purple flowers growing out of the leaf axils. The loosestrife, cattail, arrowhead, various heaths, and boggy soils make shore access next to impossible.

You can explore a few coves and islands on the western side, but during high water, dozens more coves and inlets become accessible.

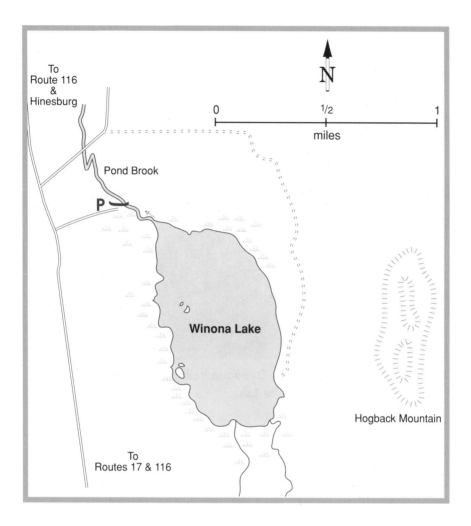

To
Route 116
&
Hinesburg

N

0   1/2   1

miles

Pond Brook

P

Winona Lake

Hogback Mountain

To
Routes 17 & 116

Feathery tamarack trees grow along the shore here and there, but most of the vegetation consists of shrubs. We found a large beaver lodge encrusted with jewelweed, swamp loosestrife, and swamp rose. Hemlock, white pine, white birch, and maple—both red and sugar— grow farther from the water and along the wooded eastern shore. Marshland and water birds include wood ducks and mergansers, but most keep to the more protected marshy pools north and south of the main lake. Also, osprey may nest here.

Strands of swamp loosestrife, *Decodon verticillatus*, cover a beaver lodge on the shores of Winona Lake.

GETTING THERE

To reach Winona Lake from the east or west, take Route 17 to Bristol. Just west of Bristol, turn north off Route 17 onto Burpee Road where Route 116 turns off to the south. Go 2.0 miles to Monkton Road. Go north on Monkton Road (left) for another 1.7 miles to the boat access on the right.

From the north, in Hinesburg, as Route 116 turns sharply left, continue straight onto Silver Street. In Monkton Ridge, go left at the Y onto Bristol-Monkton Road. The boat access on the left is about 10.7 miles from Route 116.

Wrightsville Reservoir
East Montpelier, Middlesex, and Montpelier, VT

MAPS

Vermont Atlas: Map 40

USGS Quadrangle: Montpelier

INFORMATION

Area: 89 acres

Prominent fish species: Largemouth bass, yellow perch, and brown trout

This reservoir seems larger than its 89 acres because you can paddle the inlet stream for quite a distance, back up to a scenic waterfall by an island covered with stones worn smooth by cascading water. The stones have a lot of embedded mica that causes them to shimmer in the sun. For us, paddling up to the waterfall gave us an opportunity not only to have lunch but also to see a river otter in the upper reaches. Though the reservoir may not look interesting from the boat launch, paddling up to the falls is well worth the effort. The clear water of the inlet stream, the North Branch of the Winooski River, provides habitat for numerous animals and plants. The area to the north of the access point, including all of the inflow stream, has a motorboat speed limit of 2 MPH (at our best, we can exceed this speed limit by a factor of three!).

When we paddled here at the end of May, large patches of bunchberry (*Cornus canadensis*), in the dogwood family, bloomed under a canopy of white pine, white and yellow birch, and other species that line the shores. Red-winged blackbirds sang to mark their territories in the marshy areas, while ovenbirds, black-throated green warblers, and song sparrows called from the wooded areas. We also saw five large

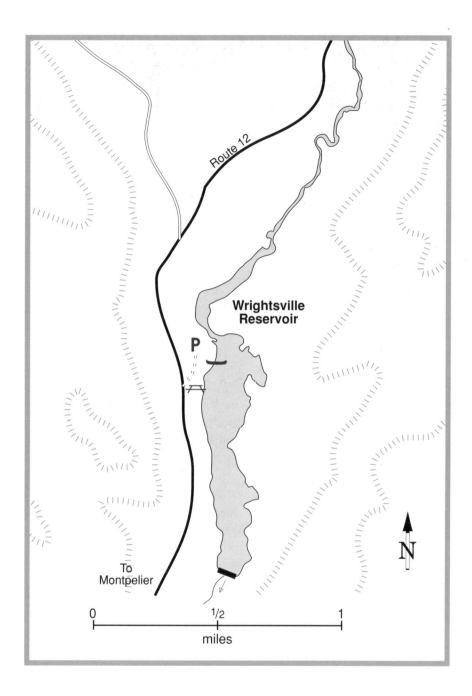

Route 12

**Wrightsville
Reservoir**

P

To
Montpelier

N

0   1/2   1
miles

A scenic waterfall on the North Branch of the Winooski River, the inlet stream of Wrightsville Reservoir.

beaver lodges and lots of cuttings stored in the water. The best time to see the resident beaver is early morning or just before closing at dusk.

Getting there
From Montpelier, take Route 12 north for several miles to the well-marked boat launch access area on the right.

Kettle Pond and Osmore Pond
Groton, Marshfield, and Peacham, VT

MAPS

Vermont Atlas: Map 41

USGS Quadrangle: Marshfield

INFORMATION

Kettle Pond area: 104 acres

Osmore Pond area: 48 acres

Prominent fish species: Kettle Pond—yellow perch and rainbow trout; Osmore Pond—brook trout

Camping: New Discovery Campground—802-426-3042; Stillwater Campground—802-584-3822; Ricker Pond Campground—802-584-3821. Register at New Discovery Campground for use of primitive camping sites on Kettle and Osmore Ponds. Register for Big Deer Campground (tents only) through Stillwater Campground. It is highly recommended that you call for reservations, especially for weekend visits.

Kettle and Osmore Ponds nestle among the hillsides of Groton State Forest. While water is the main attraction here, hiking trails travel among the peaks and skirt the edges of Peacham Bog, one of only two or three raised bogs in Vermont. If you visit the bog, expect to see rhodora, leatherleaf, Labrador tea, sphagnum, black spruce, tamarack, and many more typical bog plants.

   Kettle Pond. From an ecological standpoint, Kettle Pond is the most interesting of the bodies of water in Groton State Forest. Loons

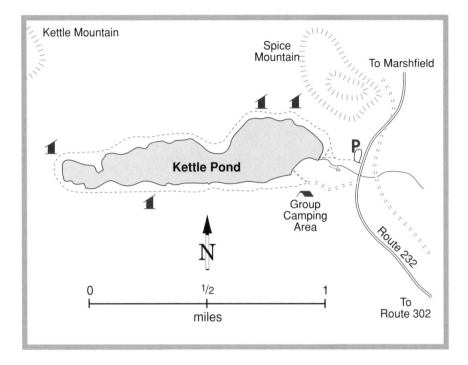

Kettle Mountain

Spice Mountain

To Marshfield

Kettle Pond

P

Group Camping Area

Route 232

N

0   1/2   1

miles

To Route 302

often nest here, and the shoreline—especially the western end—harbors a rich assortment of bog plants, including pitcher plant, sweet gale, various members of the heath family, sphagnum, and sundew. Though a group camping area exists on the east end, set back from the water, the pond has a very remote feel to it. We saw beaver and signs of otter. A hiking trail extends around the pond.

Along with the group camping area, available to organizations by reservation only, there are five primitive camping lean-tos and one tent site around the pond. We camped here in the mid-1980s and were disappointed on more-recent visits to see the area quite littered with trash (the litter bag we always carry filled right up on one visit).

Osmore Pond. Nestled beneath several small mountains, Osmore Pond is a beauty. Spruce, fir, yellow birch, and sugar maple cover the heavily wooded hills and rocky shoreline. Small, marshy areas occur at both ends. A shoreline trail extends all the way around the pond, though going might be slow during berry season—we found the pond to be a veritable treasure trove of raspberries, blueberries, shadbush,

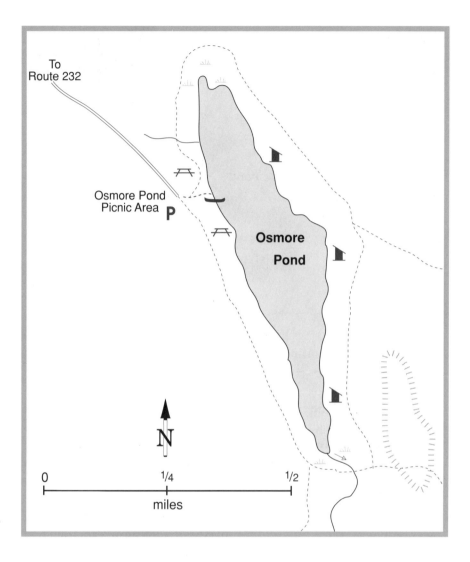

To
Route 232

Osmore Pond
Picnic Area **P**

Osmore

Pond

N

0	1/4	1/2

miles

currants, and gooseberries. When we camped here in late July, a solitary loon serenaded us late into the evening.

Small and shallow, it offers the possibility of primitive camping, with four lean-tos on the eastern side of the pond across from the access location. The lean-tos sit quite far apart, and each has a well-designed fireplace and a nearby outhouse. On the western side of the lake, groups sometimes use a large picnic shelter well into the night, but by avoiding popular summer weekends, you should find peace and quiet.

Hobblebush, *Viburnum alnifolium,* **grows in moist woods all over the Northeast.**

Register for primitive camping on Osmore Pond at the New Discovery Campground, which you must pass through to get to the pond.

Though few people realize it, the state permits primitive camping on many state lands, including most of Groton State Forest. Small groups do not require a permit. Except at designated sites, you must camp at least a quarter-mile from everything (roads, streams, lakes). If you prefer a family campground, there are several in Groton State Forest, including Stillwater, Big Deer, Ricker, and New Discovery. New Discovery is closest to Osmore and Kettle Ponds, though it is not on the water. Both Stillwater and Ricker Campgrounds are on the water; Ricker is much quieter.

GETTING THERE

Kettle Pond. The parking area is on Route 232, 1.7 miles north of the entrance to Stillwater Campground and Boulder Beach Day-Use Area on Lake Groton, just past the entrance to the group camping area. Leave your car in the parking area and carry in about 0.3 mile to the water. The trail makes a few sharp turns that can be tricky with a big canoe.

Osmore Pond. Drive through New Discovery Campground, just off Route 232, approximately 4.0 miles north of the entrance to Stillwater Campground and Boulder Beach Day-Use Area. Follow signs to the Osmore Pond Picnic Area (not Owl's Head) and park at the end of the unpaved road (about a mile from Route 232). You will see a trail down to the water from here; the carry is about 50 yards.

Peacham Pond
Peacham, VT

MAPS

  Vermont Atlas: Map 41

  USGS Quadrangle: Marshfield

INFORMATION

  Area: 331 acres

  Prominent fish species: yellow perch and brown trout

  Camping: New Discovery Campground—802-426-3042; Stillwater Campground—802-584-3822; Ricker Pond Campground—802-584-3821. Register at New Discovery Campground for use of primitive camping sites on Kettle and Osmore Ponds. Register for Big Deer Campground (tents only) through Stillwater Campground. It is highly recommended that you call for reservations, especially for weekend visits.

Situated on the northern edge of Groton State Forest and nestled beneath the rolling mountains of north-central Vermont, Peacham Pond enjoys a gorgeous setting like those seen on postcards. In the autumn, nothing beats drifting lazily, just absorbing the beauty: deep reds and yellows of the shoreline vegetation contrasting with the rich blue of the pond and sky. Even the moderate development at the western and eastern ends seems somehow all right, though on a warm summer afternoon, the motorboat, personal watercraft, and water-skiing traffic can be a bit much. We recommend paddling elsewhere on busy summer weekends.

By paddling around to the northern end, you can get away from most of the motorboats and nearly all the houses. This much shallower

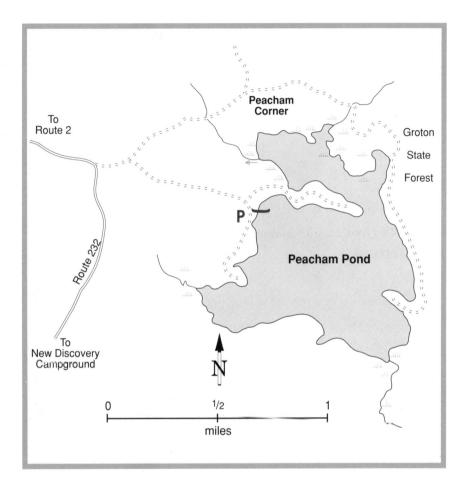

To
Route 2

Peacham
Corner

Groton

State

Forest

Route 232

P

Peacham Pond

To
New Discovery
Campground

N

0   1/2   1

miles

section has deep marshy coves, islands, and superb wildlife habitats to explore, especially the large horsetail (*Equisetum*) marsh in the north-eastern cove. Two pairs of loons regularly nest, one here and one in the south cove, and each pair successfully raised one chick in 1999. Because Peacham is one of the few Vermont bodies of water with successful loon breeding, we fail to understand why the state Water Resources Board allows personal watercraft and high-speed boating on this pond.

A marshy inlet on Peacham Pond on a quiet morning.

GETTING THERE

From the south, turn right (east) off Route 232 about 1.0 mile north of the entrance to New Discovery Campground. Take a right at the fork with a stone monument inscribed Peacham Pond.

Coming from Route 2 (Montpelier and I-89), turn onto Route 232 south just past Marshfield, go 3.0 miles, then turn left onto the Peacham Pond access road as Route 232 curves to the right.

Mollys Falls Pond
Cabot, VT

MAPS
Vermont Atlas: Maps 41 and 47

USGS Quadrangle: Marshfield

INFORMATION
Area: 411 acres

Prominent fish species: Smallmouth bass, yellow perch, pickerel, northern pike, brook trout, brown trout, and rainbow trout

Camping: New Discovery Campground—802-426-3042; Stillwater Campground—802-584-3822; Ricker Pond Campground—802-584-3821. Register at New Discovery Campground for use of primitive camping sites on Kettle and Osmore Ponds. Register for Big Deer Campground (tents only) through Stillwater Campground. It is highly recommended that you call for reservations, especially for weekend visits.

Nestled among forested hillsides, this largest body of water in the area, also known as Marshfield Lake, actually lies in the town of Cabot, not in Marshfield. Protected from development by Green Mountain Power, only one house appears along its shoreline. Though we paddled here on Memorial Day, there were only a few motorboats on the water and about the same number of canoes and kayaks. Near the access, you can hear cars and trucks on Route 2, but that soon fades as you paddle south down the lake.

Quiet coves provide protected nooks to explore, and gorgeous Mollys Creek cascades down over a boulder-strewn streambed into the

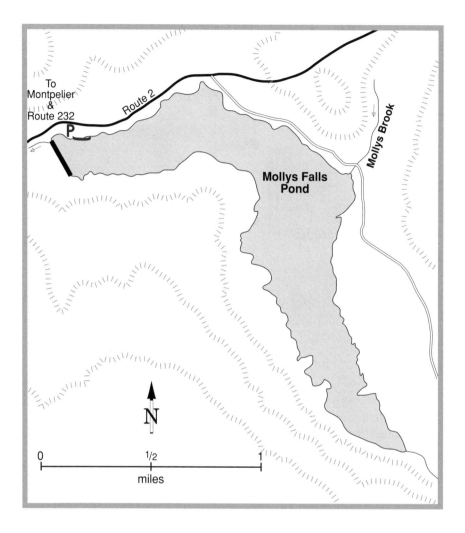

To
Montpelier
&
Route 232

Route 2

P

Mollys Brook

**Mollys Falls
Pond**

N

0   1/2   1
miles

lake. In the spring, the creek's roar, audible from afar, helps drown out road noise.

A pair of loons nested behind a closed-off section, and a solitary loon called out from another section of the lake when we paddled here. Signs warn boaters away from the loon nesting area, but we believe that speed limits should also be established.

We have never seen as much beaver activity as we saw here, with white birch appearing to be the preferred food. Given that beaver prefer deciduous trees—probably because of the resins in conifers—

Loon nesting area signs warn boaters away on Mollys Falls Pond.

one wonders why they eat so much resinous paper birch. Several massive beaver lodges poked up here and there. Seeing all of this activity, it is hard to believe that beaver were once nearly extirpated in the Northeast.

A large, conifer-clad island harbors a picnic area that has a nice view of the lake's southern end. No camping or overnight parking is allowed.

GETTING THERE

From Montpelier, take Route 2 east. The access is on the right, 1.4 miles past the junction of Routes 2 and 232.

Lower and Upper Symes Ponds

Ryegate, VT

MAPS

Vermont Atlas: Map 42

USGS Quadrangles: Barnet and Woodsville

INFORMATION

Lower Symes Pond area: 57 acres

Upper Symes Pond area: 20 acres

Prominent fish species: Pickerel

Camping: New Discovery Campground—802-426-3042; Stillwater Campground—802-584-3822; Ricker Pond Campground—802-584-3821. Register at New Discovery Campground for use of primitive camping sites on Kettle and Osmore Ponds. Register for Big Deer Campground (tents only) through Stillwater Campground. It is highly recommended that you call for reservations, especially for weekend visits.

We visited these scenic, little-used ponds twice, on weekends in June and July, and saw only one other boat. We also saw deer down for mid-day drinks, and a loon called from the far side. Bird life was incredible, including thrushes calling from the woods, lots of cedar waxwings feeding in small flocks, two kingfishers diving for fish to feed a growing brood, a great blue heron stalking the shallows, common yellowthroats calling from the dense shrubs lining the shore, a red-tailed hawk wheeling overhead, and a red-breasted merganser shooing her brood away from the intruders.

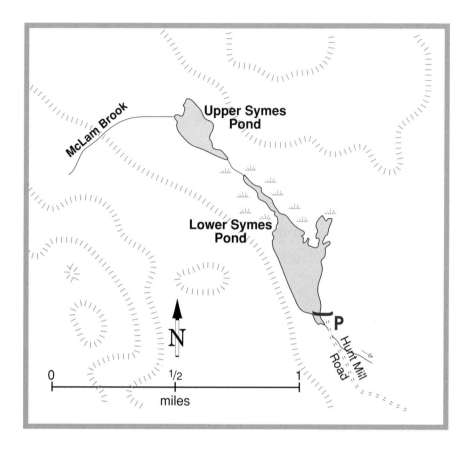

Swamp rose bloomed seemingly everywhere, including on floating islands covered with some feathery tamarack. The hillside's northern coniferous forest stood in contrast to the brushy shoreline and diverse aquatic vegetation. Spire-like balsam fir stood like sentinels as we paddled through the entrance to Upper Symes Pond, which is quite a bit smaller than the lower pond. In some places, smooth granite boulders line the shore.

This wonderful, remote setting makes getting there worth the struggle. It appears that people camp near the access. Camping is also available in nearby Groton State Forest.

Tall balsam fir spires stand as sentinels at the entrance to Upper Symes Pond.

GETTING THERE

From I-91, Exit 17, go west on Route 302 for 0.9 mile and turn right at the Curious Cow Curio Shop onto Boltonville Road. Take the left fork. After 3.1 miles, in Ryegate Center, turn right onto East Road. After 0.5 mile, veer left onto Symes Pond Road as East Road veers right; this turn is amidst the red barns of a farm, next to a huge silver maple. Take the left fork. After 1.5 miles, turn left onto Hunt Mill Road (this turn is easy to miss); the put-in is in 0.8 mile. The road has stones sticking up, especially on the uphill portion, and the last 0.1 mile, where the access road forks right, is miserable. You might want to put in by the beaver dam near this last fork rather than driving over the ruts to the access point.

Moose:
The North Woods Giant

Coming across a huge bull moose as you round the bend of a marshy stream is truly awesome—and the high point of many trips into the North Woods. The moose, *Alces alces*, is the world's largest member of the deer family. Adult males can stand seven feet tall at the shoulders and weigh up to 1,400 pounds. Bull moose range in weight from 900 to 1,400 pounds, with cow moose typically three-quarters as large. To put this in perspective, a typical bull moose weighs three times as much as the second largest land mammal in New England, the black bear. Among North American land mammals, only bison and Alaskan brown bear (a subspecies of grizzly bear) commonly exceed the moose in weight; none approaches it in height.

Well adapted to the marsh environment, its long legs allow it to reach tree branches and wade into bogs and snow. During the summer, one often can see moose in ponds, streams, and lakes, where they forage on aquatic plants. Moose sometimes stand neck-deep in water to escape hordes of biting flies, and we have even seen moose completely submerged. By late August or early September, moose generally move into the deep woods, where you are less likely to see them. The typical moose ranges over a small territory, usually just a few square miles.

Adult moose vary in color from dark brown to almost black, while calves run much lighter in color. Thick, dense fur—sometimes six inches long around the neck and shoulders—helps protect them from biting flies. Moose have a keen sense of hearing and smell but poor vision. When frightened, they can run at speeds up to 35 MPH for short distances. Their incredibly long legs help them run through bogs and muskegs. They swim slowly but have been known to swim as far as 12 miles.

Moose derive most of their nourishment by browsing on trees and aquatic vegetation but also graze on grasses, mosses, lichens, and low herbaceous plants. Because of their long legs and short necks, they often need to bend or spread their front legs or even drop to their knees to feed. They may rear up on their hind legs to feed on tree branches, and they sometimes "ride down" saplings by straddling them and walking forward to bring upper branches into reach.

The rutting season extends generally from the beginning of September through October, but may range into November and even early December. After an eight-month gestation period, cows bear one or two calves in May or June. Younger cows generally produce just one offspring. As one might expect, a correlation exists between the incidence of twins and the availability of forage.

We see most moose during the early morning and early evening hours, though one can see them at any time of day. One evening in mid-October, we saw eight moose as we drove over the Kancamagus Highway in northern New Hampshire.

The moose population in the Northeast has fluctuated considerably during the last two centuries. During colonial days, they provided an important food source for early settlers. Because they were so easily killed, populations plummeted, and by the mid-1800s, less than 15 moose populated New Hampshire, with even less in Vermont. With protection from hunting and changes in land use that have caused a proliferation of low-growing browse, moose populations have rebounded dramatically, to the point where about 200 moose die each year in collisions with cars in the two states. The moose population in New Hampshire and Vermont has reached well over 10,000.

Brainworm infestations, fatal to moose, keep populations from building in southern areas because of the presence of large numbers of deer. Though unaffected by these parasites, deer carry them and deposit them in their feces, which passes them to land snails. If moose browse on plants hosting snails—a likely occurrence at lower elevations in southern New Hampshire and Vermont—they contract the disease and die.

While countless wonderful paddling destinations exist in remote sections of New England, we prefer to paddle in the northern tier of counties with plentiful moose. We never tire of that awe-inspiring, exhilarating feeling we get paddling into a marshy cove and coming suddenly upon an enormous bull moose or a cow with a calf. We have seen dozens of these majestic mammals, and we hope you see as many on your travels. But remember, when you come across a moose or other wild creature, make sure not to disturb it with loud noises or attempt to get too close.

Shelburne Pond
Shelburne, VT

MAPS

Vermont Atlas: Map 45

USGS Quadrangle: Burlington

INFORMATION

Area: 450 acres

Prominent fish species: Largemouth bass, smallmouth bass, northern pike, yellow perch, and walleye

Ecology of the area: University of Vermont Environmental Program—802-656-4055; The Nature Conservancy—802-229-4425

Shelburne Pond, surrounded by limestone ledges and cliffs, provides a home to some very rare fern: maidenhair spleenwort, mountain spleenwort, walking fern, and purple-stemmed cliffbrake. You can see these from a boat, along the perimeter of the pond, or by exploring the surrounding area. Please do not harm any of the rare fern.

As you paddle along the shoreline of Shelburne Pond, keep an eye out for northern water snakes (*Nerodia sipedon*). Apparently thousands of these attractively patterned, nonpoisonous snakes used to appear here, but the population has declined in recent years. You may see them swimming in the water, basking on rock ledges, or way back in the limestone crevices with just their heads sticking out. We spotted at least a half-dozen in a few hours.

In addition to limestone cliffs along the shoreline, explore the extensive marshy areas, particularly at the northern end and at the

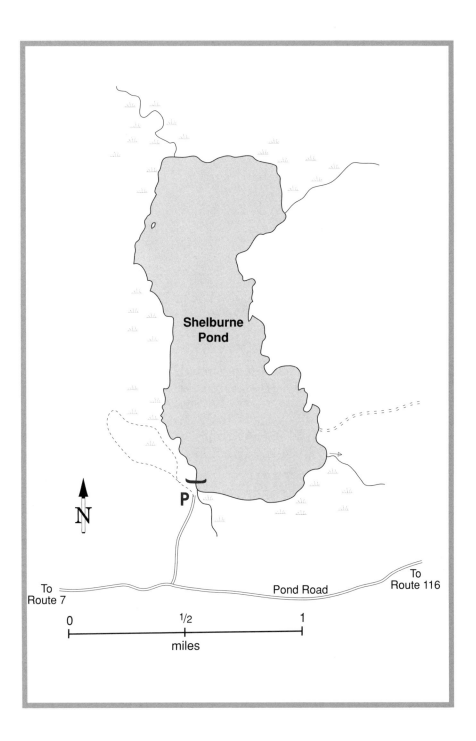

Shelburne Pond

N

To
Route 7

Pond Road

To
Route 116

P

0   1/2   1

miles

Vanessa Gray holds up a tiny painted turtle, *Chrysemys picta*, which she plucked from the pond's waters.

several inlets to the pond. Cattail, swamp loosestrife, and various rush, sedge, and grasses proliferate here. You should see great blue herons, green herons, various ducks, and painted turtles. At the northern inlet, paddle back in and explore the marsh more closely. You will see signs of beaver along the shore and piles of mussel shells scattered here and there, probably left by raccoons. Near the northern end of the pond, a small, rocky island provides a place to enjoy a picnic lunch.

Along the limestone shoreline, northern white cedar—with its lower branches sweeping out over the cliffs, dipping down to the water—predominates. On a trail extending around part of the pond from the access, you will see many other tree species: white pine, basswood, red oak, hemlock, red and sugar maple, white birch, elm, white ash, beech, hop hornbeam, a few white oak, and smooth-bark hickory.

In addition to the pond's fascinating natural history, the area harbors evidence of early human history. Dr. Hub Vogelmann, long-time chair of the University of Vermont botany department and co-founder of the Vermont chapter of The Nature Conservancy, came upon what he thought was a floating log on one of his many paddling trips to Shelburne Pond. Because he thought it looked a bit odd, he stuck his hand underneath and found it hollow—a dugout canoe. He believes that accumulating marsh gas floated it to the surface from its resting place in the mud. Radiocarbon dating showed that it had lain on the pond bottom for 4,000 years! Loads of other archaeological evidence from the pond's environs show human occupancy for at least 5,000 years. So where is the canoe? Dr. Vogelmann weighted it down and sent it to the bottom for safekeeping until the large amount of money needed to preserve it can be raised.

Shelburne Pond suffers from eutrophication caused by fertilizer runoff and augmented by limestone. The resultant algae blooms and lush aquatic vegetation eventually die, depleting oxygen as they decompose, causing anaerobic conditions. This promotes anaerobic bacterial growth and production of methane and hydrogen sulfide gas. Nonpoint source pollution—primarily fertilizer runoff—has received much attention in Vermont, and steps have been taken to reduce runoff into Shelburne Pond. Over time, eutrophication should decrease here.

Unfortunately, the pond also suffers from the use of motors. The state Water Resources Board, in its wisdom—or should we say in its inability to stand up to the consumptive-users' lobby—allows motors and personal watercraft on the pond, with no speed limit. On this eco-logically sensitive area, personal watercraft and water-skiing should be banned and a speed limit should be implemented. With Lake Champlain just next door, Shelburne Pond should be reserved for nondestructive uses.

The unique ecosystem represented by Shelburne Pond and its immediate environs remains undeveloped, protected in part by The Nature Conservancy and the University of Vermont, which own more than 1,000 acres here. When they own or have conservation easements on the entire shoreline, we sincerely hope that they will convince the state Water Resources Board to ban personal watercraft and establish limit speeds—if not ban motors altogether.

GETTING THERE

From Burlington, take Route 116 south, go 5.4 miles beyond the bridge over I-89, turn right onto Pond Road, and go another 1.5 miles to the access on the right. From the south, take Route 116 north and turn left onto Pond Road 0.7 mile past the turnoff for Route 2A.

Indian Brook Reservoir
Essex, VT

MAPS

Vermont Atlas: Map 45

USGS Quadrangle: Essex Center

INFORMATION

Area: 47 acres

Prominent fish species: Smallmouth bass, brown trout, and rainbow trout

Camping: Essex Town Office—802-879-0413

Though very small, Indian Brook Reservoir offers a nice mix of quiet-water paddling, fishing, hiking, picnicking, nature observation, and camping (with a permit from the town of Essex). Be forewarned that on warm sunny days this small pond can get overrun with people. The undeveloped reservoir's shoreline consists mostly of rock—a fine-grain metamorphic schist—with hemlock and white pine boughs overhanging the water. Many areas afford an opportunity to climb out onto rock outcroppings to picnic or bask in the sun. At the northern end, in a number of marshy inlets, look for herons, kingfishers, and beaver in the early morning and evening.

A superb trail—upgraded by the Youth Conservation Corps—circumscribes the reservoir, and several side trails provide opportunities for further explorations. One of these little trails splits off at the northern end (where it passes over a small inlet brook) and leads to a smaller and much more remote pond, where you will see nesting ducks and other wildlife—species that choose to keep their distance from people. Though it is just a short walk to the pond, to minimize

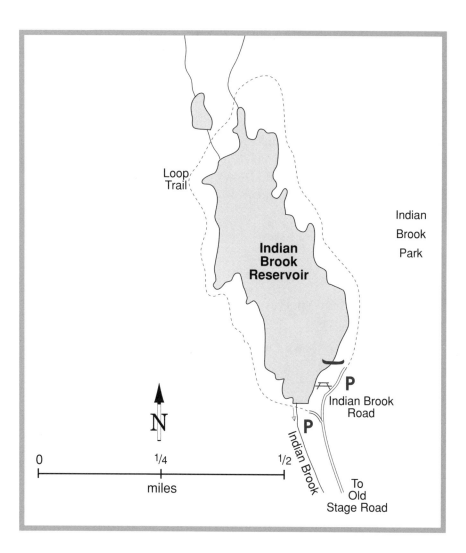

encroachment on wildlife we recommend against bringing your boat along.

The mixed hardwood and softwood forest—sugar and red maple, white and yellow birch, cherry, basswood, hemlock, and white pine—invites exploration because it is so open. Anglers enjoy fishing for plentiful rainbow trout and bass. The town of Essex owns the reservoir and surrounding Indian Brook Park, keeping them open to most uses, though it strictly forbids the use of alcohol and gasoline motors.

GETTING THERE

From Essex Junction, at the intersection of Routes 2A and 15, go east on Route 15 for 2.0 miles and turn left (north) onto Old Stage Road. Take the second left (after 0.4 mile) onto Indian Brook Road and continue 1.5 miles to the end. To get to the best put-in point, bear to the right once you get into Indian Brook Park.

Colchester Pond
Colchester, VT

MAPS

Vermont Atlas: Map 45

USGS Quadrangle: Essex Center

INFORMATION

Area: 700 acres

Prominent fish species: Smallmouth bass, yellow perch, and northern pike

Contact information: Winooski Valley Park District—
802-863-5744

At first glance, with a large power line looming off in the distance, Colchester Pond does not look all that inviting. Allowing that impression to keep one from paddling here would be a mistake. Run by the Winooski Valley Park District, with no motors allowed, this biologically productive, oblong body of water harbors an amazing assortment of plants and wildlife. Because you have to carry your boat a distance to the water, the park district has thoughtfully provided a couple of wheeled canoe carriers.

Paddling down to the cattail marsh at the south end, we watched tree and barn swallows skim the surface for a drink and listened to a bittern *oompah*ing from its concealed location in the swamp. Because of the pond's proximity to Lake Champlain, we were not surprised to see ring-billed gulls and a half dozen double-crested cormorants. Alas, there were no ospreys nesting on the provided platform. If they do nest here, there will be no dearth of fish for them to feed their young; we have rarely seen so many small fish near shore.

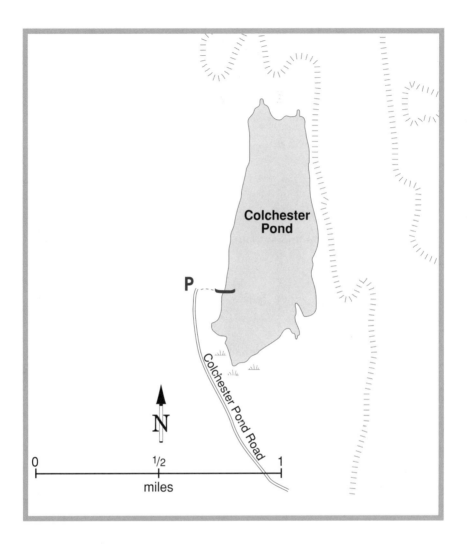

Indeed, the sheer productivity of Colchester Pond impressed us mightily. Even in May, an algae bloom and tons of aquatic vegetation covered the water's surface. We managed to pluck a snapping turtle out of the vegetation to check its underside for leeches; three had latched on. We wondered how the leeches might affect the resident beaver and muskrat population—we saw two muskrats harvesting grass and a small beaver on the bank stripping bark from a sapling. The beaver did not concern itself with our presence, but the fat raccoon we saw did amble out of sight as we approached.

Honeysuckle, in the genus *Lonicera*, grows along the shores of many ponds and lakes.

A Canada goose pair prepared to nest, and we also spotted many mallards. Columbine clung to the small cliffs along the northern shores, and droves of tiger swallowtail butterflies sipped nectar from the abundant honeysuckle that bloomed along the shore. As we listened to a hermit thrush singing off in the woods, we knew that we would come back to this wonderful spot again.

GETTING THERE

From Burlington, take Routes 7 and 2 north for about 3.2 miles beyond I-89, Exit 16, and turn right onto Route 2A. Go 1.0 mile to the stoplight, turn left onto East Road (Mill Pond Road goes right at this stoplight), and 0.2 mile farther turn right onto Depot Road. After another 1.3 miles, turn left onto Colchester Pond Road and proceed to the parking area.

Arrowhead Mountain Lake
Georgia and Milton, VT

MAPS

Vermont Atlas: Maps 45 and 51

USGS Quadrangle: Milton

INFORMATION

Area: 732 acres

Prominent fish species: Largemouth bass, smallmouth bass, yellow perch, walleye, and northern pike

We have decided to continue to include Arrowhead Mountain Lake in this quietwater guide, despite the state of Vermont's failure to protect it adequately from high-impact uses and development. Though the lake always had a few motorboats and some limited development, it had retained a certain wilderness feel, especially in the marshy northeast and in the gorgelike central section. The insidious invasion of personal watercraft, upon which the Vermont Water Resources Board places few restrictions on most larger lakes, is insult enough. But the state invited the Husky Corporation of Canada to build an intrusive injection-molding plant upon its shores and then a bridge across the lake! This seemingly constant degradation of the state's waters will not stop until the public demands better treatment for these precious resources.

A dammed-up section of the Lamoille River—which itself offers fine paddling, though with rapids (see the *AMC River Guide: New Hampshire and Vermont*)—Arrowhead Mountain Lake has much to offer. The wide, marshy northern part of the lake contains many islands and superb wildlife habitat. Ospreys have nested here since 1998, and you should see lots of water birds, including wood ducks, mergansers,

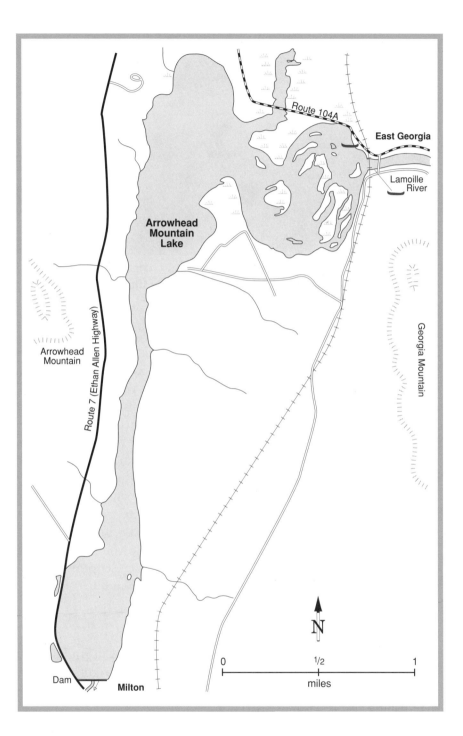

Route 104A

East Georgia

Lamoille
River

Arrowhead
Mountain
Lake

Route 7 (Ethan Allen Highway)

Arrowhead
Mountain

Georgia Mountain

N

0   1/2   1
miles

Dam

Milton

This American bittern, *Botaurus lentiginosus*, tries to look inconspicuous in the marshland grass. Normally they remain well hidden from view.

bitterns, great blue herons, green herons, and kingfishers. Anglers catch smallmouth bass and northern pike among the marshy islands and pond vegetation. Though the water remains fairly open in the spring, by midsummer you will have to restrict your paddling to the open channels that weave through the thick marshes.

As you progress south, the lake narrows and feels much more like the wide river it really is. A few houses perch along the western shore, mostly far above the water near Route 7. The formerly undeveloped eastern shore, stretching for about three miles, sports a variety of tree species: hemlock, basswood, red oak, silver maple, sugar maple, white ash, American elm, box elder, cottonwood, white pine, ironwood, beech, hickory, and alder. The banks also grow thick with fern. We saw some freshwater mussels and signs of beaver, and it would not surprise us to see mink or even otter here, who would be just as curious to know why a Husky plant has invaded this once pristine shoreline.

Getting There
From I-89, Exit 18, take Route 7 south to Route 104A. Turn left onto Route 104A and go 1.6 miles to the access on the right. There is another carry-in boat access across the Lamoille River bridge, but the state fishing access has more parking.

Waterbury Reservoir
Waterbury, VT

MAPS

Vermont Atlas: Map 46

USGS Quadrangles: Bolton Mountain and Stowe

INFORMATION

Area: 823 acres

Prominent fish species: Smallmouth bass, yellow perch, brown trout, and rainbow trout

Camping: Little River Camping Area—802-244-7103

No development crowds the shores of Waterbury Reservoir, a body of water large enough for a lot of paddling, yet narrow enough that you always feel fairly protected. The tall surrounding mountains of Mount Mansfield State Forest provide a picturesque setting. During the summer months, water-skiers and personal watercraft populate the lake, substantially detracting from its peacefulness. On the positive side, though, the lake offers both car- and primitive-camping opportunities. Also, the northern arm, starting about a mile south of Cotton Brook, has a 5 MPH speed limit, as do the far portions of the eastern arm.

The Little River Camping Area, located at the junction of the lake's two arms, sports many campsites and lean-tos, most set in deep woods, providing a fair amount of privacy—as much as one can expect in a campground. Most of the campsites perch well above the water on a wooded bluff. Unless you choose a site near the water, to launch a boat, you will need to drive or carry to one of two launching areas in the campground.

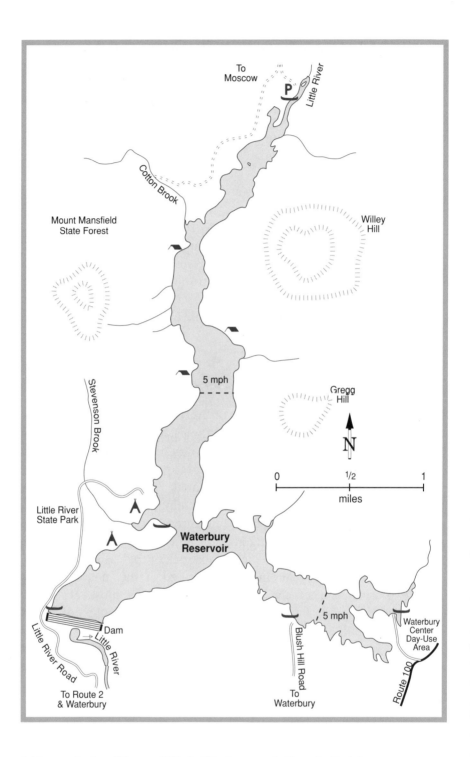

To
Moscow

Little River

P

Cotton Brook

Mount Mansfield
State Forest

Willey
Hill

5 mph

Stevenson Brook

Gregg
Hill

N

0   1/2   1

miles

Little River
State Park

Waterbury
Reservoir

Little River Road

Dam

Little River

5 mph

Blush Hill Road

Waterbury
Center
Day-Use
Area

Route 100

To Route 2
& Waterbury

To
Waterbury

Because the campground fills in the summer, you should reserve a site in advance. Primitive sites around the reservoir, some in truly gorgeous settings, should be reserved as well. The park office also rents canoes. Because of safety concerns, in 2000 the reservoir level was dropped 40 feet to begin dam repairs, which may last into 2002, with another year or more to bring the water level back up.

The water itself, unfortunately, can get somewhat dirty, probably from erosion along the shoreline caused by wakes of big motorboats. By the looks of it, this erosion occurs at an alarming rate, causing stretches of shoreline to appear very unnatural.

Deciduous trees, primarily, populate the wooded shoreline, though they give way to stands of white pine and hemlock every so often. Songbirds filled the trees as we paddled along in the early-morning light. Broad sections of mica schist protruding into the water provide dramatic rest areas and picnic locations. You will also find some quiet, protected swimming beaches along the shoreline.

GETTING THERE

From Waterbury (I-89, Exit 10) take Route 2 northwest for a couple of miles, turn right onto Little River Road, and go 3.5 miles to Little River State Park.

You can also launch from the dam off Little River Road; from the end of Blush Hill Road leading north from Waterbury; from the eastern arm at the Waterbury Center Day-Use Area off Route 100; and from the northern tip, also off Route 100. To get to the northern tip, follow the paved road west from Moscow along the river; when the road curves sharply right, continue straight on an unpaved road, bear left at the fork, and park at the end.

Green River Reservoir
Eden and Hyde Park, VT

MAPS

Vermont Atlas: Map 47

USGS Quadrangles: Eden and Morrisville

INFORMATION

Area: 863 acres

Prominent fish species: Smallmouth bass, pickerel, and yellow perch

Green River Reservoir State Park: 802-241-3655; www.parks@fpr.anr.state.vt.us

Green River Reservoir, located in north-central Vermont, remains the premier paddling destination in Vermont and a real treasure for remote-camping enthusiasts. The reservoir, formerly owned by the Morrisville Department of Water and Light primarily for power generation, was purchased by The Nature Conservancy and transferred to the state for management as a state park. The Conservancy retained a conservation easement to ensure the reservoir will remain undeveloped and wild. As of 2000, the state did not charge a registration fee, require reservations, or maintain facilities of any kind—outhouses, springs, and so forth—but that will probably change in the next few years. You might want to contact the park's office for current regulations.

The property includes 5,110 acres of surrounding forest, managed for recreation and as habitat for moose and bear. It contains deer wintering areas, and the Catamount Trail passes through. The reservoir seems much larger than its 863 acres because of its many long inlet arms and 14 islands. The total paddlable perimeter of more than 19 miles makes it Vermont's largest undeveloped shoreline. Campers concentrate

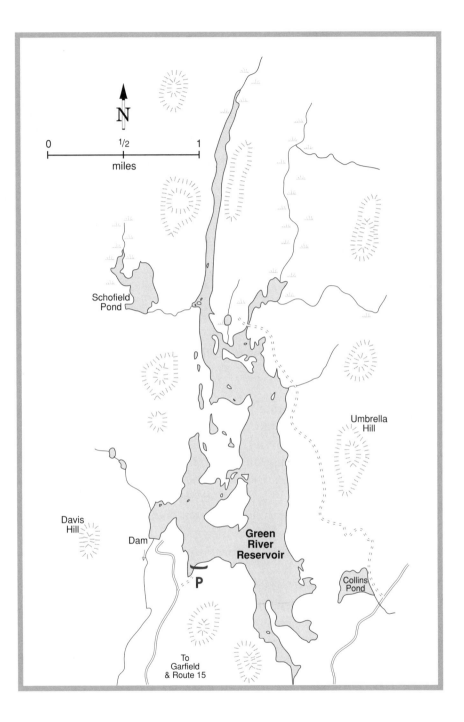

Schofield
Pond

Umbrella
Hill

Davis
Hill

Dam

P

Green
River
Reservoir

Collins
Pond

To
Garfield
& Route 15

N

0   1/2   1
miles

A beaver dam eventually blocks your passage at the far northern inlet on Green River Reservoir.

in the area on and around the large island near the center. By exploring the long fingers and inlets, you can sometimes get away from other people.

The long, northernmost arm of the lake offers especially nice paddling. We saw a family of six otter, along with several beaver and a number of wood ducks up near the northern tip, which becomes marshy and narrows to a slow-moving, winding stream. A beaver dam eventually blocks your way; we carried above the dam, but you really cannot paddle too much farther because of shallow water.

Red maple, yellow birch, white pine, hemlock, balsam fir, sugar maple, and white birch populate most of the lake's heavily wooded shoreline. Look for mountain ash, with its brilliant orange berries in the fall, and hop hornbeam, along with lots of understory viburnum and other shrubs. In the northern marshlands, tamarack and spruce mix in with the other species. In some areas, exposed metamorphic schist, usually covered with a carpet of polypody fern, forms large outcroppings.

Ospreys nest here, and a tributary creek hosts a great blue heron rookery. While Green River Reservoir is one of the few bodies of water in Vermont where loons have nested successfully since the 1970s, their future here may be in jeopardy because of the large increase in boat traffic—yes, even canoes and kayaks can disturb nesting loons. The state marks off nesting sites, and we all should stay well away from these areas.

Though the waterway does suffer somewhat from overuse—we counted 18 touring kayaks and only slightly fewer canoes on a warm, bright mid-September Saturday—at least the state prohibits personal watercraft and motors. Queuing up to unload your boat and finding a place to park along the rut-filled access road also provides a challenge. Reluctantly, we have to recommend that you stay away on busy summer weekends; better yet, visit in the spring or after Labor Day.

GETTING THERE

From Morrisville, at the junction of Route 100 and either Route 15 or 15A, go east on either Route 15 or 15A. Shortly after Routes 15 and 15A join, turn left onto Garfield Road and go 3.1 miles to a T in Garfield. Turn right and then take a fairly immediate left up a hill, following the Green River on your left. After another 1.3 miles, the maintained road bears left; go straight onto an unmaintained road that goes downhill to the access in 0.2 mile. The road was still in poor condition in 2000, so be careful.

From Hardwick, at the junction of Routes 14 and 15, take Route 15 west for about 11 miles, turn right onto Garfield Road, and continue as above.

Long Pond
Greensboro, VT

MAPS

Vermont Atlas: Map 47

USGS Quadrangles: Caspian Lake and Craftsbury

INFORMATION

Area: 97 acres

Prominent fish species: Yellow perch and pickerel

Contact information: Vermont Nature Conservancy—
802-229-4425

Northwest of St. Johnsbury, pretty much in the middle of nowhere in Vermont's Northeast Kingdom, lies undeveloped Long Pond. The Nature Conservancy protects the southern end of Long Pond as well as 1,500 feet of shoreline on the eastern side—some 454 acres total. The state prohibits gasoline-powered motors on this pristine, difficult-to-find, and hard-to-reach pond.

Northern white cedar lines almost all of the pond's perimeter and represents one of the finest cedar swamps in the state. When northern white cedar dominates the shore, it usually looks as if someone trimmed the lower branches to a perfectly horizontal plane—at least when you see the trees from a distance. Something does trim the lower branches: deer. During the winter, deer feed on the lower branches from the ice—as far up as they can reach—creating a browse line. Farther inland, the cedar gives way to balsam fir, hemlock, maple, and other deep-woods species.

Marshy areas with cattail, floating pondweed, and various grass and sedge species line the north inlet and the south outlet. Look for wood

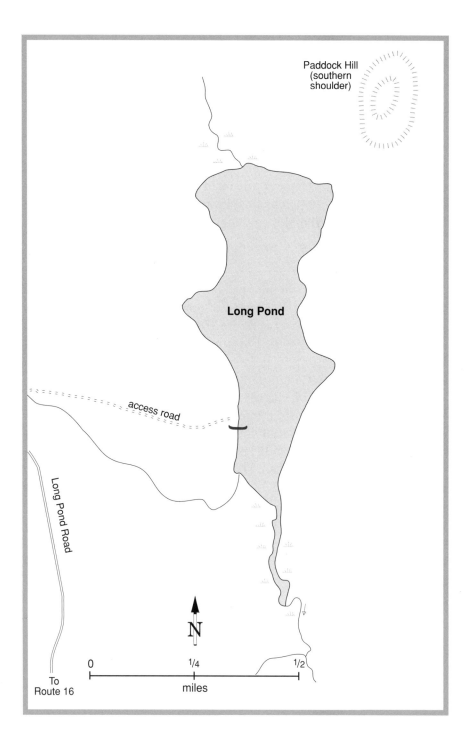

Paddock Hill
(southern
shoulder)

Long Pond

access road

Long Pond Road

N

0   1/4   1/2

miles

To
Route 16

ducks here and for the resident beaver in late afternoon. Also keep an eye out for otters. We watched one lazily fishing here on a midafternoon in September. Seeing an otter at midday gives testimony to the remoteness of this pond; usually to see otter, mink, and beaver you need to get out early in the morning or around dusk.

Loons nested on Long Pond until 1982 but remained absent for 15 years, until 1997. They now nest on the north side of the island; people camping on this privately owned island have disturbed loon breeding in the past. A game warden and some local residents routinely patrol the pond to keep people away from the nest site. Camping is not permitted anywhere around the pond.

Getting There

As of summer 2000, road-signing had not reached this area; road names come from DeLorme's atlas. From the junction of Routes 15 and 16 east of Hardwick, go north on Route 16 for about 8.6 miles; turn left onto Taylor Road (unsigned). From here, it is 3.6 miles to the Long Pond access road. Setting your trip odometer at Route 16, bear left at 0.3 mile, bear right at 1.4 miles onto Garvin Hill Road, bear left at 1.8 miles onto Hillcrest Road, and turn right at 2.5 miles. At 3.6 miles, look for a nondescript, hard-to-see track on the right that bears off steeply downhill. If you pass the access track, you will get to Skunk Hollow Road on the right, just 0.1 mile farther along.

Park along the gravel road. Do not even think about driving down the access road. Even if you have four-wheel drive and high ground clearance, you should still carry in to avoid damaging the road and the grassy area at the pond (especially in wet weather). The mile-or-so carry takes about 20 minutes if you hoof it. When you reach the pond, a nice grassy clearing beneath some large cedars makes an ideal picnic spot.

Flagg Pond
Wheelock, VT

MAPS

    Vermont Atlas: Map 48

    USGS Quadrangle: Stannard

INFORMATION

    Area: 108 acres

    Prominent fish species: Largemouth bass, pickerel, and yellow perch

Located in the heart of Vermont's Northeast Kingdom, small, out-of-the-way Flagg Pond rarely sees many visitors, even on a nice summer weekend. During a paddle here at the end of May, a remarkable number of American toads (*Bufo americanus*) inundated the shoreline, particularly at the northeast end. A veritable cacophony of high-pitched trilling greeted us, made by toads inflating their throat sacs—and this was a little past their typical breeding season! Paddling along the pond's perimeter we saw literally hundreds of toads, either clinging to the branches of shrubs along the hummocky shoreline or in the water.

As you paddle along here, notice the royal fern, sweet gale, thick hummocks of sphagnum moss, and an occasional pitcher plant, along with several members of the heath family—leatherleaf, bog rosemary, and beautiful bog laurel with bright pink blooms—that comprise the thickly vegetated shoreline. Tamarack and northern white cedar, species that do not mind getting their feet wet, also grow here. Several active beaver lodges cling to the pond's edge, and we saw a few great blue herons plying the waters for tasty fish (or toad?). Extensive stands of bulrush grow along the eastern shore.

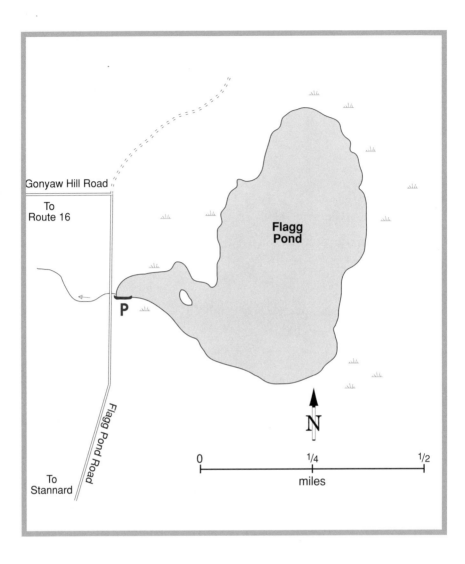

Getting there

From Hardwick, take Route 15 east. Turn left onto Route 16, go northeast for 6.5 miles, and turn right onto Gonyaw Hill Road (unmarked
when we visited). After 2.0 miles, turn right onto Flagg Pond Road.
The access is another 0.2 mile, just after the outlet brook. Park on the
left (east) side of the road.

One of the few trees that grows on boggy hummocks, tamarack, *Larix laricina*, ranges from Alaska to Newfoundland and south to northern New Jersey.

From I-91, Exit 23, take Route 5 south for a short distance, and turn right (west) onto Wheelock/Stannard Mountain Road. Continue beyond Stannard village for 0.7 mile and turn right onto Flagg Pond Road. Go 1.5 miles north to the pond.

Jewett Brook and Stevens Brook
St. Albans, VT

MAPS
> **Vermont Atlas:** Map 51
>
> **USGS Quadrangle:** St. Albans Bay

INFORMATION
> **Jewett Brook length:** 2.3 miles
>
> **Steven's Brook length:** 1.4 miles
>
> **Prominent fish species:** No game fish

Jewett Brook, flowing into Lake Champlain at St. Albans Bay, and the smaller Stevens Brook that flows into it provide a relaxing morning or afternoon of quiet paddling. The very murky water—due in part to the silty soils found in the Champlain Valley—also suffers from high nutrient loading from surrounding farmland. We suspect that it could become fairly eutrophic in late summer—with a thick layer of algae on the surface and high levels of decomposing organic matter in the water. Breakdown of organic matter robs the water of oxygen, making it uninhabitable for all but so-called coarse fish, such as carp.

Paddling north from the muddy access point, you will pass through a thick cattail marsh. The tall trees at the marsh's edge are mostly silver maple, which can survive water-saturated soils that would kill most trees. Keep an eye out for turtles here. We saw a number of common map turtles (*Graptemys geographica*)—a species that is anything but common in New England. In fact, the marshy, muck-bottomed shallows of Lake Champlain and its tributaries comprise the eastern extension of the range for this midwestern and southern species. The

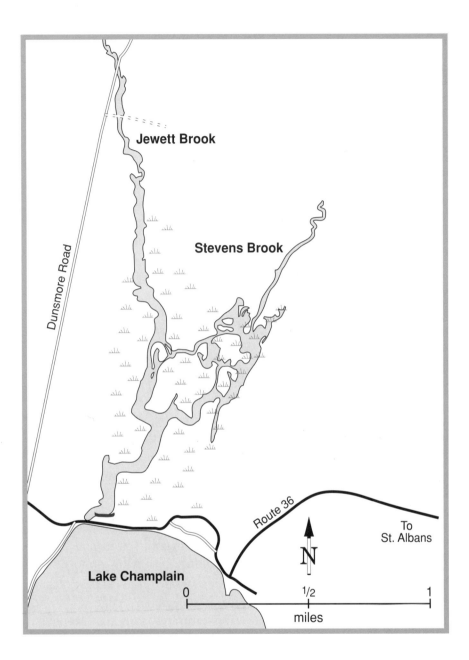

Jewett Brook

Stevens Brook

Dunsmore Road

Route 36

To
St. Albans

N

Lake Champlain

0   1/2   1

miles

females get quite large; we saw some in which the top shell (carapace) must have been nearly 10 inches in length—which is quite a bit bigger than our more-common painted turtle. To see these turtles out sunning you must be quiet, though. Map turtles are slightly flatter than painted turtles and significantly flatter than snapping turtles—the only other species here that could be as large. The rear end of the carapace flares out slightly.

We saw wood ducks in the marsh, lots of great blue herons, several black-crowned night herons, mallards, and a blue-wing teal during our midday paddle in late May. Swamp sparrows called with a metallic chip, and marsh wrens flitted about, building nests in the cattails. You undoubtedly will be startled, as we were, as you paddle over some of the huge carp that help make the water murky as they root around in the shallows.

If you stay to the left (western shore), you can follow the main channel about two miles upstream, with the marsh gradually narrowing to a creek. Downed trees might block your way here; after maneuvering around a few, a tree finally blocked our way at an old railroad-tie-and-concrete-slab bridge on a farm road.

Along the eastern shore, you can explore some marshy inlets, but the thick cattail growth restricts paddling considerably. About three-quarters of a mile from the access, the smaller (but generally clear) Stevens Brook angles off to the right (northeast); you can paddle up it at least a mile. You may pass grazing cows along the brook as you leave the marsh and get into farmland. We turned around where a pipe was spewing some foul liquid into the creek—something that we hope will have ended by the time you read this. (If it is still there, you too might want to contact Vermont environmental officials.)

Despite the nutrient loading, the mystery pipe inflow, and some smells from nearby farms wafting into the marsh, Jewett and Stevens Brooks offer pleasant paddling and wildlife-observing opportunities less than an hour from Burlington.

Getting there

From downtown St. Albans, at the junction of Routes 36 and 7, take Route 36 west for 3.7 miles. There is a pullout on the right, just before the bridge over Jewett Brook, with room for a half-dozen vehicles. This is a hand-carry access.

Fairfield Swamp
Fairfield, St. Albans, and Swanton, VT

MAPS

Vermont Atlas: Map 51

USGS Quadrangles: Fairfield and St. Albans

INFORMATION

Area: 1,293 acres

Prominent fish species: Pickerel

With their rich and varied plant life, waterfowl, frogs, and aquatic insects, one could spend days exploring each of the hundreds of underappreciated swamps and marshes of Vermont. Located just a few miles east of St. Albans and I-89, Fairfield Swamp is a great place to experience the changing of the seasons at one of these marshes.

From the boat access on Route 36, you can paddle either north or south, though the latter necessitates snaking your way through the culvert under Route 36 (this may not be possible at times of high water). If you head north (downstream) with the imperceptible current, you can paddle nearly three miles through gradually changing vegetation until you reach a small concrete dam that maintains this swamp on Dead Creek.

Cattail and the silvered spikes of long-dead trees, killed when the dam was built, dominate the swamp near the boat access. Tamarack, a conifer that loses its needles in the winter and can survive in water-saturated soils, is gradually coming in here. On higher ground, you will see hemlock, white pine, and assorted hardwood trees. Thick masses of yellow pond lily and—farther north—water shield, pondweed, and pickerelweed impede paddling. After narrowing somewhat as you

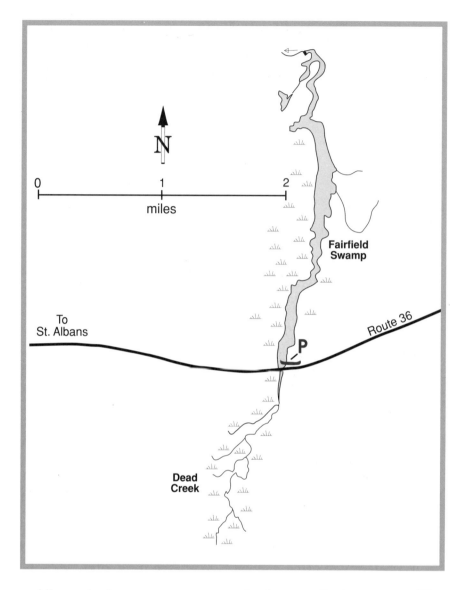

paddle north, the swamp opens up again about a mile downstream. The cattail gradually disappears, and at the north end the woodland extends right down to the water, providing suitable habitat for the resident beaver.

South of Route 36, Fairfield Swamp feels somewhat more remote, with extensive stands of cattail, black spruce, and tamarack. Wood duck

A northern leopard frog, *Rana pipiens*, eyes us warily from a lily pad.

nesting boxes represent the only evidence of humans. Yellow pond lily and pondweed cover the surface of this very wide marsh, with shores and hummocks lined with aromatic shrubs such as sweet gale. We delighted in seeing wild calla (*Calla palustris*) in bloom, the bloom spike clothed in a bright white sheath. Beaver keep the channels open, making paddling through the primordial abundance of vegetation relatively easy.

We saw frogs galore, and in some sections the late-spring chorus was almost deafening. Great blue heron, wood duck, eastern kingbird, ring-billed gull, and the ever present red-winged blackbird abound. We watched much smaller blackbirds hassle a red-tailed hawk. A handful of duck-hunting blinds argue for avoiding this paddling spot during waterfowl-hunting season in the fall.

GETTING THERE

In St. Albans, from the junction of Routes 36 and 7 take Route 36 east for 4.8 miles to the parking area on the left (just after crossing the open water). A wildlife-observation sign marks the access. Floating vegetation sometimes blocks the access; push it out of the way to gain easier access.

Missisquoi National Wildlife Refuge

Highgate and Swanton, VT

MAPS

Vermont Atlas: Maps 50 and 51

USGS Quadrangle: East Alburg

INFORMATION

Area: 6,500 acres

Prominent fish species: Largemouth bass, smallmouth bass, yellow perch, pickerel, northern pike, walleye, brook trout, brown trout, and rainbow trout

Contact information: Missisquoi National Wildlife Refuge— 802 865-4781. At the headquarters, pick up a map of the refuge and brochures on birds, mammals, hiking trails, and fishing.

On Lake Champlain, even a relatively light wind can produce swells of a foot or more, and a breeze more than 15 MPH can produce dangerous whitecaps. But the lake should not be considered totally off-limits either. A few places on the lake—including Missisquoi Bay and Missisquoi River delta—offer protected areas for open-boat paddlers.

Way up in the northwestern corner of Vermont, virtually a stone's throw from Canada, sits the Missisquoi National Wildlife Refuge, established in 1943. The Abenaki word Missisquoi means "great grassy meadow." Over the years, at least 20 different spellings of the word have appeared. Two paddlable channels exist here: Missisquoi River proper, which divides into several different branches near its terminus,

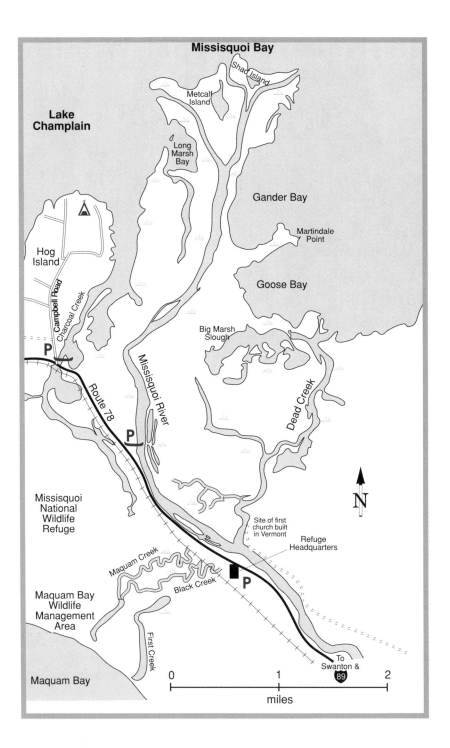

Missisquoi Bay

Shad Island

Lake
Champlain

Metcalf
Island

Long
Marsh
Bay

Gander Bay

Martindale
Point

Hog
Island

Goose Bay

Campbell Road

Charcoal Creek

Big Marsh
Slough

P

Route 78

Missisquoi River

Dead Creek

P

Missisquoi
National
Wildlife
Refuge

Site of first
church built
in Vermont

Refuge
Headquarters

N

Maquam Creek

Black Creek

P

Maquam Bay
Wildlife
Management
Area

First Creek

To
Swanton &
89

Maquam Bay

0   1   2

miles

Thick silver-maple swamps lend an eerie feeling to the Missisquoi River where it flows into Lake Champlain.

and Dead Creek, which branches off the Missisquoi near the refuge headquarters.

On a calm day, you can make a nice loop of these channels; on a windy day, stick to the channels. From the boat access on Route 78, paddle downstream along the Missisquoi River, then around the eastern side of the peninsula and up Dead Creek to its intersection with the Missisquoi and back to the boat landing. One could also make the trip in the opposite direction.

On Shad Island, notice the several hundred large great blue heron nests in the trees, belonging to one of the largest rookeries in New England—you may hear loud croaking in spring and early summer. Look for cormorants off Shad Island point. Missiquoi harbors one of the largest nesting black tern populations in New England, and it is one of the few places in Vermont where you can see threatened common terns and find soft-shelled turtles.

While motorboat traffic can be heavy on the Missisquoi River on a busy weekend, Dead Creek can be much quieter. On a windless May afternoon we watched a mink move furtively along the bank of Dead Creek—with one eye on us. Nearby we watched a deer splash through the shallow water.

Silver maple dominates the Missisquoi River and Dead Creek shores; its winged seeds—the largest of any maple—serve as an important wildlife food source. With the maple growing right out of the water, the area reminds us of a Louisiana cypress swamp. Out near Lake Champlain—depending on lake water level—you can actually weave a twisted course through these trees, encountering an occasional wood duck. Be sure not to paddle in restricted areas.

When we paddled here in late summer, we saw clematis, butter-and-eggs, and a vinelike yellow aster in bloom. Arrowhead bloomed along the banks, and we reveled in the abundance of birds. One other area worth paddling, on the south side of Route 78, is just across from Campbell Bay Road. The broad expanse of marsh here, while home to a lot of waterfowl, has somewhat lower species diversity than the delta on the north side of the road.

If you care to hike, two short trails leave from park headquarters and pass along Black Creek and Maquam Creek, covering roughly 1.5 miles. Just across from the refuge headquarters, where Dead Creek splits off from the Missisquoi River, is the site of the first church in Vermont.

GETTING THERE

From I-89, Exit 21, take Route 78 west (make sure you stay on Route 78 as you jog through Swanton). Missisquoi National Wildlife Refuge headquarters is on the left, 3.5 miles from I-89. Access to the Missisquoi River is another 1.3 miles on the right.

The access to the marsh south of Route 78 is from Campbell Bay Road, another 1.1 miles west on Route 78.

Rock River
Highgate, VT

MAPS

Vermont Atlas: Map 51

USGS Quadrangle: Highgate Center

INFORMATION

Length: 3.5 miles

Prominent fish species: Largemouth bass, smallmouth bass, yellow perch, pickerel, and northern pike

This meandering tributary to Missisquoi Bay, on Lake Champlain, can provide hours of secluded paddling away from the clamor, bustle, and wind that can beset an outing on the big lake. We paddled about three miles upriver, though one could go farther by portaging around a logjam. As with most bodies of water in the lowland North Country, the shores are lined with silver maple that forms a canopy over this wide, slow river. A consequence of the canopy, however, is that it provides an infinite number of launch pads for deerflies, a dipteran predator (genus *Chrysops*) that locates its prey by sight. We strongly recommend wearing a hat when you paddle here to reduce the aggravation.

Some enormous bur oak appear here and there, along with a very occasional shagbark hickory, both near the northeastern extent of their ranges here. We were surprised at finding bur oak; we would have expected to find swamp white oak on this flood plain.

We listened to hermit thrushes whistling their flutelike notes from the forest floor, and Baltimore orioles (*Icterus galbula*, recently once again split off from Bullock's oriole, *Icterus bullockii*, with which it had been lumped into northern oriole) sang melodious song from the tree-tops. In the spring, the woods here were alive with a chorus of bird

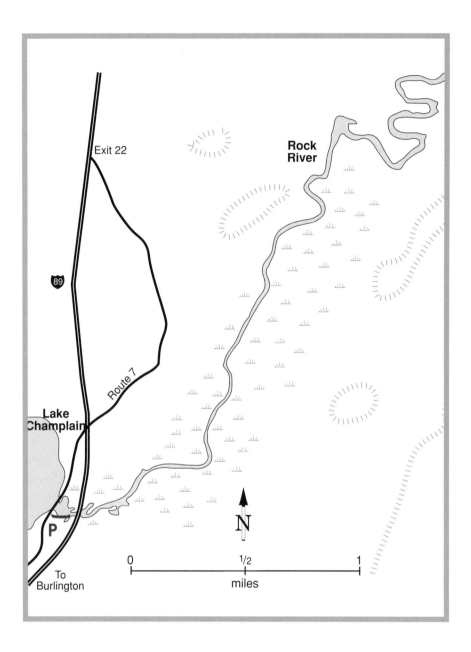

Exit 22

Rock
River

89

Route 7

Lake
Champlain

P

N

0   1/2   1
                    miles

To
Burlington

Northern Vermont **291**

Silver maples, *Acer saccharinum*, form a canopy over the wide, slow Rock River as it meanders down from Canada to Lake Champlain.

songs. Barn swallows nested under the bridges, and great blue herons and red-winged blackbirds patrolled the marshlands where the river spilled over into the adjacent lowlands in the spring.

We also saw several raptors, including red-tailed hawks, osprey, and turkey vultures. If you have time, visit the nearby Highgate Cliffs Natural Area, where turkey vultures nest and you can explore an undisturbed cobble beach.

Getting there
Take I-89 to Exit 22, the last exit before Quebec. Take Route 7 south 1.7 miles to the access on the left, just after crossing I-89.

Great Hosmer Pond and Little Hosmer Pond
Albany and Craftsbury, VT

MAPS

Vermont Atlas: Maps 47 and 53

USGS Quadrangles: Albany and Craftsbury

INFORMATION

Great Hosmer Pond area: 155 acres

Little Hosmer Pond area: 183 acres

Prominent fish species: Great Hosmer Pond—largemouth bass, smallmouth bass, yellow perch, and pickerel; Little Hosmer Pond—smallmouth bass, yellow perch, and pickerel

Camping and lodging: Craftsbury Outdoor Center— 800-729-7751 or 802-586-7768, or www.craftsbury.com

Looking for a pleasant weekend of paddling but prefer to be pampered a bit with hot meals, showers, and lodging? Consider the two Hosmer Ponds, located in scenic Craftsbury in the heart of Vermont's North Country. Great Hosmer Pond and Little Hosmer Pond offer great paddling and lodging. The Craftsbury Outdoor Center started out as a cross-country ski area but expanded into various summer sports to make it a year-round operation where people can hone their rowing, mountain-biking, and running skills. Guests can camp or stay in simple lodging with shared baths and have access to a workout room, sauna, massage therapist, and expert instruction in running and sculling—in numerous camps for all levels of skill. Wholesome buffet-style meals include vegetarian dishes.

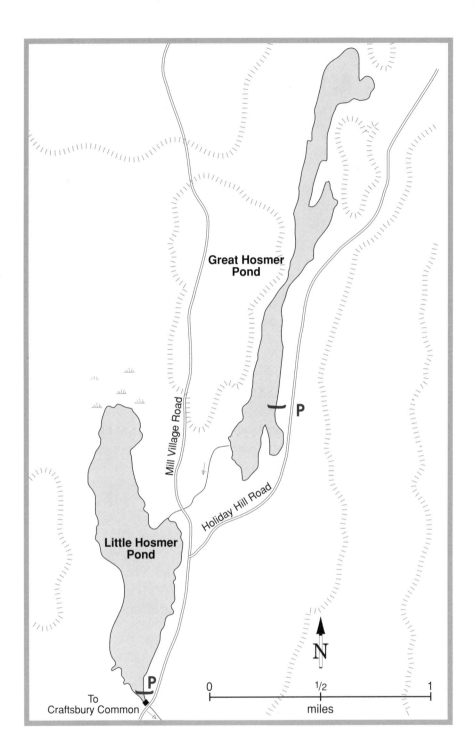

Great Hosmer
Pond

Mill Village Road

P

Holiday Hill Road

Little Hosmer
Pond

P

To
Craftsbury Common

N

0   1/2   1

miles

A conspicuous browse line on Great Hosmer Pond's shore-side northern white cedars, *Thuja occidentalis*.

Great Hosmer Pond. About a dozen cottages dot the shoreline of this two-mile-long, quarter-mile-wide pond, but most activity is connected with the Craftsbury Outdoor Center. During an early-morning paddle, a flotilla of rowing shells passed us by as if we were standing still. Of course, we had more interest in listening to the ovenbird, white-throated sparrow, and winter wren calling from the undergrowth than in a keeping up with these sleek craft. We also wanted to appreciate a major caddis-fly hatch, as thousands of these flies flew in an erratic mating dance. The larvae (the aquatic stage) build a cylindrical case of twigs, leaves, sand, or small stones cemented together, from which they feed on vegetation. When it is time to pupate, they attach the case to an underwater rock, close the open end, pupate, and then climb out of the case and out of the water as adults, with tentlike wings folded over their backs.

Paddling up the shoreline, one cannot help but notice the dominance of northern white cedar, *Thuja occidentalis*, a type of arborvitae. Arborvitae means "tree of life"; apparently, French settlers gave the tree that name after learning from Native Americans that it is a cure for scurvy. Note the conspicuous browse line on the cedars that hang out over the water. Deer often yard up in cedar stands in winter, and they browse the shoreline cedars up to head height as they walk along the frozen pond surface. The seeds and cones are important winter food for pine siskins and red squirrels.

Little Hosmer Pond. Located just a few miles away, Little Hosmer is wider but shorter and has more surface area than Great Hosmer; it also boasts more varied habitat, with marshy areas to explore and a shoreline dominated by northern white cedar and tamarack, giving the pond a wild northern feel. The shoreline vegetation consists mostly of sweet gale and fern, and yellow pond lily covers the shallows with a fairly thick mat. As with Great Hosmer, the dozen or so cottages do not intrude too severely into the pond's solitude. We saw mallards, wood ducks, loons, and a pair of ring-necked ducks here in late May. During a September visit, we watched a muskrat in one of the cattail marshes on the pond. We saw old evidence of beaver activity here, but nothing current. The state limits motorboats to 10 horsepower and 5 MPH.

GETTING THERE

To reach the Craftsbury Outdoor Center and the access on Great Hosmer Pond, head north from Hardwick on Route 14. From the intersection of Routes 14 and 15, go about 7.0 miles north on Route 14, and turn right onto South Craftsbury Road, following signs to Craftsbury. Continue north through Craftsbury and through Craftsbury Common. Follow signs to the Craftsbury Outdoor Center. In Mill Village, you will pass the Little Hosmer Pond boat access on the left.

If you are not staying at the Center, be sure to ask permission to launch your boat there. Canoe rentals are available.

May Pond
Barton, VT

MAPS

    Vermont Atlas: Map 54

    USGS Quadrangle: Sutton

INFORMATION

    Area: 116 acres

    Prominent fish species: Brook trout

    Contact information: Vermont Nature Conservancy—
802-229-4425

Located in Vermont's Northeast Kingdom about a half-hour drive from
Lake Willoughby, this little-known pond offers great wildlife viewing
in a relatively pristine environment. Though small, the pond sports a
highly varied shoreline and seems much larger. Try to visit here early
morning or late afternoon, when wildlife-viewing opportunities peak.
We watched a family of four otters here for about an hour one August
evening around dusk, diving for crayfish and munching on them at the
surface. Look for beaver, nesting loons, and osprey.

    The two cabins located near the access and the nearby rolling
farmland do not spoil the remote feeling of the pond. The marshy
shoreline supports lots of pond vegetation (water shield, waterlily,
cattail, sedge, and the like), backed by densely grown and fairly impenetrable shrubs (heaths, winterberry, and alder). Farther back on solid
ground grow red spruce, balsam fir, white and yellow birch, red maple,
and hemlock. At the shallower, more fenlike southern end of the pond,
tussocks of sphagnum moss, sundew, and the thick muck of
decomposing vegetation stirred up by your paddle stand ready to greet

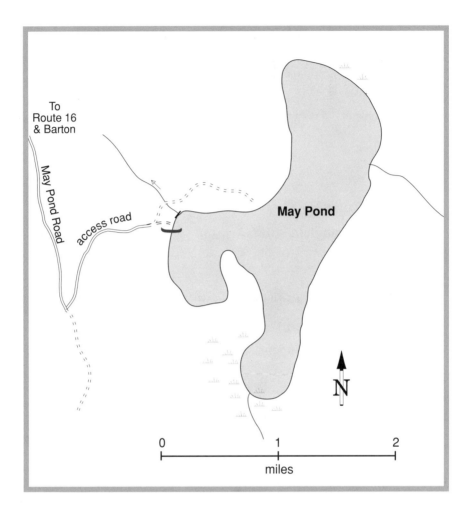

you. In the springtime, laurel blooms in the understory, and in mid-summer you may be able to enjoy a snack of wild blueberries. Look for the huge beaver lodge here—likely the home of many generations of beaver.

Recognizing May Pond's pristine ecological character, the Vermont Nature Conservancy has purchased 740 acres around the pond, including 5,000 feet of frontage. The state prohibits gasoline motors. As you paddle around May Pond, respect its fragile character and avoid disturbing nesting loons, otters, and other wildlife.

Bunchberry, *Cornus canadensis*, grows in boggy woods.

GETTING THERE

From I-91, Exit 25, take Route 16 north toward Barton. From the junction with Route 5, continue on Route 16 for 1.6 miles and turn right onto May Pond Road. The road forks after 1.4 miles—stay to the right. After driving 2.1 miles from Route 16, turn left into the access, which is about a quarter-mile down this road. From the east on Route 16, the dirt road leading to the pond is 5.7 miles from the intersection of Routes 16 and 5A at the northern end of Lake Willoughby.

South Bay, Lake Memphremagog
Newport and Coventry, VT

MAPS

Vermont Atlas: Map 54

USGS Quadrangles: Newport and Orleans

INFORMATION

Area: 745 acres

Prominent fish species: Largemouth bass, yellow perch, pickerel, walleye, and rainbow trout

The South Bay of Lake Memphremagog is an interesting body of water and much more appropriate for paddling than Lake Memphremagog proper. At the northern end, in the city of Newport, South Bay feels quite urban. You can hear sirens, trucks, heavy equipment, and cars on the nearby streets. But as you paddle south into the long, sinuous channel that extends three or four miles, most of that noise fades away.

From the fishing access on the western shore, not too far from the northern end, as you paddle south the water remains quite open for a distance. When it is windy, it might make sense to put in at the boat access off Glen Road or off Airport Road on the Black River.

You can paddle up the meandering Black River, which flows into South Bay about a quarter-mile below the primary fishing access, or you can paddle it down from Airport Road. Silver maple and willow dipping their lowest branches into the water line parts of the shore, while other stretches are marshy.

As you paddle farther south on South Bay, the open water disappears into thick marshes of pickerelweed, waterlily, water shield, rush,

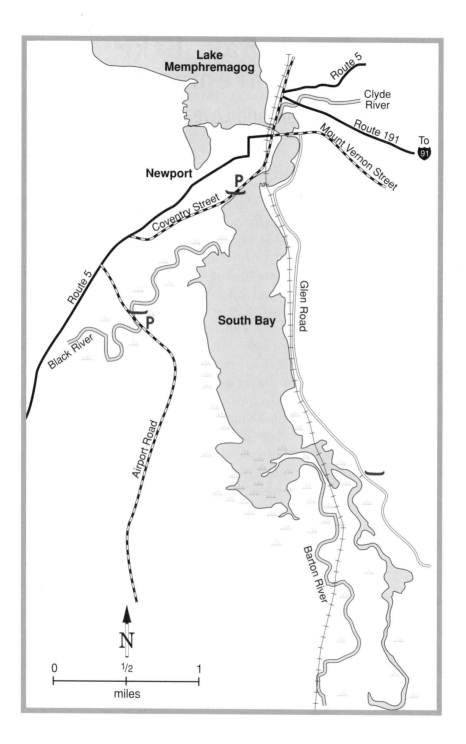

Lake
Memphremagog

Route 5

Clyde
River

Route 191

Mount Vernon Street

To
91

Newport

Coventry Street

P

South Bay

Glen Road

Route 5

P

Black River

Airport Road

Barton River

N

0   1/2   1

miles

sedge, grass, and cattail. In fact, most of the southern part of the bay is not even paddlable by midsummer. Wending your way through marshy islands, you may find yourself in the winding, slow-moving Barton River, lined with silver maple. While you might have difficulty paddling here, at least you will be a lot farther from the city—out with the wood ducks, not the pigeons. There are also many signs of beaver.

Curiously, the Barton River roughly parallels another, much wider channel leading to the south. Follow either one through the South Bay State Wildlife Management Area (a portion protected by the Vermont Nature Conservancy), one of the few sites in Vermont where black terns nest and a great haven for wood ducks. We have not explored much of the Barton River, but we have paddled all the way down the more eastern channel. To get to this channel from the Barton River, you may have to paddle back to the main lake and then north a bit; the marshes vary so much that it is hard to give precise directions. But you should recognize this wide and relatively deep unnamed channel when you get to it. We found it lined with marsh plants and home to a wide assortment of water birds. Fairly soon after getting into the channel you will pass under a railroad bridge (some of the cut-off older wooden posts lurk just below water level—paddle slowly through here).

From the railroad bridge, you can paddle several miles south through increasingly beautiful country. We rarely have seen as many wood ducks in one place—maybe a hundred, mostly in groups of a half-dozen or so. We saw bitterns, black ducks, kingfishers, great blue herons, a northern harrier, lots of painted turtles, and a few snapping turtles—just the triangular noses sticking up above the water. Feathery larch mix with silver maple, white birch, spruce, and other trees along the shores.

Duck blinds hidden among the marsh plants indicate that duck hunters use the area in the fall. We recommend avoiding this place during duck season.

GETTING THERE

From I-91, Exit 27, take Route 191 west to Route 5 south. After crossing the bridge between South Bay and Lake Memphremagog, turn left onto Coventry Street and follow the water for 0.5 mile to the access on the left.

To reach the southern inlet access to South Bay, go east across the northern tip of South Bay on Mount Vernon Street, turn right onto Glen Road, follow it down the eastern side for 2.7 miles, and look for a dirt track leading down to the water on the right.

To reach the Black River access, turn off Main Street in Newport onto Routes 5 and 105 south and west. Follow signs for the airport. After 1.3 miles, turn left onto Airport Road. The access point at the bridge is 0.4 mile down Airport Road; parking is on the right 0.1 mile farther.

Clyde River and Pensioner Pond
Charleston, VT

MAPS

 Vermont Atlas: Map 54

 USGS Quadrangles: Island Pond, West Charleston, and Westmore

INFORMATION

 Clyde River length: 8 miles

 Pensioner Pond area: 170 acres

 Prominent fish species: Pensioner Pond—yellow perch and pickerel

The Clyde River section covered here courses northwest from East Charleston to West Charleston in the heart of Vermont's Northeast Kingdom. The best access point lies along the northeast shore of Pensioner Pond, though alternate put-ins are at the bridges southeast of the pond, at Center School Road and Cross Road. Pensioner Pond itself, totally visible from the road, round, and relatively uninteresting, serves primarily as an access to the Clyde River at its southwest corner.

 The river winds through farm country, with silver maple and alder dominating the shoreline. Northern white cedar, an occasional willow, and a variety of shrubs line the 40-foot-wide waterway, and vegetation dips right into the water. Even during spring high water, the barely perceptible current presents no obstacle. The same cannot be said for the beaver that undercut the stream-side silver maple, toppling them into the water to make logjams. Be prepared to portage around their handiwork.

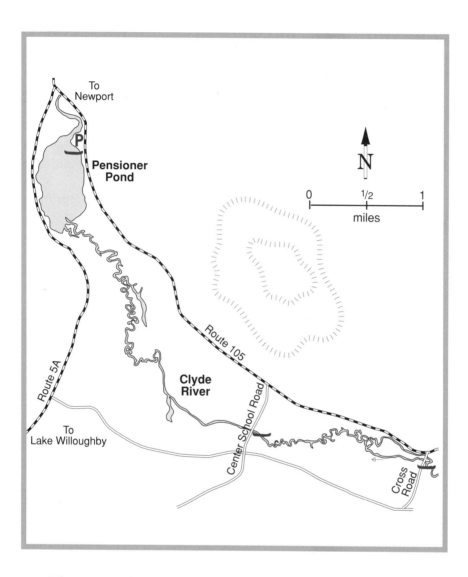

The surrounding marshland and side coves support large numbers of wood ducks and black ducks. We also saw tree swallows, red-winged blackbirds, great blue herons, a red-tailed hawk, and many other birds. Besides the beaver activity, we spotted a mink moving furtively along the shore and many piles of mussel shells—leftovers from raccoon or otter feasts.

GETTING THERE

From Newport, take Route 5 north; turn south on Routes 5A/105, passing through Derby Center and West Charleston. When Routes 5A and 105 split, take Route 105 to the left. From the split, the boat access on Pensioner Pond is 0.7 mile south on the right.

From the north end of Lake Willoughby, at the junction of Routes 5A and 16, take Route 5A north for about 8.0 miles to the junction with Route 105. Turn right onto Route 105; the boat access on Pensioner Pond is 0.7 mile south on the right.

Alternate access points are at bridges on Center School Road and Cross Road.

Dennis Pond
Brunswick, VT

MAPS
 Vermont Atlas: Map 55

 USGS Quadrangle: Maidstone Lake

INFORMATION
 Area: 185 acres

 Prominent fish species: Yellow perch and pickerel

A few rather unobtrusive hunting cabins huddle along the northeastern shore of Dennis Pond, land once owned by International Paper but now protected by The Nature Conservancy and other conservation organizations. Despite the cabins' presence, this boggy pond exudes an essence of the northern coniferous forest. Access to the pond, unfortunately, requires carrying about 100 feet over a rather spongy sphagnum bog. If you want to keep your feet dry and unmuddied, stay away from Dennis Pond.

A paddle here is worth it, especially in the early-morning or evening hours when you have the best chance of spying moose. Sphagnum hummocks, many sporting stands of stunted tamarack, occur everywhere out in the water and along the shore. Typical bog plants abound, including leatherleaf, sheep laurel, cattail, and yellow pond lily; nodding flower heads of pitcher plants poke up everywhere.

As you dip your paddle in the water, note the brownish yellow cast from tannic and other organic acids arising from decaying vegetation. This very shallow lake is filling in; even if you push your paddle down very lightly into the silty bottom, it will penetrate quite far. It will not be long before this pond fills in completely; indeed, it would be best to

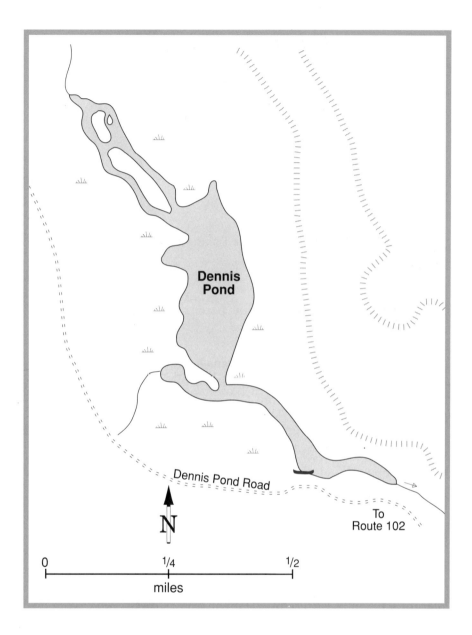

paddle this shallow pond in spring, during high water and before emergent vegetation takes over.

We spent a lazy afternoon here in June, enjoying the scenic hillsides all around, along with myriad wildlife: tree swallows, kingfishers, wood

Tiger swallowtails, *Papilio glaucus*, congregate on a wet road.

ducks, red-winged blackbirds, beaver, kingbirds, painted turtles, cedar waxwings, bittern, and great blue heron. Tiger swallowtail butterflies were in abundance, and two osprey fished the shallow waters.

GETTING THERE

From the junction of Routes 105 and 102 in North Stratford, take Route 102 south. In a couple of miles, turn right at the signs for Dennis Pond Road and Wheeler Ponds Road. Take Dennis Pond West Side Road at the Y at 0.3 mile. (Ignore Wheeler Ponds Road as it goes left at 0.6 mile.) Just after the bridge over the Dennis Pond outlet stream at 0.8 mile, turn right. From the bridge it is 0.5 mile to the small clearing in the roadside brush that leads out over the bog to the pond. There is enough room for two cars to get fully off the road, but because the road has little traffic, several more cars can park partially off the road.

Nulhegan Pond
Brighton, VT

MAPS
>**Vermont Atlas:** Map 55
>
>**USGS Quadrangle:** Spectacle Pond

INFORMATION
>**Area:** 37 acres
>
>**Prominent fish species:** Pickerel
>
>**Camping:** Spectacle Pond in Brighton State Park—802-723-4360 (summer); 802-479-4280 (winter)

Nulhegan Pond, though very shallow and small, presents a wonderful place to study aquatic and bog plant life. Its two entrance streams provide more habitat to explore and make the pond seem much larger. When we paddled here in mid-July, two species of orchid were in bloom along with rafts of pickerelweed, water shield, sundew, pitcher plant, and yellow pond lily. We also found a white waterlily with very small blossoms, perhaps the smallest we have seen on a plant of this type. This could be dwarf waterlily, *Nymphaea leibergii*, recently split off from *N. tetragona* of the Northwest. It is critically imperiled in the Northeast.

We also enjoyed identifying bog rosemary, leatherleaf, sweet gale, and a yellow pea that bloomed in profusion. In addition to exploring the pond, take some time to explore the two outlet channels, but watch out for submerged logs.

As in much of the Northeast Kingdom, northern boreal forest surrounds Nulhegan Pond. Balsam fir, red spruce, northern white cedar, white birch, and red maple dominate, while tamarack and black spruce tolerate growing on the sphagnum hummocks. Northern white cedar is also called arborvitae—the tree of life. Historians believe the French

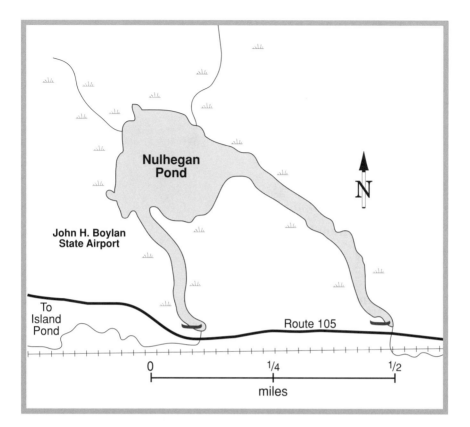

Nulhegan
Pond

John H. Boylan
State Airport

N

To
Island
Pond

Route 105

0   1/4   1/2

miles

explorer Jacques Cartier, who made a tea from the tree to cure his men of scurvy, named it.

The Northern Forest is also moose country. If you do not see moose standing in the local ponds and streams, you can often see them by the road in the early morning and evening.

GETTING THERE

From Island Pond at the junction of Routes 105 and 114, take Route 105 east. After 3.5 miles, pass John H. Boylan State Airport. The access is at either of the next two bridges, just past the airport, at 4.2 and 4.7 miles from Island Pond. We prefer the second bridge, as the first is on a curve and has a narrow shoulder.

To get to Spectacle Pond Campground, turn right off Route 105, 1.7 miles east of the junction of Routes 105 and 114, and follow signs to Brighton State Park.

Norton Pond
Norton and Warren Gore, VT

MAPS

Vermont Atlas: Map 55

USGS Quadrangles: Morgan Center and Norton Pond

INFORMATION

Area: 583 acres

Prominent fish species: Northern pike

Norton Pond, less well known than the Averill Ponds, Lake Willoughby, and some of the other lakes in the Northeast Kingdom of Vermont, has some real advantages for paddlers. The pond stretches out in a southwest-to-northeast direction, providing many coves and inlets to explore. Some—but not much—development mars its otherwise wild and remote-feeling shoreline. Islands, deep coves, and long, winding inlet brooks fill the entire southern end of this large pond. Be sure not to disturb the nesting loons; the chicks have a hard enough time evading the large northern pike that inhabit this pond.

While we enjoyed paddling the northern reaches of Norton Pond, we much preferred the southern end and especially the marshy inlet to the west, where Hurricane Brook and Coaticook Brook flow in. Wildlife abounds here; we saw wood ducks, black ducks, herons, and deer. Look carefully for otters cavorting along the banks. Judging from tracks along the swampy shores, moose must browse this area in considerable numbers.

Even in late summer, with water levels down and pond vegetation at a peak, you can paddle surprisingly far up the inlet creeks. Higher water in late spring makes the area much more accessible. Where the

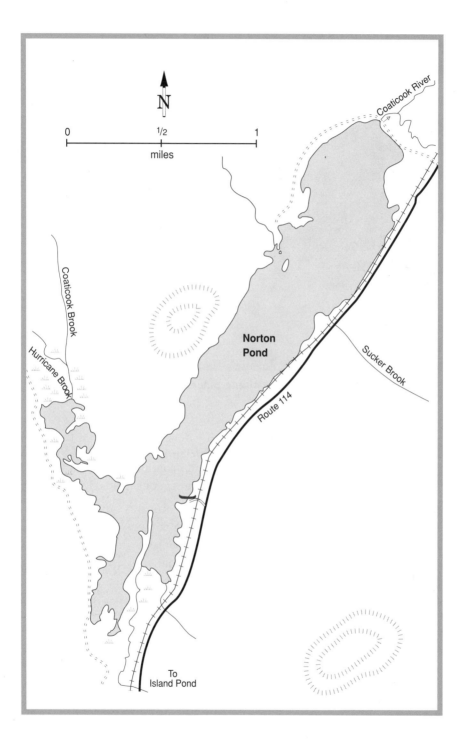

N

0   1/2   1
miles

Coaticook River

Coaticook Brook

Hurricane Brook

Norton
Pond

Sucker Brook

Route 114

To
Island Pond

Stumps and deadfalls provide hiding places for the large northern pike that inhabit Norton Pond.

Hurricane and Coaticook inlet joins the main pond, you can explore a number of different channels through and around the various islands. At the far southern end you will find some gorgeous little coves and just a few summer cottages.

GETTING THERE

From Island Pond, go north on Route 114. Stay on Route 114 when Route 111 forks left; from this fork, the access road is 6.3 miles north on the left. Coming from the north, the access road is 7.3 miles from Route 147 at the Canadian border. The put-in is 0.25 mile from Route 114, across the railroad tracks.

Holland Pond and Turtle Pond
Holland, VT

MAPS

   Vermont Atlas: Map 55

   USGS Quadrangle: Morgan Center

INFORMATION

   Holland Pond area: 334 acres

   Turtle Pond area: 27 acres

   Prominent fish species: Holland Pond—pickerel, brook trout, and rainbow trout; Turtle Pond—brook trout

Holland Pond sits less than a mile, as the crow flies, from the Canadian border, in the Northeast Kingdom. The pond has moderate development along its western shore, but these summer cottages (approximately 40) are much different from the ones farther south. Few big docks and few huge motorboats loom in front, and little new development is in evidence. As long as the camps remain small and unpretentious, the pond will likely remain a nice place to visit, though you may want to time your visit to avoid popular summer weekends.

   Both the northern and southern ends provide more interesting areas to paddle than the rest of the pond. Two inlets at the southern end, as well as a fairly extensive marshy area, await exploration. You can paddle a short distance into the inlets, amid the alders and sphagnum- and grass-covered tussocks—though because of nesting loons access to this marshy area may be restricted from May through July.

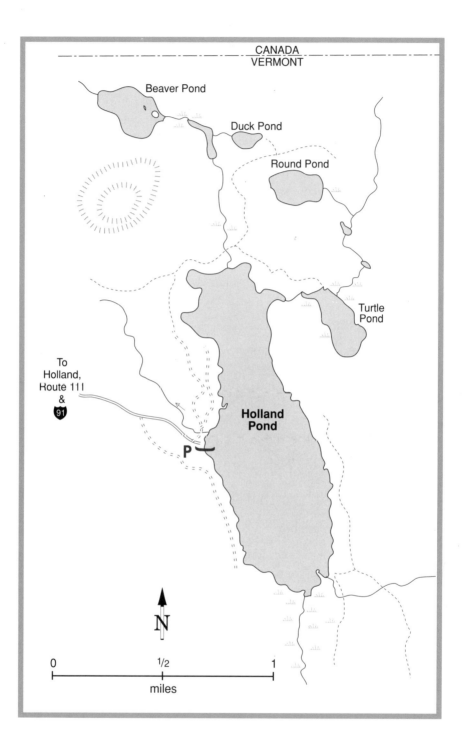

CANADA
VERMONT

Beaver Pond

Duck Pond

Round Pond

Turtle
Pond

To
Holland,
Route 111
&
91

**Holland
Pond**

P

N

0   1/2   1
miles

The northern end feels a little more remote and wild. You can paddle into the northeast inlet a little way, and if you feel really adventurous, you can carry your boat from here a couple hundred yards into small, beautiful, totally remote Turtle Pond. The trail to Turtle Pond starts on the northwestern side of the inlet, where the inlet narrows to a rock-strewn channel. Judging from the tracks, moose do most of the trail maintenance.

Farther around the northern end of Holland Pond to the west, there are two nice picnic spots, one on a large, flattish rock protruding into the pond and another where the other inlet creek flows in. Here the small creek flows over huge, flat rocks beneath a stand of large northern white cedar. You may find trails here to several other small ponds to the north. Dense stands of cedar, balsam fir, larch, white and yellow birch, and red spruce grow along the rest of the shoreline.

GETTING THERE

From I-91, Exit 29 (at the Canadian border), turn onto Holland Road toward Holland and Morgan Center. After passing Holland Elementary School on the left, keep an eye out for unpaved Holland Pond Road on the left. The turnoff is 5.3 miles from I-91, just as the paved road curves to the right. Follow the unpaved road for 5.3 miles to the pond (bear to the right at 3.0 miles and bear left at 5.0 miles, staying on the main road).

Coming from Island Pond, take Route 114 north; turn left onto Route 111. In 6.7 miles, turn right onto Valley Road across from the Seymour Lake boat access. Go 4.7 miles, turn right onto Holland Pond Road, and continue as above.

Little Averill Pond
Averill, VT

MAPS
>**Vermont Atlas:** Map 55
>
>**USGS Quadrangle:** Averill

INFORMATION
>**Area:** 483 acres
>
>**Prominent fish species:** Smelt, landlocked salmon, lake trout, brook trout, and rainbow trout

Little Averill Pond lies just south of the Canadian border, in the Northeast Kingdom of Vermont. Like its larger brother to the north, Great Averill Pond, Little Averill sits in a deep boreal forest of spruce, fir, cedar, red maple, white birch, and yellow birch. Beautiful Brousseau Mountain, with an extensive cliff area, overlooks the pond from the northwest. Some development has occurred around the pond, though much less than at Great Averill.

A round, deep pond, Little Averill boasts excellent fishing for landlocked salmon, and lake, rainbow, and brook trout. The densely wooded and generally rocky shore includes a few sandy beaches. The Nature Conservancy manages a tract of land around the pond's northwestern end, including a deep inlet, to protect loon nesting habitat. You will see wispy horsetails and grasses in the water in this gorgeous inlet, amid the whitened snags of long-dead trees. From May through July, this area often has remained off-limits to paddlers to protect nesting loons; however, since 1994 the resident loon pair has used an artificial nesting platform in the south cove.

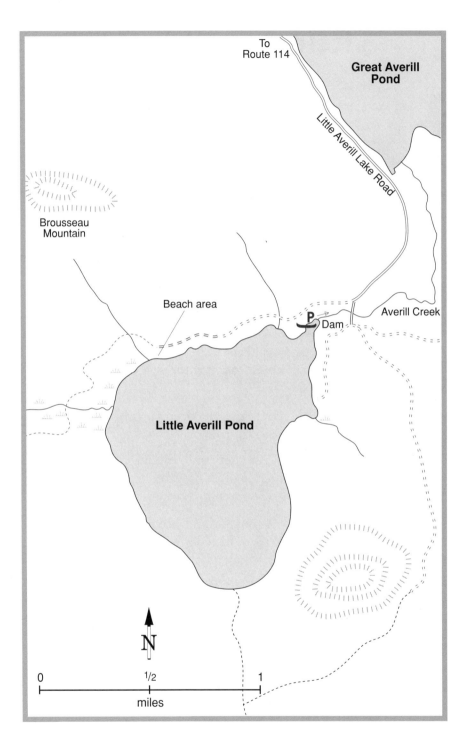

To
Route 114

Great Averill Pond

Little Averill Lake Road

Brousseau
Mountain

Beach area

P

Dam

Averill Creek

Little Averill Pond

N

0   1/2   1

miles

Watch for signs on Little Averill Pond indicating loon nesting habitat, and keep away from these areas from May through July.

A trail extends west from the boat access, around the northern end of the pond, south to the Black Branch of the Nulhegan River, and northwest toward Norton. Another trail extends south from the southern tip of the pond, along the East Branch of the Nulhegan River (see the *Vermont Atlas and Gazetteer* or, better yet, use the USGS topographical map).

GETTING THERE
From Norton, where Route 147 enters from Canada, take Route 114 east for 3.4 miles and turn right onto Little Averill Lake Road. Drive southeast along Great Averill Pond for 3.1 miles. Take the right fork and continue another 0.2 mile to the access. Coming from the east, Little Averill Lake Road turns off Route 114 1.0 mile west of the Lakeview store, near the access to Great Averill Pond.

The Playful River Otter

If you paddle the more remote lakes, ponds, marshes, and rivers of New England, and if you get out on the water early in the morning or remain out as dusk approaches, sooner or later a river otter—or perhaps a family of these sleek mammals—will bob into view. We have seen dozens of otters throughout New Hampshire and Vermont, mostly in the less-populated North Country but some near the Massachusetts border. Their playful antics, friendly facial expressions, and masterful swimming make them one of our favorite species to observe.

The river otter, *Lutra canadensis*, once inhabited virtually every U.S. watercourse, from sun-warmed southwestern rivers to icy far-northern lakes and streams. Today, because of two hundred years of trapping, water pollution, and encroaching development, the otter has retreated to the far corners of its former range. Because they eat at the top of the food chain, otters also suffer from pollution and toxic chemicals in the environment, such as heavy metals, DDT derivatives, dioxin, and PCBs.

The river otter, with its long, thin body and relatively thick, sharply tapered tail, can reach four feet in length and weigh up to 25 pounds. Long prized by trappers, its dense dark-brown fur above gives way to lighter colors on the belly and throat.

Otters are well adapted to aquatic environments. Their noses and ears close when under water, and their webbed toes aid in swimming. Though otters swim fast enough to catch trout in open water, they usually opt for slower-moving suckers, minnows, crayfish, tadpoles, and salamanders. When hunting, otters come up for air every 30 seconds or so, though they can remain underwater for up to two minutes. When they surface, their heads generally pop way up in the air as they look around—quite different from beaver and muskrat, which barely rise above the water's surface.

Though adapted for water, otters do pretty well on land as well, their undulating gait typical of weasel family members. Clocked at up to 18 miles per hour on land, they can travel 100 miles overland in search of new territory. Otters generally place their dens—abandoned beaver lodges or natural cavities under tree roots—at the water's edge, with an underwater entrance.

Otters consume smaller fish and crayfish in the water, while they take larger prey to shore or to a protruding rock. In shallow water, look for an otter's tail sticking out of the water as it roots around in the mud for food. Ingenious hunters, otters sometimes herd fish into shallows, making prey capture easy. They may even puncture a beaver dam, then wade in and feast on fish flopping in the receding water. Because otters hunt so successfully, they have plenty of time to play—a famous otter trait.

The young of many mammal species play. Animal behaviorists believe such play provides practice for future hunting, territorial interactions, and courtship. But otters do not stop playing when they reach adulthood. They roll in the water chasing one another or repeatedly climb up on a snow- or mudbank and slide down into the water. Animal behaviorists have not yet found reasons for otters' play, other than simply to have fun.

Otters mate in the late winter or early spring, but birth does not follow until almost a year later. As with many members of the weasel family, implantation of embryos is delayed in otters, and development stops until the following fall or winter. Otters give birth to two to four cubs in a well-protected den anytime between November and April (usually February to April). The cubs emerge fully furred, but with eyes closed and no teeth. They will not venture outside the den for about three months, remaining completely dependent on their mother for at least six months. Though the mother provides all care for the young cubs, the father may rejoin the family and help with care and teaching after they reach about six months of age. Otters become sexually mature after two years.

Though otters are curious animals and relatively bold, keep your distance when observing them. Interference from humans may cause them to move away and search for more-remote streams or ponds.

Alphabetical Listing of Lakes, Ponds, Reservoirs, and Rivers.

VERMONT

About the Appalachian Mountain Club

Since 1876, the Appalachian Mountain Club has helped people experience the majesty and solitude of the Northeast outdoors. We offer outdoor skills workshops, guided trips, and lodging options for all levels of outdoor adventuring. Our conservation programs include trail maintenance, air and water quality research, and conservation advocacy work to preserve the special outdoor places we love and enjoy for future generations.

Take a hike, ride a bike, paddle a canoe. We believe that people who enjoy breathing fresh air, climbing mountains, splashing in streams, and walking on trails have more fun and take better care of the outdoors. Join the fun today. Call 617-523-0636 for membership information.

From beginner backpacking to advanced backcountry skiing, we teach outdoor skills workshops to suit your interest and experience. If you prefer the company of others and skilled leaders, we also offer guided hiking and paddling trips. Our outdoor education centers guarantee year-round adventures.

With accommodations throughout the Northeast, you don't have to travel to the ends of the earth to see nature's beauty and experience unique wilderness lodging. Accessible by car or on foot, our lodges and huts are perfect for families, couples, groups, and individuals.

We can lead you to the best hiking, biking, skiing, and paddling destinations from Maine to North Carolina. With more than 50 books and maps published, we're your definitive resource for discovering wonderful outdoor places. For ordering information call 800-262-4455.

Check us out online at **www.outdoors.org** for lots of great information. Appalachian Mountain Club, 5 Joy Street, Boston, MA 02108-1490; 617-523-0636

About the Authors

John Hayes is a professor of biochemistry and environmental science at Marlboro College in Marlboro, Vermont. He has canoed and kayaked in Minnesota's Boundary Waters Canoe Area, in Georgia's Okefenokee Swamp, and in Florida's Everglades, as well as throughout the Northeast. When he is not in the classroom, he often leads natural history field trips to Central America, Africa, Borneo, the deserts of the Southwest, the Rockies, and the Everglades. He is co-author with Alex Wilson of two other canoe guides for the Appalachian Mountain Club: *AMC Quiet Water Canoe Guide: Maine* and *AMC Quiet Water Canoe Guide: New York*.

Alex Wilson is a writer in Brattleboro, Vermont. He is an avid canoeist and naturalist, and has co-written with John Hayes the two canoe guides for Maine and New York, mentioned above, as well as the *AMC Quiet Water Canoe Guide: Massachusetts/Connecticut/Rhode Island*. He is the publisher of *Environmental Building News*, and is a widely published freelance writer on energy, building technology, and environmental issues for such magazines as *Architecture*, *Progressive Architecture*, *Fine Homebuilding*, *Popular Science*, *Home*, and *Consumers Digest*.

Leave No Trace

The Appalachian Mountain Club is a national educational partner of Leave No Trace, Inc., a nonprofit organization dedicated to promoting and inspiring responsible outdoor recreation through education, research, and partnerships. The Leave No Trace Program seeks to develop wildland ethics—ways in which people think and act in the outdoors to minimize their impacts on the areas they visit and to protect our natural resourcses for future enjoyment. Leave No Trace unites four federal land management agencies—the U.S. Forest Service, National Park Service, Bureau of Land Management, and U.S. Fish and Wildlife Service—with manufacturers, outdoor retailers, user groups, educators, organizations such as the AMC and the National Outdoor Leadership School (NOLS), and individuals.

THE LEAVE NO TRACE ETHIC IS GUIDED BY THESE SEVEN PRINCIPLES:

- Plan ahead and prepare.
- Travel and camp on durable surfaces.
- Dispose of waste properly.
- Leave what you find.
- Minimize campfire impacts.
- Respect wildlife.
- Be considerate of other visitors.

The AMC has joined NOLS—a recognized leader in wilderness education and a founding partner of Leave No Trace—as the only sole national providers of the Leave No Trace Master Educator course through 2004. The AMC offers this five-day course, designed especially for outdoor professionals and land managers, as well as the shorter two-day Leave No Trace Trainer course, at locations throughout the Northeast United States.

For Leave No Trace information and materials contact: Leave No Trace, P.O. Box 997, Boulder, CO 80306; 800-332-4100; www.LNT.org